D0826501

Coming Out
of Shame

Coming Out

of Shame

TRANSFORMING GAY AND LESBIAN LIVES

Gershen Kaufman, Ph.D.
and
Lev Raphael, Ph.D.

MAIN
STREET
BOOKS

DOUBLEDAY/*New York London Toronto Sydney Auckland*

A Main Street Book
PUBLISHED BY DOUBLEDAY
a division of Bantam Doubleday Dell Publishing Group, Inc.
1540 Broadway, New York, New York 10036

Main Street Books, Doubleday, and the portrayal of a building with a tree
are trademarks of Doubleday, a division of Bantam Doubleday Dell
Publishing Group, Inc.

Coming Out of Shame was originally published in hardcover by Doubleday in 1996.
The Main Street Books edition is published by arrangement with Doubleday.

The Library of Congress has cataloged the Doubleday edition as follows:

Kaufman, Gershen.
   Coming out of shame: transforming gay and lesbian lives / Gershen
Kaufman and Lev Raphael. —
      p.   cm.
   Includes bibliographical references.
   1. Gays—Psychology.   2. Shame.   I. Raphael, Lev.   II. Title.
HQ75.25.K38   1996
305.9'0664—dc20   95-16870
                                                            CIP

ISBN 0-385-47796-1
Copyright © 1996 by Gershen Kaufman and Lev Raphael

*"If we could talk about shame,
we could build a language of pride."*

LESLIE FEINBERG,
AUTHOR OF *STONE BUTCH BLUES*

To Our Families

ACKNOWLEDGMENTS

We'd like to thank Harold Dennis Schmidt for believing in this project from the beginning. He never lost faith that this book would be born.

We'd also like to thank our editor at Doubleday, Charles Flowers, whose editorial vision and insight made this work blossom and grow.

Contents

Coming Out
of *Shame*

Divided from Ourselves

You're on the playground during recess. You're about nine years old. You see a group of kids playing and you walk over to join their game. As you approach—half-expectant, half-apprehensive —one of them sneers at you and another laughs. You hesitate a moment, wanting to move forward, but wanting to retreat. They decide to let you play after all. Later, you blunder badly and several of them call you "Faggot!" Not knowing what that means, you look down anyway, hanging your head for a moment, feeling despised. Everyone standing around begins to mock you.

You're older now, thirteen, just on the threshold of adolescence. Everything about you is changing. Your face, your body, even your feelings. Inside, you feel different from everyone you know. You just don't seem to fit in anymore. But did you ever fit in? Even the way you look at people has changed. You find yourself staring at someone you like until suddenly you're noticed. Then you quickly lower your eyes and look away, off to the side, embarrassed at being caught. Other kids don't seem to stare the same way you do. Sure, they stare too—but not at the same indi-

> *viduals you stare at. And you don't particularly notice the ones*
> *they do. Something's different about you. Something seems wrong.*
> *Better not let anyone find this out about you. It's safer to hide.*
>
> *Remember that time in class when everyone crowded around*
> *the big table for the science demonstration, and you actually got*
> *to press against that certain person you'd been staring at? But you*
> *were noticed—you'd been* seen. *Then, later, in the hallway be-*
> *tween classes came the crash: "You're a queer! Look at the*
> *homo!" Instantly, everyone's eyes were on you. The silence was*
> *deafening and you just wanted the floor to open up so you could*
> *disappear—vanish from sight. The world was spinning. You*
> *wanted to get out of there, escape, find somewhere to hide. But*
> *you couldn't. There was nowhere to go—you felt trapped and*
> *exposed.*

These experiences are universal scenes of shame, of being exposed as
something lesser and despicable. Shame is one of our most powerful emotions and, until recently, one of the least understood. This is especially true
in contemporary American society, where we overvalue competition, success, achievement, and perfection. We are taught that we must be flawless. A
culture that worships achievement brands anyone who falls short of the
mark as imperfect.

One thing that makes shame so crippling is that it usually feels impossible to talk about, to express openly in words. That's because of the inevitable shame *about* shame. Simply revealing our shame, and thereby exposing
the way in which we feel lesser, deficient, or inferior, can actually cause us to
reexperience the very shame we long to hide, disown, or anesthetize. In a
competitive society, telling someone we feel inferior can seem like opening
up the castle gates to the besieging enemy.

> *You're fourteen now and you've found a best friend. You go*
> *everywhere together, share everything. You tell your friend your*
> *deepest secrets and feel closer because of the revelations. You like*
> *to touch, even hug each other occasionally—when no one's look-*
> *ing. You feel a rush inside, a thrill you don't fully understand, or*
> *want to understand. One day you're out walking, arm in arm,*
> *oblivious to the world, when all at once your serenity is shattered:*

A group of kids walks by and suddenly begins to jeer, "Look at those homos! They're sick." Instantly your head goes down, involuntarily. Both of you silently drop your arms to your sides. Neither of you speaks about what happened. But your friend suddenly becomes busier, has less time to spend with you. Something is wrong, and also feels wrong inside—but neither one of you can talk about it. Gradually, you're surrounded by a deepening silence, and that silence also spreads within you. You begin to hide more of yourself.

You sleep over at your friend's house, you know, that one. The one you've been staring at and have even imagined touching. You're older now, fifteen. It's quite dark and you're both under the sheets—sleeping in the same bed. You want to reach over and touch, feel, caress—but you're afraid. So you hope your friend reaches for you instead. You pray for it. You lie there listening to your own breathing, listening to your friend's breathing as well. At last you summon up your courage and you do it—you actually reach over, holding your breath, praying that your friend is sound asleep. Hesitantly, your fingers explore. You caress softly, hoping your friend doesn't wake up. The next day in school, you notice your friend whispering to everyone as you come in. They're all staring at you, pointing, sneering. Something's up. Then, later that day in gym class, one of those tough kids walks over to you while you're all sitting on a bench and looks down at you, sneering, "I know what you want. I know what you are. You're a faggot, a queer!" The words scream in your mind. Everyone is watching, hushed, while you're paralyzed, trapped, exposed to all those watching eyes. All that day, you're followed around, taunted, jeered at. As much as you try to hide, to escape, you can't. Afterward, the watching eyes are inside of you as well, as if you're jeering at yourself.

In this book, we'll be exploring what it's like for men growing up gay and women growing up lesbian in contemporary society. In particular, we'll examine how experiences of shame can become embedded in our emerging awareness as lesbians and gay men, and thereby shape our eventual lesbian or gay identity. It is virtually impossible to be different, particularly in this culture, and not feel deficient for the difference, because any awareness of difference inevitably translates into a devaluing comparison. First we are devalued by others, and then we devalue ourselves. Certainly, there are degrees of difference. Some people are left-handed, others are extremely overweight, some are short, others very tall. Other differences—of ethnicity, religion, color, and sexuality—are more problematic. While the culture rewards certain differences like athletic achievement and heroism, it unequivocally punishes many others—signaling the danger of appearing too different. In such a climate, differences almost automatically translate into deficiencies.

Just as there are degrees of difference, there are inevitable degrees of shame. Certain differences are more shameful than others, either in the eyes of the culture or in our own eyes. But differences don't even have to be significant, just perceived that way, particularly in a culture that prizes social conformity. Being *seen* as different can be a sufficient and equally potent source of shame. Because of the close connection between the awareness of difference and shame, being gay or lesbian inescapably marks us as lesser. That is always true in the culture at large. Often, being lesbian or gay is to be not only shamed, but shunned and actively renounced. We become outcast in our own culture—and in some instances demonized. Think of all the times you've heard people say that being gay or lesbian is not only sick or unnatural, but actually *evil*.

Embedded in these judgments are distinct, though sometimes hidden, expressions of shame. To be sick, to be unnatural, to be judged evil—these are beyond question shameful. Herein lies one of the deepest sources of the equation that being gay or lesbian *equals* being shameful. Being seen as gay or lesbian therefore unavoidably targets anyone for shaming. Examining the lesbian/gay experience inevitably brings us face to face with shame because that experience has been inexorably infused with shame across cultures and centuries. To fully comprehend the nature of the contemporary lesbian/gay experience, we must confront the problem of shame while also furthering the task of enlarging lesbian/gay consciousness.

What do we mean by a lesbian consciousness or a gay awareness? What is a gay identity or a lesbian identity? How does a lesbian or gay identity develop? How is self-esteem influenced by the intimate knowledge of being gay or lesbian? How does our experience translate into intimacy and sexuality? These are the central questions we'll be examining as we consider gay life for both women and men. Shame is deeply rooted in self-esteem, identity, and intimacy, which are vitally important to each of us, and shame is the most disturbing of human emotions. Because shame is so acutely disturbing, we quickly try to escape the feeling, mask it from view, or even deny its existence. And it is shame that we must carefully examine as well as counteract in the journey toward individual *and* societal change.

If we are to effect substantive, lasting change in the personal lives of gay people, then we must begin with a searching inquiry into shame that expands our knowledge of this misunderstood human emotion. The key to building self-esteem is understanding shame and its profound hold on us, because shame is the source of low self-esteem. Shame is equally central to the development of identity for all people, gay and non-gay alike. No other emotion is more central to our emergent sense of identity. Further, if we are to become successful in the pursuit of intimacy, we must understand shame's disruptive interpersonal impact. Shame is the single greatest barrier to the realization of intimacy. Developing self-esteem and a secure, self-affirming gay identity, along with integrating intimacy and sexuality, are central developmental tasks for gay individuals.

Andrew Holleran once wrote in *Christopher Street* that "only by dealing with Gay Shame will we ever get to a definition of Gay Pride."[1] Otherwise, all we have is just a cheerleading slogan. To extend his formulation, only by confronting and *transforming* gay shame can we achieve gay power. Gay pride is to gay power what individual growth is to societal change.

But we are seriously mistaken if we believe we can achieve that power without first recognizing and ultimately mastering the dynamics of shame that operate on a broad societal plane. We cannot sustain gay power without moving through and ultimately dissolving the shame surrounding being gay, any more than we can sustain gay pride without examining gay shame.

Unexamined shame on either the individual or societal level becomes an almost insurmountable obstacle to the realization of inner wholeness and true connection with others, because shame reveals us all as lesser, worthless, deficient—in a word, profoundly and unspeakably inferior. People of difference—women who love women and men who love men—become people haunted by shame, not because of particular actions but, more profoundly, because of who they *are*.

Silence reinforces that shame, and we know that silence is the distinctive way for the wider culture to oppress lesbians and gay men. How does that silence operate? Until very recently, there has been too little public discourse about homosexuality. The lives and experiences of millions of gay people have been invisible in many ways. Historians, of course, recognize this invisibility. Works like *Hidden from History* by Martin Duberman, Martha Vicinus, and George Chauncey, *Odd Girls and Twilight Lovers* by Lillian Faderman, and *Invisible Lives* by Martha Barrett, among numerous others, reflect this aspect of the gay experience, and gay scholars have begun the difficult task of speaking our history and reclaiming our lives. But for the most part, scholarship in various fields has proceeded with scholars remaining essentially silent about, if not openly hostile to, the homosexuality of people and times under the particular lens of their inquiry.

Historically, films and television are other major medias from which gay experience has largely been excluded. Simply playing the role of a gay character has been viewed as potentially stigmatizing, to say nothing of the fact that gay characters have been too often portrayed stereotypically and negatively. Even Paul Rudnick found it difficult casting the movie of his hit play *Jeffrey* because it was so openly gay.[2] Dramatizing gay life and gay relationships has never been a media priority, nor has including gays and lesbians been commonplace.

While the media once colluded in creating silence about this profound aspect of human experience, that is slowly changing. Films depicting gay lives or television shows that include gay or lesbian characters are now appearing with increasing frequency. In the movie *Philadelphia,* for example, celebrated Hollywood actor Tom Hanks played a gay character with AIDS and won an Oscar for his role—the ultimate public acclaim. But because there are so few gay films or films with gay characters, any film that does get produced has far too many expectations riding on it. In a way, we want our images to be perfect since they are so rare. Hence we become hypercritical of gay images that reach the mainstream.

When gay themes do become the focus of visual artistic expression, they are invariably laid open to charges of obscenity and pornography. The controversy surrounding exhibits of Robert Mapplethorpe's photography several years ago is a case in point. More recently, the lesbian kiss on *Roseanne* and PBS's airing of *Tales of the City* ignited national controversy. People killing one another remains a staple of movies and TV, but two men or two women simply kissing or expressing affection is seen as abhorrent and subject to censorship.

Gays and lesbians are certainly more visible now—in all the media. But in spite of our increased visibility, we are still stigmatized. The source of our difference, our sexuality, is *still* not openly discussed, *still* considered unnatural and shameful. Yes, we're visible at the March on Washington or in an IKEA ad, but we're not seen talking about our emotional and sexual lives. By focusing on what's *not* talked about, and by revealing the hidden operation of shame, this book will enable us to create *whole* selves that we can present to the world and finally allow us to assume moral parity with heterosexuals.

Our religious institutions have been another source of stigma because organized religions have judged homosexuality to be against both God and nature. Organized Christian religion, in particular, has been a major source of shame and contempt for homosexuality. It is the Christian clergy who most often quote from both the New Testament and the Hebrew Bible, inveighing against homosexuality with frequent citations of Leviticus 18:22, commonly translated as "You shall not lie with a man as with a woman; it is an abomination." Yet such condemnations ignore the context and invariably fail to mention that the word used for "abomination" in this passage is elsewhere used to denounce men and women wearing each other's clothing and disobedience in sons.

Some biblical scholars believe that the prohibitions in Leviticus are warnings against practices associated with cult worship in societies surrounding ancient Israel and are thus not *inherently* abhorrent—but to be shunned because of their idolatrous association. There are still other interpretations of these injunctions, which demonstrates that no one knows exactly what they meant at the time, nor what their actual purpose was, nor what relevance they may have for us today.

From the perspective of theology, the homosexual has been invariably judged as a contaminant to be condemned, permanently distanced, and inexorably punished. Like the leper of years past, the homosexual will contaminate others who are healthy and pure. This is the ideology of group hatred, not of love and forgiveness. What has been the solution? Silence, so that the pollution of homosexuality remains buried, out of sight. If a religion doesn't denounce homosexuality, it usually denies its presence.

Closer to home, our educational system has also remained virtually silent on the subject of homosexuality, as though everyone were presumed heterosexual, save for this unfortunate, aberrant subset of the human species. But ten percent of the population—or even the five percent figure reported in certain recent surveys—is no small subset.[3] In a country of 250 million citizens, we're talking about 15 to 25 million people. When the topic is even broached within the educational system, gay people are perceived as "recruiting" others to their "deviant" lifestyle or of having a demonic "agenda." The fact of the matter is that gay and lesbian teenagers do exist, and they are at high risk for suicide and addiction because of self-hatred. So we cannot even educate our young people about what homosexuality is without bringing down the gavel of retribution. Given the volume of society's antigay rhetoric, it's no surprise that gay people have often been overwhelmed by silence.

How does that silence originate? Shame itself is the source. What cannot be openly expressed is perceived as too shameful to speak about. It is shame that bars the tongue from speaking. When parents either fail or refuse to speak openly about some subject, whether sexuality or a family secret, shame forges the chains of their silence. When a culture's media, churches and synagogues, as well as its schools all fail to engage in frank discourse about homosexuality, that deafening silence only strengthens and validates shame. Besides, how are we to express a perceived flaw openly? Hiding and covering yourself—not openness—are the natural responses to shame. Silence is simply the inevitable *aftermath* of hiding and, in turn, further confirms shame. The deep historical and cultural shame about homosexuality is the source of the widespread societal silence that has been governing gay experience and distorting gay life. That silence functions as a form of oppression, as Michael Denneny has described it.[4] When societal silence only reinforces shame, the circle of denial and shame becomes complete.

Even a much-quoted phrase used in connection with homosexuality bespeaks the close historical association between silence and shame: "It is the love that dare not speak its name." Consider what happened not too long ago when the director of the Jewish Book Fair in a major midwestern city was asked by a newspaper editor about the glaring lack of inclusion of new gay and lesbian Jewish authors. That person's response was telling: "It's not a problem we have to deal with."

So we have been a people without either a recorded or a recognized history, without even a visible presence as a cultural group (until quite recently), without the acknowledged language, traditions, and customs of a valued culture; for many years driven by necessity and oppression to meeting secretly, always living in dread of exposure, a people who have been kept invisible; a people who, when discovered, have been ridiculed, publicly humiliated, and actively repudiated, often threatened and beaten, even killed; a people who have been forced to live imprisoned by silence. Breaking that silence means emerging from the closet of shame. To proclaim oneself openly as gay is, above all else, to come out of shame—profoundly, to break the silence. This is why the term "coming out" is a shame metaphor.

But coming out only partially breaks the cultural hold of shame because we have been bombarded by negative cultural stereotypes, loathing, and hatred all our lives, an onslaught that has left its mark in the form of *internalized* shame. Fully coming out of shame requires something more than merely coming out to others. Many gays are out to their friends or at work; they feel happier than they ever have felt before; they have no shame —or so it may seem. Just as there is shame about shame, there is denial of shame. And that can prevent its recognition. Although gay men and lesbians may be out, their lives can still bear the signs of shame: silence in the family around being gay, a lack of political consciousness, compulsive or addictive behaviors, a life bleached of intimacy. We believe that only by examining shame can we change these aspects of gay identity. Shame can be so deeply buried, so rooted in our being, that we are blind to its presence in our lives. Internalized shame can completely capture us, yet we can still believe we have no shame. We have certainly never developed the words to describe that emotion, either to others or ourselves. That's what this book is partly about—learning a language for shame so that we can finally begin to see it.

Shame is the most disturbing emotion we ever experience directly about ourselves, for in the moment of shame we feel deeply divided from ourselves. Shame is like a wound made by an unseen hand, in response to defeat, failure, or rejection. At the same moment that we feel most disconnected, we long to embrace ourselves once more, to feel reunited. Shame divides us from ourselves, just as it divides us from others, and because we still yearn for reunion, shame is deeply disturbing.

This is a book about probing, understanding, counteracting, and healing shame for lesbians and gay men. We'll explore the sources of shame directly connected to being gay. We'll examine how shame becomes internalized, thereby crippling our identity and fomenting inner division and self-hatred. We'll explore homophobia in terms of shame, disgust, dissmell, and contempt—four critical emotions—whether directed at anyone suspected of being gay or instead turned inward against ourselves. Finally, in coming out of shame, our focus will be on strengthening self-esteem, creating a self-affirming identity, and securing intimacy.

Chapter One presents the main features of *shame theory* in its more general form in order to outline the framework that we'll be applying in subsequent chapters to the gay and lesbian experience. Here we'll focus on the nature of shame, what it is, and how it develops. We'll also explore shame in connection with identity, gender, and interpersonal relations.

Chapter Two applies this shame theory specifically to the lives and experiences of lesbians and gay men. We'll consider the unfolding historical context in which homosexuality has been viewed and then consider the various sources of gay shame. Here we'll consider homophobia in terms of the specific emotions at its heart. We'll also explore characteristic shame situations for lesbians and gay men.

Chapter Three examines how shame and identity can become inextricably interconnected for lesbians and gay men. Here we'll explore the nature of gay shame and how it arises in the lives of men and women. We'll also focus on the process of healing shame for lesbians and gay men, along with creating a self-affirming gay identity. Only by examining gay shame can we develop the necessary principles and strategies for securing gay pride.

Chapter Four explores affect, sex, and relationships for gay men and lesbians. All of our relationships are governed by emotion, and through examining the impact of different emotions, both our sexual and relationship patterns will become more visible and ultimately understandable. Sexuality itself is always under the sway of emotion, and we'll explore how to release sex from shame. We'll also look at how to match our individual needs and expectations with the reality of the person who interests us. Only then will the relationships we seek meet our needs. We'll also explore how to release intimacy while keeping shame's potential to a minimum.

Chapter Five focuses directly on the unique factors that come into play when two women or two men become partners. We'll explore how attitudes about emotion surface in couples and how to handle anger effectively; we'll also consider the question of sexual monogamy. Of utmost importance in creating committed relationships that endure is consciously matching expectations. When the two individuals' separate expectations of their relationship either collide or diverge, then their ability to sustain intimacy is in jeopardy. We'll look at how shame influences our expectations, both for our partners and for ourselves.

The Epilogue extends shame theory from the individual to the wider societal level. Here is where the pride-to-power transformation takes place. New models are emerging for gay life as we approach the close of the twentieth century, and we all need to participate actively and directly in creating those patterns. We are engaged in a profound process: reinventing ourselves.

As we proceed, we'll use the term "gay" to include both women's and men's experience when we are referring to both or when the particular example or issue includes both men's and women's same-sex experiences. But we'll also use the term "lesbian" when we refer specifically to women's experience and "gay men" when we address men's experience separately. We recognize the importance of not burying women's experience within the domain of men's experience, just as gay experience has been made invisible in the larger non-gay world. However, we feel there are times when using the term "gay" can legitimately include the experiences of both gay men and lesbians.

Because this book is our personal contribution to transforming gay and lesbian lives, let us tell you a little about who we are, and why and how we came to write this book. Gershen is a psychologist, psychotherapist, writer, and teacher; Lev is a writer and educator. Together we developed a psycho-educational curriculum, beginning more than ten years ago, which Gershen now teaches as an undergraduate psychology course at Michigan State University. We specifically designed that program to actively promote psychological health and self-esteem and coauthored two books based on the program, one for adults and the other for children.

Gershen is one of the early pioneers in the study of shame as it relates to personality, psychopathology, psychotherapy, gender, and culture and has been publishing articles and books on the subject since 1974. Lev's fiction has appeared since 1978 in many Jewish, gay, and non-gay publications and in a wide array of American and English anthologies. He has published a novel, an award-winning collection of stories, a book of literary criticism, a mystery, and an essay collection.

But beyond the professional scope of our work, there is a much deeper connection. This book is born of our firm conviction that loving and lasting relationships are attainable for gays, that shame, fear, and loathing about being gay—which we have both struggled with in our professional and personal lives—can be confronted and integrated. The journey out of shame, for us as for any individual, never occurs without struggle and pain. We must all discover two fundamental qualities in ourselves—the courage to suffer and the determination to endure—before we can *triumph* over shame.

The journey toward wholeness must first take us deeper into shame before bringing us out of shame—with pride reaffirmed, power restored, and hope for the future renewed. For Gershen, the vision that the two of us were brought together to create new models dissolved doubt and conflict. For Lev, it occurred with the awareness that there comes a time when love is stronger than fear and shame. These realizations did not eliminate further struggle—they transformed it.

CHAPTER ONE

A Sickness of the Soul

To be human is to be vulnerable to shame. Everyone has experienced shame in some form and to some degree. That's normal. And there are times when shame is even appropriate and necessary, though at other times it can be truly overwhelming. That's when shame has the potential to be crippling. While we have all known failure in our lives, the feeling of inferiority is not always conscious because of the denial of shame. In this culture, particularly, we learn to deny the existence of shame—so we fail to recognize shame for what it is. Think of all the ways shame can occur: being laughed at, mocked, or ridiculed; suffering the belittling scorn of a parent or the biting mockery of peers; enduring humiliation from a father or mother, an older sister or brother, a bully, or even a teacher at school; appearing foolish, clumsy, or stupid; feeling embarrassed, shy, or tormented by self-consciousness; criticizing or blaming yourself for a mistake; retreating from a challenge because going ahead would leave you feeling foolish or expose you to ridicule. Even if you don't remember any of these situations happening to you, you've probably seen them happen to others.

By its very nature, shame is both multidimensional and multilayered. It is first of all an individual phenomenon that everyone experiences. No one is immune to the sting of shame. But shame also occurs on much wider planes as well, most notably within the family and culture. Our family is where we first learn to hide, to disconnect from ourselves, where we first feel divided from others and alienated. The individual experience of shame is directly reproduced within every family, and each culture has its own distinctive sources of shame, particular targets for shaming, as well as prescribed remedies for returning from shame to honor.

Shame is a deeply disturbing human emotion that becomes triggered anew throughout the life cycle, from birth to death. Shame is by no means confined to just one time of life. During each successive, unfolding phase of development, from childhood and adolescence to adulthood and old age, there are distinctive sources of shame. It is ever-present in our lives, however masked it may be. This perplexing emotion is also passed from each generation to the next; the transfer is mediated directly by critical scenes of shame which become internalized through imagery but which then are reactivated and reenacted with others. Shame is therefore an intergenerational phenomenon of central importance, causing such conditions as physical and sexual abuse, which are recycled from generation to generation in the family, peer group, and society at large. Finally, shame invariably plays out between countries—making it an international problem of unrecognized significance. The mistrust and hatred observed between various ethnic groups and also between nations is always fueled and magnified by shame. This is as true today in the Balkans as it is in the Middle East, and wherever racial, ethnic, or religious tensions exist.[1]

Understanding the intricacies of shame will illuminate recurring ethnic violence on a wide societal plane, just as it will illuminate the cycle of abuse that plays out less conspicuously in the privacy of the family home. Each is governed by shame. We're not implying that shame by itself is the entire cause of violence, but rather that shame invariably fuels the recurring cycle of violence in ways that have gone unrecognized. We have also lacked a precise *language* for describing shame, one that accurately describes our inner experience, a language that will enable us to reveal shame everywhere it operates.

Where do we begin? Our perspective on shame is grounded in the seminal work of Silvan S. Tomkins, the pioneer and foremost theorist in the study of human emotion. He was the first to offer a comprehensive theory of the psychological role of each of the major emotions, and he did so with precision and detail. Beginning in 1955 and continuing until his death in

1991, Tomkins originated and expanded a startlingly new theory of the human being—as revolutionary in our day as when Copernicus theorized four hundred years ago that the planets actually revolve about the sun, not the other way around as previously supposed. Tomkins viewed people as governed by emotion or feeling rather than by sexuality and aggression as Freud had conceived half a century earlier. To this newly conceived dimension of human beings Tomkins gave the name *affect,* and we'll be using his terminology in this book. Tomkins's paradigm has also yielded essential tools for examining the realm of inner experience more precisely than ever before. Though complex at first acquaintance, Tomkins's theory is like a deeply veined mine that is rich in ultimate benefits if we persevere in probing each new layer.

Our main focus in this chapter is how shame impacts self-esteem, identity, and intimacy for women and men in general. Then we'll focus on lesbians and gays in the following chapters. First we'll briefly define shame; next we'll look at Tomkins's overall formulation more closely before exploring the dynamics of shame in greater depth.

DEFINING SHAME

To experience shame is to feel *seen* in a painfully diminished sense. Our eyes turn inward in the moment of shame, and suddenly we've become impaled under the magnifying gaze of our own eyes. Even when other people are present and watching, we are watching ourselves; but we actually mistake the watching eyes as belonging only to others. Exposure is what we feel in the instant shame strikes: our face burns hot, we blush, we lower our head or eyes, yearn to disappear, to escape all those watching eyes, to find cover. But we can never hide from ourselves, from those watching eyes *inside,* not entirely.

Exposure, the central characteristic of any shame experience, can be of two distinct forms: exposure to others *or* exposure only to ourselves. We will experience shame when we unexpectedly feel exposed before an audience of some kind, whether stumbling in a crowd, falling on the ice, becoming tongue-tied when introducing someone to a friend, or being criticized by a parent or supervisor in the presence of others. We will feel equally exposed in the moment of shame even in isolation, when no one else is present and the watching eyes belong only to ourselves—like the first time you masturbate, damage someone's borrowed property, or imagine injuring someone you love out of hurt and rage. We must distinguish the experience of shame on two levels—being seen by others and being seen by yourself—because they are typically confused. Many people therefore fail to realize that shame can be experienced when no one else is watching. This sudden, unexpected sense of exposure is inherent in the experience of shame: we stand revealed as lesser. Shame instantly calls attention to our face, heightening both self-awareness and visibility to others. That is why we immediately become so aware of our face in the moment of shame. We are unexpectedly visible when we wish most to disappear from sight. Caught like a deer in an automobile's headlights, we are frozen by our own inner gaze. This acute inner scrutiny, in turn, generates the torment of self-consciousness as a by-product of the heightened visibility created by shame.

> *I was in my high school's chorus, and during our last performance my senior year I went blank in the middle of my solo. I couldn't remember anything. The concert went on for another hour, and I felt trapped, like nobody in the auditorium was paying attention to anyone but me. I felt pinned down, barely able to open my mouth.*

Tomkins describes the shame experience in poignant terms that capture the felt experience of this deeply disturbing affect:

> If distress is the affect of suffering, shame is the affect of indignity, of defeat, of transgression, and of alienation. Though terror speaks to life and death and distress makes of the world a vale of tears, yet shame strikes deepest into the heart of man. While terror and distress hurt, they are wounds inflicted from outside which penetrate the smooth surface of the ego; but shame is felt as an inner torment, a sickness of the soul. It does not matter whether the humiliated one has been shamed by derisive laughter or whether he mocks himself. In either event he feels himself naked, defeated, alienated, lacking in dignity or worth.[2]

For Tomkins, shame is always tied to the loss of dignity and honor, and therefore to fallen pride. Shame is a disease of the spirit that is without parallel.

THE BUILDING BLOCKS OF PERSONALITY: AFFECT, SCENE, AND SCRIPT

Before we can understand the full impact of shame on lesbian and gay lives, we have to know how shame influences the development of personality, gender, and identity in more general terms. We need to examine the ways we collect and store experience within ourselves, for these processes give shape to the emerging self and to identity. Three fundamental concepts originally formulated by Tomkins will focus our discussion: *affect, scene,* and *script.*

Affects are the set of emotions that we all experience, regardless of culture, because we inherit them. Everything that happens to us becomes amplified by affect, causing us to care deeply about what happens. Of course, different affects do cause us to feel quite differently, but we *care* nonetheless—enough to do something. Thus, anger feels different from fear, and both feel different from excitement. Yet each motivates action. Conversely, even boredom is a consequence of affect—the absence of sufficient interest. If we don't feel enough interest in someone, then we aren't likely to pursue a relationship. Affect makes anything matter to us because we feel more urgently about it, whether it's an accomplishment, a disappointment, or a danger. Events become amplified in their urgency by affect, and these affective experiences then become stored in memory in the form of *scenes,* which is a more dynamic way of conceiving of memories. Scenes can also fuse directly together and when they become interconnected, they take on a life of their own, growing by magnification. *Scripts* arise next; these are the rules that govern scenes—the rules for predicting, interpreting, responding to, and controlling a magnified set of scenes.

Affect

Tomkins has identified nine innate affects and described them in terms of their corresponding facial responses.[3] The affects have been cross-culturally validated as well. People living in both Eastern and Western cultures, as well as in both literate and preliterate societies, display identical facial signs for each of the affects.[4] Since affects are experienced along a continuum from mild to intense, the name for most of these affects is designated by two terms that represent the range of intensity.

The three innate positive affects are Interest—Excitement, Enjoyment —Joy, and Surprise—Startle. Surprise—Startle is actually a *resetting affect;* it clears the way for important new information to be received. The six innate negative affects Tomkins identified are Distress—Anguish, Fear— Terror, Anger—Rage, Shame—Humiliation, Dissmell, and Disgust. (These last two lack a double name because Tomkins was never able to come up with a satisfactory one.) Conceived by Tomkins to be universal, these affects are the irreducible building blocks of all of our more complex emotional experiences. Each of the affects is displayed on the face in a characteristic pattern:

POSITIVE AFFECTS

Interest—Excitement	Eyebrows down, eyes track, look, listen
Enjoyment—Joy	Smile, lips widened up and out
Surprise—Startle	Eyebrows up, eye blink

NEGATIVE AFFECTS

Distress—Anguish	Cry, arched eyebrows, mouth down, tears, rhythmic sobbing
Fear—Terror	Eyes frozen open, pale, cold, sweaty, facial trembling, hair erect
Anger—Rage	Frown, clenched jaw, red face
Shame—Humiliation	Eyes down, head down
Dissmell	Upper lip raised
Disgust	Lower lip lowered and protruded

While Tomkins distinguishes the two classes of affects as positive and negative, the terms "positive" and "negative" are not judgments. Rather, they refer to differences in the feel and operation of these two classes of affects. First, positive affect feels rewarding and we are encouraged to maximize the experience—we want *more* of it. Negative affect, in contrast, feels punishing and we are encouraged to minimize the experience—we want *less* of it. Second, negative affect spirals more rapidly and can quickly overwhelm positive affect. That is why, for instance, one disappointment, even a relatively minor one, can completely overshadow the preceding hours or days of enjoyment or excitement, eclipsing your general happy mood.

> *I was having a perfect day. I got to work on time, finished a project sooner than I expected and my boss was really pleased, had lunch with an old college buddy I really missed. All of this good stuff was buzzing through my head on the drive home. I was so happy I wasn't paying attention to the speed limit and I got a ticket. I was furious and it felt like my day was a disaster.*

In reality, at times like this your day hasn't been ruined, and the good news or events haven't been entirely wiped out, yet it certainly *feels* that way, and the feeling can persist for hours or days. That's the power of negative affect: it casts a long shadow.

According to Tomkins, affect is the primary innate biological motivating mechanism, more urgent than the drives or even pain.[5] Tomkins was the first to distinguish the *affect system* from the *drive system*. The drive system is made up of universal physiological appetites, including such innate drives as hunger, thirst, sleep, warmth, oxygen, and sex. Related to the drives is the pain mechanism, which motivates action for the relief of pain. These constitute our biological requirements. In terms of gender socialization and shaming, the ones that are most important to examine are the sexual and hunger drives. Though we have not understood that even the drives become fused with various affects, the drives are more familiar to us than the affects. That's in part because our language is already more precise ("I am hungry"; "I need sleep") and the "solutions" more obvious.

Affect is primary over the drives because the drives actually require fusion with affect in order to function. Just as it powers decision, action, and cognition, affect powers the drives. Consider the sexual drive. When we're sexually excited, as we usually describe it, the *excitement* we're experiencing is not actually occurring in our genitals, even though specific bodily changes are happening there. We're excited because we're breathing hard in our chest, face, and nostrils. The excitement we experience during sex is an affect; it is no different from excitement at a political rally or football game.

"At the first sign of affect other than *excitement*, there is impotence and frigidity," Tomkins argues.[6] Thus, shame, dissmell, disgust, fear, or boredom will immediately disrupt the functioning of the sexual drive, ruining sexual pleasure.

> *Micky and I were having a great time in bed—at least I thought so. Then he said, "Can't you be more aggressive?" Instantly, I lost my hard-on and felt terrible. I just wanted to get out of bed and go home. Sex just wasn't appealing anymore.*

Our sexual pleasure can also be disrupted by feeling afraid of an interruption or being discovered by someone. The drive must borrow its power from the affects.

Two of the affects, dissmell and disgust, originated to protect the oxygen, thirst, and hunger drives from noxious, poisonous substances. That was their evolutionary significance, their distinct survival value. Dissmell, the first line of defense, is the innate smell response to bad odors. The upper lip raises on both sides of the face and the face pulls back from whatever smells so foul. Watch parents' faces when they are changing their infant's dirty diapers. Watch children who are three or four years old walk up to each other and say, "Stinky" or "Smelly." In disgust, the lower lip protrudes and the face spits out whatever tastes bad. As an early warning response, dissmell reduces or counteracts smelling, thereby protecting the oxygen drive from toxic odors, and the next level of response, disgust, comes into play when something foul is taken into the mouth. If something toxic has been swallowed, disgust produces nausea and vomiting, protecting the hunger and thirst drives.

But dissmell and disgust are no longer limited to these functions, though that was why they first evolved. We no longer have these affective responses only to "substances" we smell, taste, or ingest. Dissmell and disgust have been evolving from responses that specifically protected drives to motivating affects that communicate feelings of rejection both to others and to ourselves. We can pull back in distancing dissmell or spit out in disgust from many things: other people we consider smelly or dirty, greasy food, movies that are foul, even "dirty" thoughts or feelings. When artistic creations trigger intense dissmell, like Robert Mapplethorpe's controversial photograph exhibit did for many people, then we respond to them like rotten eggs. We want to permanently distance them, reject them utterly. That is the affective source of judgments against pornography.

> *When I came out to her, my sister was really supportive and even curious. She didn't know anybody who was gay and had lots of questions. I lent her books I thought would help her understand what it was like for me to be attracted to men and not women. Everything went fine until she talked me into letting her look at one of my jack-off magazines. It was a real mistake because she came storming out of her room, saying, "This is so gross! How can you look at it!"*

Like the primary colors, the innate affects are the building blocks for all of our more complex emotions such as compassion, love, and ecstasy (positive), or jealousy, envy, and hatred (negative). Depression, which is a continuing mood, is produced by the dual magnification of shame and distress over time; that is why in depression we feel both sad and worthless. The combination of these two affects, brought to peak intensity and extended together over time, results in the depressive mood. Contempt, another complex affect, is actually a learned blend of anger combined with dissmell; hence the sneer, which is produced by the lip raised on one side of the face. In contrast to the innate affects, only affect blends are learned. Jealousy is the result of shame tinged with anger in the particular context of an unwanted rival who has suddenly appeared. Envy further tinges jealousy with contempt. As these brief examples suggest, our emotional experience is the result of combinations or blends of the various innate affects which evolved originally because they had definite survival value.

While dissmell and disgust evolved to protect the oxygen, thirst, and hunger drives, anger and fear are emergency responses. Distress, less toxic than fear, signals suffering and motivates us to do something about the cause of our suffering. Excitement is the source of all passion, sexual and otherwise. If we didn't smile into each other's faces in mutual enjoyment, infants would never develop an emotional bond with their mothers and fathers. And if we did not lower our eyes and head in shame, we would never know that our social bonds had ruptured.

We *inherit* these innate affects; we do not learn them. Upon birth, the infant cries, displaying what Tomkins has labeled distress affect. The infant has not learned to appraise the world as something to be sad about, as Tomkins sees it; crying or distress affect is innately triggered by the sheer density of stimulation that bombards the infant at birth.[7] We no more learn to be afraid, to cry or to be startled, than we learn to feel pain or gasp for air.

Affects are correlated sets of responses, occurring in the face, glands, and muscles, which are first triggered in the brain where specific programs for each affect are stored. We are born already equipped to respond with these innately endowed affects. Affect can simultaneously capture the face, heart, and endocrine glands, though we experience affect primarily on our face and only secondarily in our body. The face actually leads the body in the experience of affect.[8] Think of the blush that often accompanies shame. The facial response is quicker, more immediate, than the slower-acting bodily responses. When we become aware of our facial responses we become aware of our affects, and the feedback we receive from those facial responses produces the distinctive feel of affect. Affect, in short, is primarily facial behavior.

But affect also has a distinct function: to amplify other responses. Affect first amplifies your awareness of whatever triggered the affect in the first place, forcing you to pay attention, to be immediately concerned, and to do something about it. Only affect makes you feel any urgency about a situation that confronts you. Fear, for instance, makes anything dangerous a matter of utmost concern to you, just as enjoyment both relaxes and quiets you.

Something always first triggers an affect: a rapidly approaching automobile will trigger terror if you're crossing a street, while someone unexpectedly stepping hard on your toe triggers anger, and a lover's caress triggers enjoyment. In terror, your hair stands on end and you sweat. In anger, your face frowns and reddens as your blood pressure rises. In enjoyment, your blood vessels dilate and your face becomes pleasantly warm as you smile. These various affect receptors are what enable you to experience affect.

Because affect amplifies and extends both the duration and the impact of whatever triggers it, affect will either make good things better or bad things worse. A pistol shot, for example, is a triggering event that starts and ends abruptly—with a bang. The pistol shot actually triggers the startle affect, and this affect now "mimics the pistol shot by being equally sudden in onset, brief in duration, and equally sudden in decay."[9] The affect of startle is *analogous* to the pistol shot in how it responds over time. The startle response first triggered by the pistol shot now makes the prior bang actually feel even more disturbing. Moreover, the startle response exaggerates any additional responses that follow it, whether thoughts or actions, like jumping up and running to look. The startle response makes both the pistol shot and our actions feel more alarming. In the absence of a startle, there is simply no alarm.

In exactly this way, affect joins together its own activator and the response that follows. Affect amplifies both at once—activator and response—by *imprinting* each with the same amplification pattern. Why is this important? Because the imprinting process is the source of so many of our more complex experiences, particularly ones that come to have a life of their own. Phobias are one example. Any object, situation, or person can become imprinted with intense, enduring affect. When that affect is fear, shame, or a combination of the two, and avoidance becomes the preferred response, then the pattern is being set for the eventual emergence of a phobia. Sexuality is another example because it is so easily disturbed by negative affect as well as imprinted with affect of any kind. But sex can actually be heightened instead of disrupted by negative affect, depending on whether fear, for example, further amplifies excitement or interrupts it.

> *I really get off on sex in public—the riskier the better. Parks are great, but bathrooms or stairwells are the best because there's so much more chance of someone finding you. Even if I had the shades up and the lights on, a bedroom is a complete turn-off to me. It's just way too ordinary and dull.*

The range of sexual desires that we experience—from preferring sex after a candlelight dinner to preferring it in dangerous situations—is a direct result of how sex becomes imprinted with enjoyment, fear, or other affects and also how those particular affects join sex together with different triggers and responses.

The sequence of activating trigger, followed by affect, followed by response, results in these three events becoming interconnected in a *coassembly*. Such a connection arises simply from the overlap in time of the particular affect with whatever precedes and follows it.[10]

Our responses to affect are not only observable ones, like motor responses or actions. The responses evoked by affect also include memories and constructed thoughts, no less than physiological drives and even pain. We make this distinction between observable and unobservable responses because it is especially crucial in regard to shame, an affect that can result in primarily psychological crippling.

Consider the following examples, which illustrate the range of responses to affect on these different levels. When you feel excitement affect, your thoughts race, and if you're walking, your pace quickens. If it's in response to good news, you might give a shout and jump up and down. If you've made a personal or creative discovery, your mind will feel on fire with insight. Any response you have to excitement will amplify in exactly the same way—by accelerating quickly. If you experience fear instead of excitement, then the pace of your thoughts or actions is even faster. You're terrified, not excited—you've got to get away. Panic. Now the acceleration exerted by affect increases sharply. When you feel enjoyment affect, however, your pace slows in relaxed contentment, as do your thoughts. You slow down. Now the amplification pattern changes in the opposite direction, producing calm. Enjoyment is a relaxing, quieting response. But when you feel shame affect, your eyes and head lower and you retreat from your sense of heightened visibility; you long to cover yourself, to hide, to disappear from sight.

According to Tomkins, natural selection has favored distinct classes of affect for the preservation of life and for people. Tomkins argues that the "human being is equipped with innate affective responses which bias him to want to remain alive and to resist death, to want sexual experiences, to want to experience novelty and to resist boredom, to want to communicate, to be close to and in contact with others of his species and to resist the experience of head and face lowered in shame."[11]

Scene

Our affective experience becomes stored in memory in the form of specific *scenes*. The scene, according to Tomkins, is the basic element in life as it is lived—the psychic equivalent of a photographic slice of life, except that, unlike photographs, scenes are dynamic, not static. Playing contentedly on a sunny beach, winning a race, being slapped across the face, being laughed at, losing a game, being awarded a prize, breaking a window, and attending a funeral are all examples of distinct scenes that are created by the experience of affect about those particular events. A scene must include at least one affect and one object of that affect, which can be a person or the event itself. In order for any scene to be experienced instead of ignored, an event must be "amplified in its urgency by affect."[12] The affect we experience—whether enjoyment or excitement, fear or shame—makes us immediately aware of the event, causing us to notice it sharply. The affect then makes us care enough to do something, if only to pay even more attention to the event. That event has now become more urgent in our awareness, much as an injury is made urgent when we experience pain.

> *I was sitting in my room, just reading. Suddenly, the door opened and my father barged in, shouting, criticizing me for my lousy grades at school—blaming me over and over. He was livid— his face blazing red. First I was startled, wondering what the hell was wrong—then I just felt mortified and crushed into silence. I couldn't say a word. I couldn't look him in the face.*

If an event is intense enough, or lasts for long enough, that scene will be seared into memory. Given the tendency of negative affect to overwhelm positive, we typically remember moments of shame or fear longer than moments of joy.

The perception of any scene involves a separation of a particular event from surrounding events, just as figure and background become divided in awareness. To become separated as a scene, the event first must be amplified by sufficient affect, positive or negative. Only then does a scene stand out from the stimuli surrounding it before and after, like a figure in bold relief. In this way, the scene becomes partitioned from the perceptual field and stored in memory.

Affect first imprints and amplifies individual scenes, but those unrelated scenes subsequently become interconnected with and magnified by other affect-laden scenes. This is the process that Tomkins refers to as *psychological magnification*.[13] Distinct scenes previously separated by time and place become fused into families of scenes that are now permanently interconnected. If you experience a series of unrelated fear scenes over a period of time, for example, there comes a point when those scenes actually grow together, fusing into one interconnected family of fear scenes. That's how a

27

phobia based on fear eventually develops and takes hold of a person. And the identical thing happens with any affect, shame included. Through this process of psychological magnification, scenes grow in their power to capture and dominate us. They take on a life of their own.

Script

These scenes next generate *scripts*. Scripts comprise rules for action, for cognition, and for decision. These are rules for predicting and interpreting scenes; for responding to scenes by escaping, avoiding, or celebrating them; and for controlling any magnified set of scenes. Whereas the scene is a happening perceived with a beginning and an end, the script encompasses our emerging rules for dealing with scenes. Consider the following examples. Just as the yearly birthday or anniversary rituals represent a celebratory script of an individual or a family, the chronic avoidance of a particularly dreaded scene represents a phobic script, as when people refuse to engage in public speaking or compete in sports. Holidays, even birthdays, can be both celebratory and dreaded—lots of fun, but lots of pain too.

It's weird—I always look forward to going home for the holidays because it's great seeing everybody again, but it's such a hassle too because I hate the arguments. I imagine talking with my Mom in the den, shooting some hoops with my Dad, playing Scrabble with my brother. But even though all that stuff happens, by the end of the visit, no one's talking to anyone else. We've all ended up pissed off at each other about something.

Scripts can operate on the individual or even family level as well as on the wider cultural plane. Gay Pride Day is an example of a celebratory script embraced by gay men and lesbians in the effort to increase visibility while transforming gay shame. Many nations have national celebratory scripts. The annual ritual of Independence Day observance in the United States, for example, represents a national script celebrating a particular event in our nation's history. The yearly commemoration is replete with marches, bands, fireworks displays, and often dramatic reenactments of historical events that further magnify this particular scene.

Initially, the scenes that are first stored in memory and that later become magnified determine exactly which scripts eventually arise. But once scripts take root, they determine which scenes we'll seek and which we'll avoid. In the case of phobias, for example, the phobic avoidance script first arises in response to a magnified set of fear or shame scenes but then becomes entrenched, increasingly dictating how the phobic person lives. By making us avoid situations that have not yet occurred, the phobic script actually limits the various kinds of future scenes we'll experience.

Similarly, an equally entrenched celebratory script guarantees that any individual governed by such a script will continue to celebrate memorable events that have not yet happened, anniversaries of all kinds, future life transitions, and significant encounters or relationships.

I was raised really different than my girlfriend Karen was. In my family we were always told not to make a fuss about things, even birthdays. But anything was an excuse for Karen to buy flowers, balloons, bake a cake, go out for dinner. I was uncomfortable at first, but after a while I started getting into the mood, and now I really enjoy doing all of that with her.

In contrast to the phobic individual who scans present and future events for similarities to prior fear or shame scenes precisely to avoid them, the individual governed by a celebratory script is destined to seek out new scenes to celebrate.

Reactivation of Scenes

In addition to shaping our future scenes, scripts also reactivate old scenes. Three distinct processes interact in the initial construction and subsequent reactivation of scenes: *affect, imagery,* and *language.* Just as any affects present during the actual event become imprinted in the scene, both images and language also become embedded in the scene. Images include any people who were present, their facial expressions, or actions they performed, and language includes even spoken words, sounds, or smells. Consider again our example of the father barging into the room. The look on his face, his snarl, and everything he screamed became imprinted into the scene. Another example:

> *My first day in second grade I needed to go to the bathroom*
> *really bad, but my teacher was kind of mean, and I was too*
> *embarrassed to raise my hand. I tried to hold it in until recess, but*
> *I couldn't and I pissed in my pants. The other kids went berserk*
> *and I got teased all through second grade. After the summer kids*
> *forgot and I just blocked it from my mind.*

Years later, when a scene like that finally returns to full consciousness, it may come with the distinctive smell of urine that was embedded in the original scene.

In this way, affectively charged events become stored in memory in the form of discrete scenes, and these scenes also comprise important visual, auditory, and kinesthetic features. In most cases, the scene itself recedes from our full conscious awareness, increasingly operating at the periphery of consciousness. To illustrate: an adolescent girl is talking to her mother about her closest friend when her older brother walks past, behind her, and in a singsong fashion begins mocking her, "You have a girlfriend, you have a girlfriend, you have a *girlfriend!*" In the instant the teasing occurs, the young girl is paralyzed. As an adult, whenever she sees an interesting woman whom she'd like to approach, she immediately begins to hear the sound of mocking laughter inside of her—and she freezes, unable to approach. She has no memory of the prior scene because it has disappeared beneath the surface of awareness. The sound of mocking laughter is the trace of the scene that is conscious, but the scene itself has slipped out of awareness.

Scenes are reactivated by the occurrence of new situations that are sufficiently similar to those original scenes, but also different from them in one or more important ways. If instead of containing critical differences, the new situations were always exactly identical to the original scenes, then their reactivation and further magnification would simply not occur. The sheer repetition of exactly similar scenes would cause them to weaken, not magnify. The pistol shot is a case in point; after the third or fourth shot rings out, the startle response simply decreases, reduced to just a trace. We get accustomed to it. The identical process would happen if the very same scene were repeated over and over with absolutely no change. It is repetition with a *difference* that is decisive in Tomkins's view.[14] When old scenes are reactivated silently just by their similarity to new situations, what happens is like a "real" déjà vu. We simultaneously relive the old scene right along with the present situation that prompted its return.

Language is another way we reactivate old scenes and reproduce the feelings originally experienced in those scenes. We can synthesize new repetitions of old scenes through language, as when we say the identical phrases to ourselves now that others said to us before. If your mother or father, for instance, said "You never do anything right" over and over to you as a child, then when you're an adult you're apt to say the identical phrase to yourself, typically in very much the same kind of circumstance. Your parent's phrase became embedded in the original scene, and by repeating that phrase to yourself as an adult you are actually reactivating that scene in the present.

When reactivated through either mode—sufficiently similar scenes or language—an old scene intrudes directly into present consciousness, usually with little or no awareness that it's happening. Then we relive that scene, in the present, with all the force of its original affect. Scenes invade consciousness and transport us completely inside them like emotional tornadoes. What we more typically think of as memories are also scenes, but ones in which the affect has been at least partially digested and the scene integrated, making it tolerable to consciousness. Memories are conscious; scenes remain on the edge of awareness.

For many people, only the language component of the scene remains available to conscious awareness. These individuals typically experience an *inner voice,* which is the scene's conscious residue, the language or auditory component of the scene. The inner voice that some people experience in this way can be the actual voice of a particular person embedded in the original scene. Or it can be a particular word or phrase permanently attached to the scene that is repetitively spoken internally.

> *When I was growing up my mom was always calling me "Stupid" when I tried to help her in the kitchen or around the house. It seemed like no matter what I did, she'd say, "You're so stupid." And when I'd look down at the floor because I couldn't stand seeing her look at me that way, she'd say it again. When I grew up, the same thing happened even without my mother there. I'd say to myself, "You're stupid," whenever I made a mistake at work or was clumsy putting a meal together.*

That inner voice this woman must now live with once belonged to a particular face—her mother's—which looked angry, disgusted, and contemptuous while it was speaking. The voice she hears inside that calls her disparaging names, thereby reproducing shame, is the conscious remains of a scene operating beneath the surface of consciousness.

For individuals like this, therefore, only the language channel remains both open and connected. Their experience of scene reactivation is primarily auditory. Through this channel, which is mediated by the inner voice, the entire scene itself can be reactivated, and they can experience all the affect embedded in the scene without being fully aware of the scene itself.

People in a second group actually hear no inner voices but have full visual recall of the scene. Their images of earlier events can be crisp and vivid, but they lack any feeling when picturing those events. For these individuals the imagery channel remains open and connected, while the affect and language channels are blocked. These people are able to vividly recall and describe, often in precise detail, even the most traumatic or shaming events without any affective experience connected to those events. Able to picture disturbing events they had previously experienced but without feeling disturbed in the present, they appear numb and affectless. When new repetitions of old scenes occur, generated by new situations sufficiently similar to them, their experience is equally bleached of affect.

Steve illustrates this form of scene reactivation. While he recently began to come to terms with being gay, he was also plagued by a set of abuse scenes from childhood. A male babysitter had molested him sexually. This did not *cause* his homosexuality, but it branded those scenes into memory. The way he coped was by disconnecting himself from his feelings. He still remembers the scenes in detail, and whenever he becomes sexual with another man, the old abuse scene returns. During sex with a lover, the image of his old babysitter's face suddenly reappears and is superimposed over the face of the man he is with—startling him and disrupting sex.

A third group of people don't hear inner voices and don't experience visual images, yet these people become overwhelmed by intense affect often for no apparent reason. For them, the process of scene reactivation is essentially silent because the language and imagery channels have both been disconnected. Any new situation sufficiently similar to an old scene can prompt its immediate reactivation and return. When that occurs, these people hear no inner voice and have no visual recall of the old scene, but the affect embedded in the scene forcefully intrudes, as if these individuals had been swept away by affect storms.

Linda's situation is an example of this particular form of scene reactivation. She is in a mutually satisfying relationship with her lover, Sandra. Whenever Sandra behaves in ways that are sufficiently similar to how her mother behaved to her when she was a child, Linda reacts by feeling criticized or judged. No specific scenes come back to her, no visual images of early interactions with her mother—just the feelings return.

> *I can't believe how pissed off I get when Sandra tries to be helpful. I know she means well—but I always get defensive and hostile. Like last weekend when I was trying to do our taxes and she kept hovering at my desk and making suggestions. I just felt like pushing her away and I didn't know why.*

Psychological health depends on the conscious recovery of scenes and the *complete* reconnection of all three channels—affect, imagery, and language—by which scenes become reactivated. In furthering this objective, it is necessary to utilize whatever channel initially remains connected or open for each of us, thereby gradually working toward reconnecting the blocked channels.

OUR BASIC HUMAN MOTIVES

What are the primary human motives? The essence of all of motivation lies in the answer to a single question: What do human beings *want?*

Extending Tomkins's formulation of the affect system, we conceive of the human being as governed by four distinct yet interrelated sets of motives or systems of motivation: *affects, physiological drives, interpersonal needs,* and *future purposes.* These four classes of motivators actually govern all of our thoughts and actions, but affect is still primary because the remaining systems require fusion with affect.

Interpersonal Need System

We have already considered the affect system and drive system as motivators. A third important motivational system is the interpersonal need system. In our earlier work we have identified seven basic interpersonal needs: for relationship, touching/holding, identification, differentiation, nurturing others, affirmation, and power.[15]

The *need for relationship* is a need to be in relationship with anyone significant to us, beginning with our parents and extending to siblings, peers, and teachers. It is the need to feel wanted and special—a need to feel convinced we are loved as a separate person—and therefore is the most basic need of all. The evolving bond between child and parent (and between adults) must be genuinely desired, expressed in word and action, and also lived out consistently over time. These conditions create secure relationships.

The *need for touching/holding* is a need for tactile touch that we experience in infancy and throughout our lives. At certain times touching is our way of expressing affection. At other times it is a need for security holding, particularly in response to distress or shame. On these occasions, holding communicates protection and safety—the basis for trust. Physical contact in the form of touching or holding, while pleasurable, is *not* inherently sexual.

The *need for identification* is a need for fusion or merging. To identify is to feel *one* with another person. One of the earliest identification scenes involves infant and parent smiling into each other's faces during feeding, but they are also gazing deeply into each other's eyes for an extended period of time, well past the point that hunger has been satisfied. They are locked in a facial embrace. We first experience fusion through gazing directly into one another's eyes—mutual facial gazing. Later, we identify with anyone whom we admire sufficiently, even groups and eventually causes. Identification is the source of belonging and connectedness, through which loyalties and allegiances evolve.

Balancing this need is the *need for differentiation,* a need to define ourselves as different from others with whom we've previously identified. First we identify and then we differentiate. This is also a need for separateness from others, for independence and autonomy, and for mastery over our own lives. We actually develop into distinctly separate and different individuals, each possessing a unique self, through the operation of this need. The needs for identification and differentiation in particular shape identity.

The *need to nurture* is a need to give to others, to offer comfort or aid, express affection, and offer service, gifts, even love. Young children need to give to their parents, just as they need to be taken care of. Our need to nurture others is as fundamental as our needs to merge with others and to separate from them. All of altruism begins in this basic human need.

The *need for affirmation* is a need for valuing, recognition, and admiration from others. This is a need to feel affirmed as a person. When a child is admired by a parent, that child feels affirmed inside. To be admired by another is to be gazed at with deepening enjoyment, to be openly smiled upon. Admiration mirrors back to us our own joy. Just as children need to be singled out and openly valued, so do adults. Thus the need to be openly admired by others extends from parents and older siblings to peers and teachers. As adults, we seek out mentors who can affirm us.

The *need for power* is fundamentally a need for inner control over our own lives. A sense of inner control is the felt experience of power. This is a need to predict and control events in our lives, in our immediate surroundings, and thereby experience inner control. We need to be able to influence our environment and other people, to feel consulted, to have an impact, to feel heard. Whenever we are able to see choices or make choices in any situation confronting us, we experience a measure of power over that situation. This need is not inherently for power over others, but for power *in relation to* others, that is, equal power. Any life event that thwarts our ability to predict and control, to make choices, robs us of inner control and triggers powerlessness.

We conceive of these seven primary interpersonal needs as innate and universal, just like the affects and drives. Having those needs responded to in our family relationships is necessary for the optimal development of all individuals. To argue for inclusion of an innate factor in how we formulate these interpersonal needs does not preclude the importance of how different cultures shape their expression. The identical point, for example, can be made about affect: the innate affects are inherited in the form of specific programs stored in the brain that control each of the affects along with their corresponding, uniform facial expressions, yet each culture *socializes* the *expression* of affect in a distinctive fashion through that culture's particular affect display rules.[16] Those affects that are approved for display in various social contexts are indeed culturally determined and vary from culture to culture.

Similarly, we conceive the interpersonal needs to be equally innate and universal, as biologically given, but culture certainly places an equally distinctive stamp on their expression as well. The power of particular cultures, such as Asian, French, or Native American, to regulate expressions of mutual facial gazing (need for identification) or expressions of physical contact (need for touching and holding) between their members does *not* mean that there is no innate dimension to what is being regulated. Likewise, the physiologically based drives are also considered biologically given and unequivocally inherited. Thus, the sexual drive, amplified as it must be by excitement affect in order for sexual pleasure to occur, is nevertheless open to great variation in when, how, and with whom it becomes expressed—largely the result of how different cultures shape its expression.

The affects, drives, and interpersonal needs are distinct systems of motivation that embody both innate and learned components. Each is biologically endowed as well as culturally patterned, with neither precluding the other. The fundamental question concerning the nature and origin of any of the basic human motives, sexual orientation included, can only be framed meaningfully in terms of *how* nature and nurture interact, rather than *if*. Neither biology nor culture may be excluded in the search for knowledge.

Purpose System

The fourth and final motive is the *purpose system*, which comprises those deeply compelling, enduring scenes we first imagine in the future with ever-deepening enjoyment and excitement. All of us operate with images in the mind of things that aren't actually present to our senses. As children, we conjure up images of ourselves in the distant future, enacting specific parts or roles in our imagination that we envision ourselves someday actually living out.

> *I've always felt so hemmed in by my work, by where I live, by pretty much everything. It's like I never have enough time to be by myself, to reflect. What I dream about all the time is finally escaping this dreary life and sailing all the way around the world*

*in a boat I built by myself. I'd finally have the chance to discover
who I really am and feel free.*

Every individual eventually develops a set of future scenes that function as guiding purposes, giving meaning and direction to life. Dreams are
always conceived in imagination, and we are instantly transported forward
in time—to a scene in an imagined future. In effect, we are the heroes of our
own dreams. But we are also the script writers and directors of our dreams:
through imagination we envision ourselves in the future, inventing parts in
our mind that we long to play in reality. Then we try to make these scenes
happen, to command them into being. In this way, we are always reinventing ourselves.

While such a system of purposes is innate in human beings, the purpose system is quite variable across individuals because the *particular* future
scenes of purpose are not innate. They vary from person to person and are
also partly determined by the culture in which we live. For example, marriage and children have been compelling dreams guiding many people living
in different cultures over a span of centuries. As one instance of a particular
future purpose, however, marriage and children are historically and culturally determined desires. Even though they are widely shared, such specific
dreams are not innate in the same way that specific affects, drives, and
interpersonal needs are innate.

The range of possible options for living that are available to any individual is indeed a function of culture, which presents a predefined, socially
approved, and therefore limited set of possibilities. But each individual's
own imagination produces an expanded set of received alternatives for living. Where culture may be constricting, imagination can set us free; but the
dynamics of shame play out even as imagination invents new possibilities
and new relational forms. This fluidity and great variability in the spectrum
of our future purposes allows certain individuals to conceive of living life
radically differently from others—with another man or with another
woman.

*I was married for ten years, and had a little girl, a home, and
a good job. Everyone knew me in our town. But I always sensed I
was attracted to other women, and sometimes I even did things
with them—secretly. I was terrified of being found out and I al-*

ways promised myself I'd never do it again. God, how I hated myself. But what was I supposed to do? The only life I ever dreamt of was getting married and raising a family. That's how I grew up. But then I met Jeannette—and everything changed. It's like I finally felt free inside. For the very first time in my life, I could picture living with another woman.

Such a startlingly new vision of life, though culturally disallowed, is constructed directly in imagination and desire and fueled by the interplay of specific affects, drives, and interpersonal needs. Those affects, drives, and needs that make up our loving and erotic desires can be directed either toward our own sex, the other sex, or both sexes. As a central human motive, sexual orientation can become a profound source of shame, especially when it encompasses homosexuality.

THE IMPACT OF SHAME

The principal effects of shame on the self are *hiding, paralysis,* and a feeling of being *transparent.* The urge to hide and disappear from view immediately follows shame because we desperately want to reduce that agonizing scrutiny. All hiding behavior therefore originates in the necessity of "covering" the self. A second important effect of exposure is experiential paralysis: speech is silenced, movement is interrupted, the self becomes frozen.

I was about to give a prepared talk to this group and right before starting, I stumbled in front of everybody present. I looked around, trying to compose myself, but my mind went blank. I felt stared at, pierced by all those eyes. I couldn't think, not one word came to mind. Then I started stuttering. I felt dumb, such a fool. I wanted to flee—but I couldn't even move.

Even our thoughts and feelings can become erased by the sense of exposure inherent to intense shame, sometimes culminating in the eventual repression of whatever has become associated with shame. The final key effect of exposure is to leave us feeling *as if* we were transparent. Because we feel painfully revealed in the moment of shame, it feels as if other people can see inside of us and know our innermost being, our secret flaws. Shame therefore leaves us perpetually feeling like impostors, waiting to be found out and unmasked.

Shame is self-validating because in the moment of shame we believe we deserve to feel so bad. Equally important, the distinction between the subject and object of shame, a distinction present with all other affects, is experientially lost. "In contrast to all other affects," argues Tomkins, "shame is an experience of the self by the self."[17]

What Shame Looks Like

If the inner experience of shame is exposure, the outer view of shame is revealed by its characteristic facial signs: eyes down, head down, eyes averted to the side, and blushing. These universal facial signs signify the experience of shame for people in all cultures. They communicate shame both to the person who is feeling it and to anyone else who is present or watching.

Shame turns the attention of the self as well as of others directly to the face. The shame response of lowering the eyes or head is a direct consequence of this heightened facial and self visibility. But lowering your head or eyes also reduces that painful visibility, thereby producing the universal symbol of the head hung in shame. From this poignant image comes the historical equation of shame with "loss of face," the equivalent of dishonor in any culture that prizes "face." Shame always damages self-esteem, which is what we feel when we hold our heads upright.

Reactions to Shame

Shame is typically followed by various secondary reactions, most notably other affects that generate quickly and further mask shame from view. The three most frequent reactions are *fear, distress,* and *rage.* Fear, which often takes the form of anxiety, frequently functions in anticipation of further shame or additional encounters with shame. If we've been repeatedly shamed, then we'll become fearful of new shame encounters; we're often anticipating shame without knowing it when we feel anxious, nervous, or tense. Much that is ambiguously labeled anxiety or nervousness is on closer inspection shame. While fear may be present along with shame, these two affects are distinctly different in their impact on us.

Another affective reaction widely observed to follow shame is distress—the crying response. Both children and adults often respond secondarily to the awareness of shame by beginning to cry. The simple intensity of shame can trigger the crying response. In this case, what other people usually notice and respond to is the crying, and the shame underlying those tears goes unrecognized and unacknowledged.

Contributing to this quandary of recognition on all levels is the inevitable shame that surrounds even the *awareness* of shame, which has produced as strong a taboo as the one surrounding sexuality observed in Freud's day.

One of the most common secondary reactions to shame is rage, an inflation of the affect of anger. When the intensity of shame reaches the highest levels, rage is triggered. Rage serves a vital self-protective function: it shields the exposed self. At certain times, rage actively keeps everyone away, covering the self. We refuse further contact because rage has shut us in and others out. But at other times rage in response to shame may make us invite or seek direct contact with whoever has humiliated us—if for no other reason than to strike back. Thus, a young woman who has been repeatedly humiliated by her father will at certain times inwardly seethe in a hatred that bars everyone's approach, her father included. But this same woman may strike out at last, directly attacking whoever has deeply humiliated her or someone else if the humiliator is unreachable. Whether expressed openly or not, rage insulates the self against further shame. That is why if we feel worthless or inadequate as a parent, spouse, or lover, we often mask our deeper shame with surface rage.

Forms of Shame

Shame typically appears in a variety of forms that are universal and distinctive, but that have also created confusion about exactly what shame is. The principal forms of shame are discouragement, embarrassment, shyness, self-consciousness, inferiority, and guilt. The affect of shame is present in each one, along with certain additional features that together make the overall experience actually *feel* distinctly different. These experiences do not reflect different affects, but rather the same affect differently coassembled.[18]

As we mentioned earlier, *coassembly* is a process of combining additional factors along with the particular affect we are experiencing at the moment. It's analogous to the way we arrange and connect words to form a sentence. While the overall arrangement of various sentences will be different, the same verb may be present in each one. In exactly this fashion, we combine particular affects with their perceived activator and response, with whatever precedes or activates the affect along with whatever follows or reduces it. The total complex of affect, source, and response determines our overall experience—and we give that complex a distinctive name. Failure and transgression are different sources of shame, and combining each of these causes with the identical affect, shame, produces such diverse experiences as inferiority and guilt.

Thus these various emotional states that combine shame with different causes and consequences are, more precisely, *shame complexes.* They ought to be viewed as examples not of innate shame affect alone, but of various complexes in which shame is combined with different sources and responses.

Embarrassment is shame in front of an audience of some kind, while *shyness* is shame in the presence of strangers or at the thought of approaching a stranger. *Discouragement* is shame about temporary defeat and is not necessarily focused on the self as a whole but can be limited to specific actions, while *inferiority* is shame that is permanent and localized directly within the self. *Self-consciousness* is shame about performance, such as public speaking, athletics, or dancing, while *guilt* is shame about moral transgression. An ethical judgment of immorality must be added to shame in order to produce the distinctive feeling of guilt, which Tomkins therefore calls "immorality shame."[19]

The common distinction, still made by many, that guilt is about actions whereas shame is about the self is actually a mistaken one because shame can just as easily be about actions and guilt about the self. You can feel ashamed of a specific action like having stolen something, and you can also feel completely guilt-ridden as a person. Like shame, the feeling of guilt can infuse the self.

It's not immediately apparent, however, that shame and guilt do not differ in terms of affect per se. That's because our perception of inner experience is profoundly shaped by language and the culture-bound categories we are taught for describing ourselves both to ourselves and to others. But if we look more closely at presumed differences in the experience of these various affect complexes, then what has remained hidden from view and obscured by linguistic categories for describing the inner life can be brought into sharper focus.[20]

In American and Western European cultures, beginning largely in this century, we began to label such experiences of immorality shame with the term guilt—even though the core affect is still shame. Among Asian cultures, in contrast, an immorality is usually still referred to as shame, felt as shame by the transgressor, and described as shame to others. A transgression is also more apt to be labeled as shame among certain cultural groups living in contemporary American society, for example, Native Americans.

Just as there are cultural differences in how we are taught to label immorality shame, there are important historical differences as well. If we examine the literature of Western Europe as well as America in previous centuries, even continuing into the early decades of this century, we will discover infinitely more references to shame than to guilt—and specifically shame over immorality.[21]

The gradual infusion of Freudian thought into contemporary Western society early in this century undoubtedly played a role in shifting the focus away from shame to guilt. Freud viewed human beings "as the battleground for their imperious drives, which urge them on blindly to pleasure and violence, to be contained only be a repressive society and its representations within—the ego and the superego."[22] As Freud's view rooted itself more deeply in our culture, it hindered the recognition of affect while also orienting us more toward the study of guilt. When people are thought to be gripped by imperious drives that are in perpetual conflict with reality and society, shame is of little consequence.

In the classic American novel *The Scarlet Letter* by Nathaniel Hawthorne, Hester Prynne was forced to wear the letter *A*, boldly embroidered in scarlet on her bosom, thereby publicly branding herself an adulteress. She was shamed for her transgression. Not only was she required by Puritan justice to wear the scarlet letter, prominently displayed, but she was also required to stand upon the platform of the pillory before the assembled crowd. There she was displayed to the multitude, forced to endure a thousand unrelenting eyes. That is a shame scene of enormous power—and one specifically about immorality, transgression. Nowhere is guilt even mentioned. In fact, one of the townsfolk cries out, "This woman has brought shame upon us all, and ought to die."

Was Hester Prynne "guilty"? Was she blame-worthy? The word *guilt* once was used principally to refer to responsibility for wrongdoing—the determination of a particular individual's guilt or innocence. It is still used that way in criminal proceedings: the accused must be tried before a jury and found guilty or innocent of the crime. In this sense, Hester Prynne was guilty —of *committing* adultery. But the word guilt has since evolved from its original use to also refer to the actual inner experience *felt* by the transgressor. Using the same word—guilt—to name these two very different events masks the underlying experience of shame felt in connection with any transgression.

But there is even further ambiguity in how we commonly use the word *guilt.* Shame about immorality can additionally be combined with any of the other negative affects, thereby producing quite a range of ambiguously described "guilt complexes." A transgression usually results in immorality shame about the misdeed. But it can also produce immorality anger at the self in the form of punitive self-blame, immorality fear of retribution, immorality distress at having violated one's moral code, immorality disgust at the self for behaving so reprehensibly, or immorality contempt at the self for behaving so criminally. When combined with the ethical judgment of immorality, each of these affects actually produces a distinctly different guilt complex.

Guilt certainly feels quite different from other forms of shame. Guilt also usually "appears" more connected either to specific acts instead of the self as a whole or to the particular control of sexuality and aggression. Whenever we are judged to have harmed another, we will usually label what we experience as guilt—but only in Western cultures. Among Asian cultures, harming another is a source of shame and the inner experience is also labeled shame.

> *In China, we're taught obedience above everything else. I must obey my father—even when he beats me. Once he was so angry at me—I remember I was lying on the floor while he kicked me. But I could not resist. I had to obey—unless I thought he might kill me. Then, I could disobey him—but only to spare him the shame of killing me.*

What we ambiguously call guilt can be composed of any of the negative affects—fear, anger, distress, dissmell, disgust, contempt—either in addition to or instead of shame. The various additional affects that may be present in any particular instance of guilt also help determine whether the apparent focus of guilt is on specific actions or on the self as a whole. Connecting guilt to actions is more likely when other affects constitute the experience of guilt instead of shame. Immorality anger or contempt at the self, for example, actually shifts the apparent focus away from the self onto our actions, whereas shame reveals the self even when shame is *about* failed or immoral actions. Anger, disgust, and contempt always produce a heightened awareness of others instead of ourselves—so our actions loom before us.

When guilt is composed of shame and fear of retribution, or shame and distressing remorse, or shame and anger at the self, then the changing affect complex, in turn, alters the way "guilt" is actually perceived. If you harm someone you love, you might hang your head in immorality shame, or you might fear retribution, or you might feel deeply distressed with remorse, or you might accuse yourself in anger over and over, or you might reproach yourself viciously with contempt. Thus, there are many different kinds of guilt, and each is determined by a particular combination of affects. Depending on which affect blend is operating, the overall experience of resulting guilt is more likely to appear focused on discrete actions instead of on the self as a whole. But in every instance of guilt, regardless of its particular affect blend, there will always be an ethical judgment of transgression; that is its defining feature.

In addition to the various affect combinations that create different kinds of guilt, how children are socialized concerning their misdeeds also plays a role in determining their later perception of guilt. When children learn, for example, that specific actions can atone for their guilt, they are actually being taught to focus attention directly on actions. However, when children are not given such redemptive acts to perform, acts that also return them to parental favor, then the focus of attention is turned away from actions.

The apparent focus of shame on the self and guilt on actions also has to be reconsidered in the light of shame always beginning as partial and temporary. For all children the experience of shame is *initially* focused in their failed actions, as when a younger child cannot match an older sibling in skill or accomplishment. At that moment you hang your head in shame, even though your shame is about a temporary defeat. Shame therefore always grows from very specific and limited moments to an experience about the whole self.

There are still other, more or less ambiguous experiences that we are apt to describe to ourselves or to others which are equally rooted in shame: alienation, failure, worthlessness, feeling unlovable, and defectiveness. Though these appear to fall under the inferiority shame complex, they are generated by additional factors combined with shame, most notably various kinds of negative evaluations of ourselves in the context of our jobs or our personal relationships. While inferiority might capture the felt experience of shame for one person, feeling unlovable does so for another.

Shame and Privacy

The question of the forms in which the affect of shame appears brings us to one further manifestation. Shame is directly connected to privacy, modesty, and humility. By revealing us in the moment of exposure, shame violates privacy. Paradoxically, shame is also the foundation of privacy. The need for privacy and the urge to remain private are molded in the crucible of shame. That is particularly true, for example, with regard to nudity. Being naked alone is one thing, but being naked with others is another matter. Privacy, particularly about the body, takes root in late childhood, somewhere around eight years of age. At exactly this point, being naked with others becomes a source of shame. Self-consciousness about our bodies is the key. Ingrained attitudes about being seen naked are revealed when we're faced with a situation in which we have to be naked in the presence of other people, like taking showers in high school or even at the gym in adulthood. Comfort with nudity in the presence of others versus a need for complete privacy about the body is itself a shame dynamic.

Shame calls attention to the self within each individual; it's often unwanted attention, leaving us in a state of heightened self-awareness and exposure. Even when we may have initially wanted that attention, however ambivalently, shame will cause us to hang our head and lower our eyes, seeking cover. The urge to cover ourselves and, in so doing, to hide is deeply felt and universal in response to shame. In covering ourselves, we are drawing a curtain about us and shutting out the watching eyes that belong to other people. In effect, we create privacy, which can be defined as an absence of exposure and visibility.

The *right* to privacy is usually linked to things like telephones, mail, off-hours behavior, abortion, and sex. Telephone calls, particularly from strangers selling products or wanting donations, can feel like an unwanted intrusion, a violation of privacy. What we do on our own time, after hours, is our own affair. Similarly, what we do in the privacy of our own home is nobody's business but our own. The home is the bastion of privacy. Yet *Bowers v. Hardwick* proved that gays do not have a right to privacy in our own homes. In 1986, the U.S. Supreme Court ruled that the right to private, consensual behavior between adults does not extend to gays. In this case, Michael Hardwick was arrested when police entered his home and found him engaged in sex with another man.

We have been gripped in national debate about extending privacy to the body—to women in the case of reproductive rights and to gays and lesbians in the case of sexual rights. Privacy is the issue, but of course there are degrees of privacy, and any violation of privacy will therefore yield a comparable degree of shame. By recognizing an individual's right to privacy, we acknowledge respect for the power of shame.

Modesty and humility are additional, everyday forms of shame. When we're feeling modest, we are expressing a measure of shame. Is modesty an appropriate degree of shame? The issue is not a question of appropriate versus inappropriate. The issue is rather that modesty is a universal manifestation of shame, but one that we have not previously viewed as such. Modesty in public is even seen as a virtue. When modesty occurs in response to a compliment from a friend or stranger or is specifically about our own accomplishments, it is still an expression of shame. Modesty can be mild or intense, only occasional or pervasive. The same is true in the bedroom, where sexual modesty can be an endearing quality to some people, but seen as shameful by others.

Humility, long held to be a virtue, is itself an expression of shame, though not of crippling and debilitating shame. The humble person will bow the head in shame in the presence of others or before God. The experience of awe is itself formed of shame, as in the presence of great beauty or natural wonder. Our capacity for modesty and humility itself entirely depends on our willingness to surrender to shame, to hang our head, for we cannot be truly humble without it.

This, of course, brings us to the question of individuals who appear shameless—as though they had no shame or behaved in ways that shame others but feel none themselves. These are individuals who violate convention, manners, or social norms without chagrin. They act with evident ease in ways that put *us* to shame. Shamelessness can be a strategy that is learned in order to overcome shame that's been experienced to an inordinate degree. Like the person who is driven by fear but then attempts to master fear by behaving fearlessly, the shame-driven individual adopts a similar strategy: counter shame by being shameless.

> One of my cousins was always surprising me by how nothing seemed to embarrass him. He'd fail classes, get into car accidents, get caught shoplifting, but he was still the same cheerful guy. He'd come by our house uninvited and even if anyone else would have realized they were in the way, he was oblivious. Nothing worked—not even asking him to leave. And he was always borrowing stuff of mine like books or shirts without mentioning it. It's like he was following his own set of rules and there was no way you could make him feel bad if he did things that embarrassed you.

The seeming absence of shame may actually point to the powerful grip shame has upon a particular individual. Shamelessness is only apparent; we are biologically equipped to respond with shame to both innate and learned circumstances.

There have been changes at work within our culture that revolve directly about this whole question of shame and privacy. Examples include the paradoxical display of once private matters in very public situations, like television, and the increasing intrusion of the media into the private lives of individuals. Earlier we noted that shame itself has been under strict taboo in contemporary society, but that taboo has been gradually lifting over the last ten years. In saying this, we are not overlooking the fact that we have all witnessed the emergence of a unique phenomenon: "shame-athons" on television. Various daytime television talk shows now bring on a parade of shame, a veritable circus of shame performers. We're not minimizing the legitimate pain felt by individuals who, paradoxically, display their shame before the viewing public instead of withdrawing in privacy. They are, in effect, willingly inviting total strangers to intrude on their privacy—hardly the act of someone steeped in shame.

So how can we describe our culture as one in which shame is under taboo when that taboo appears inoperative in this particular context? Shame *is* under taboo because it is still shameful to announce it. These television shame fests—featuring addicts, survivors of abuse, perpetrators of abuse, prostitutes—are providing a kind of therapeutic experience for the masses, just as twelve-step groups do. The recovery movement is almost a mirror image of these television shame-athons in one important respect: each provides a validating experience for people who publicly expose their shame. But there is an important difference because there's often a sense of exploitation and spectacle when shame is seen on television rather than in the relative privacy of a room of people.

What exactly is being validated in both contexts? Shame, of course. Consider the recovery movement more closely. That movement, evolving in the early 1980s, has begun to lift this culture's long-standing taboo on shame. What the movement has given people is a language with which to name their shame, a ladder by which they can begin to pull themselves out of shame and out of hiding. By identifying yourself as a recovering alcoholic, recovering drug addict, recovering bulimic, recovering sex addict, and so on, you move out of hiding and gradually out of the prison of shame. The recovery movement certainly releases shame, but what it actually releases is the secondary shame surrounding such syndromes as alcoholism, addiction, bulimia, physical abuse, and sexual abuse. Continuing to identify yourself as a *recovering something* yields only an incomplete identity. Becoming a whole self means eventually transcending shame, and so a completely integrated identity can never be based on a perceived wound. Television has simply generated new variations on the theme—yielding a phalanx of individuals willing to expose their shame and promising validation to people on stage and off, who often live lives of desperation.

One further dimension of the cultural change at work in regard to shame and privacy concerns the news media. Beginning with Gary Hart in 1984, and seen more recently with Gennifer Flowers and Bill Clinton in 1992, the private lives of public figures, particularly politicians, have come under increasing surveillance by the press. This expanding intrusion into what was previously considered private and off limits has itself become a matter for public debate by members of the press and others. There is now growing recognition that a border has been crossed, that the dividing line between the private and public domains is no longer sure and firm, no longer even generally agreed upon.

This intrusion into the private, as though the simple fact of being a public figure robs one of the luxury of privacy that others enjoy, reveals a loss of connection with shame in the sphere of public life. Culture does not change consistently at all levels, however, but in fits and starts. Just as we can gain greater awareness of shame in certain spheres (on television, in the recovery movement), we can lose connection with it in others. Only when we bury shame within ourselves do we become equally unaware of or insensitive to shame experienced by others, particularly when shame is felt at our hands. Shame guards the boundary of privacy for a politician or celebrity, just as it does for any other individual. Publishing intimate details of the private lives of public figures robs them of their privacy. Whenever we cross that boundary and violate another's privacy, we inevitably expose them to shame. That can happen even unintentionally, but it can happen only when we have lost connection with shame itself.

Our society began to bury shame a century ago and, despite its recent appearance on television, we have lost connection to the downtrodden and disadvantaged, the feeble and sick, the hungry and homeless, the poor— anyone who suffers from shame. In every city in the nation, the homeless are increasing, intruding, invading our serenity. They are poignant reminders. But do we act? Only when sufficient shame becomes widely shared among us will it call us to remedy such outrages.

Without shame we can have neither privacy nor humility, but with too much shame we can have neither pride nor self-esteem. We must balance shame as if walking on a tightrope, so we can walk humbly with pride.

The Positive Significance of Shame

Why is shame so central? What value does it have? All of our affects evolved because they have evolutionary significance: they are necessary for survival. The affect of shame is essential to the development of conscience, dignity, identity, and intimacy. Shame is the principal source of conscience. In order to develop conscience, we must experience sufficient but appropriately graded doses of shame. A child who has transgressed must experience sufficient shame to feel bad, if it is to correct behavior, but not so much shame that conscience becomes overburdened. Conscience will misfire in response to either too little or too much shame.

When we teach children right from wrong, and thereby instill conscience, we invariably do so by shaming them. We insist that they hang their head in shame for having done something morally wrong—ideally, with a dose of shame graded according to both the age and offense of the child. Without appropriate doses of shame, there would be no conscience. Some cultural commentators are now advocating increased public shaming to suppress undesirable behavior like teenage pregnancy.[23] Their assumption is that somehow shame has completely disappeared from American life as a source of social regulation. And they seem fueled by anger and powerlessness over what they see as social breakdown—their intent is to use shame to control others.

Our sensitivity to human dignity and to violations of dignity is itself founded in shame. Without shame we would have no means of alerting one another to indignities suffered by individuals or groups. Shame is a call to action. When the plight of the Kurds in northern Iraq went unheeded after the Gulf War ended in 1991, the media denounced their treatment as shameful, humiliating. Action was taken, however belatedly. Closer to home, the way rape victims have typically been treated by police has been widely decried as shameful—as a second violation and further humiliation. This awareness has led to growing reforms in police and trial procedure.

Paradoxically, we come to know ourselves most intimately during encounters with shame, which makes this affect absolutely central to our emerging sense of identity. In failure, we know the agony of defeat. In rejection, we know the torment of feeling abandoned. These experiences of shame tax our ability to recover, to endure, but we see deeper into ourselves. We come to know ourselves differently than before, more completely. We have had an experience of ourselves *by* ourselves unlike any other. The development of identity is propelled by encounters with this alienating affect, provided that the shame we feel can be neutralized and counteracted.

In moderation—and only in moderation—shame is necessary, positive and adaptive, and healthy from the perspective of optimal development. It is certainly not inherently crippling. Countless people experience shyness, for example, which is shame in the presence of strangers, but only occasionally or rarely; and when it does recur, they're readily able to counteract or neutralize their shyness and then interact freely again. Other people are chronically shy to the point that encounters with strangers in almost any social setting become agonizing, impossible to tolerate. Shame poses difficulties for us only to the degree to which it becomes internalized and magnified; then it begins to capture and dominate us.

There is still a further reason for shame's evolutionary significance, and it concerns the development of the social bond. Human beings would not bond together emotionally if they did not smile into each other's face. Smiling, the facial expression of enjoyment affect, is the source of the social bond. That is true between infant and mother and equally true between strangers. But without the affect of shame, there would be nothing to alert us to ruptures in our relationships. In moderation, shame can even motivate us to restore those severed connections, to once again smile as we gaze deeply into each other's face and eyes. That is intimacy, and shame and intimacy go hand in hand.

Technology has added a new wrinkle, first with telephones and now with electronic mail, so that we are no longer entirely dependent on the visual presence of smiling for even the creation of a social bond—at least after childhood. Electronic communication simply challenges us to evolve comparable expressions of enjoyment, such as smiling faces added to electronic messages. But children do require visible smiling in order for any bond to develop, just as the deepest form of intimacy occurs when two individuals gaze into each other's eyes for an extended period of time.

SHAME AND IDENTITY

We have so far considered shame as an innate affect which has various critical effects upon the self, notably hiding, paralysis, and transparency. Once triggered, shame can be followed by any of several secondary reactions, the principal ones being fear, distress, and rage. Shame is overtly displayed on the face in characteristic ways—eyes down or averted, head down, blushing—and also manifests in the form of various shame complexes like discouragement, shyness, embarrassment, self-consciousness, inferiority, and guilt. Now we'll consider critical features of the developmental process by tracing the impact of shame on the growing individual.

Shame Amplifies Our Experience

As an innate affect, shame is activated and then passes, generally rather quickly. But we all show considerable variation in our actual tolerance for shame as well as in our ability to effectively counteract this deeply disturbing affect. Some of us are even likely to be born with a greater susceptibility to shame because shame is stronger in us relative to other affects, or because our threshold for activating shame is substantially lower.

> *It amazed me how different my sons were. If Jason was acting up at the dinner table, all I had to do was just fix him with a stare and he simmered right down. He looked so crushed. But Patrick was incredibly defiant from an early age. Giving him a disapproving stare didn't do a thing; he just stared right back. Even criticizing him to try to get him to stop wouldn't work; he'd mouth off at me. I finally had to use force before he'd behave— and then he became furious.*

If two different children were exposed to an identical shame experience, they would show marked differences in how well they tolerated shame and how quickly they recovered from it. While one child is easily shamed into stopping undesirable behavior, another child becomes even more oppositional. Some children actually react to insult with anger, not with shame at all. It simply takes more to shame certain people when shame is weaker in comparison to their other affects.

Conversely, for other individuals, fear or anger—or even excitement— may be stronger. Two brothers in a family, for example, might display very different affect patterns from birth. One brother is quick to feel anger and equally quick to feel excitement; when this child was first examined by the family pediatrician at the age of only *ten days,* the diagnosis was made: "This boy has a temper." When excitement generates in this boy, it does not abate—he is the kind of child who must be made to sit down every half hour on the day of his birthday or made to run around the house ten times in the evening to exhaust him before bed. For this boy, excitement simply runs wild.

The other brother, in contrast, readily reacts with fear and shame and has visibly done so from about a year of age, often at a heightened intensity. This brother is a fearful child, reacting with fear to any novel situation, not only to real dangers. He is the kind of child who, at the age of three or four, is intensely fearful of crossing the street even while holding his parent's hand whenever an automobile has been spotted as much as a block away. This second brother also reacts quickly with intense shame to a cross word, a disapproving look, not just to insult or disparagement. Such differences are widely observable among children. These varying tendencies to respond more with one affect than another, though initially the result of innate differences in affect intensity and threshold, can still be modified greatly through later experiences.

How Shame Is Triggered

There are both innate and learned activators of shame. We do not *learn* to respond with shame because that potential is present from birth. But we do learn numerous ways of *generating* shame.

Tomkins argues that shame is innately activated whenever we encounter barriers that prevent our continued expression of the positive affects, interest or enjoyment.[24] Whenever our excitement or joy is thwarted, we will naturally experience shame, however briefly. Disappointment of any kind therefore activates shame. This means that if you hope for or expect something to occur which does *not* occur, then your reduced interest or enjoyment itself spontaneously triggers shame. As Tomkins puts it, shame becomes possible whenever desire outruns fulfillment enough to reduce desire without completely destroying it.[25]

> *Last weekend I was doing some shopping and thought I saw my favorite niece. I was surprised because I didn't know she was back from school, and I shouted out, "Hi, Kath!" She turned around—and it was someone else. I was so embarrassed. I apologized profusely.*

When the happy expectation of being greeted by the familiar face of a friend turns suddenly to disappointment, excitement automatically turns to shame. Instantly, your head or eyes are lowered. That's not a learned reaction, but an innate one.

This all too familiar example is a reenactment in adulthood of a comparable scene from earliest childhood: the seven-month-old infant cries out for its mother after a nap and smiles, expecting its mother's smiling face to appear, but is greeted instead with the face of a stranger—prompting shame. This is not stranger anxiety or fear as it has previously been interpreted, but *stranger shame*. The infant, in fact, displays many of the usual signs of shame: lowering its eyes, covering them with its hands, or hiding its face— refusing contact. As soon as the infant learns to distinguish mother's face from the face of a stranger, which happens at approximately seven months of age, he or she is then forever vulnerable to shame. After the first experience in which a strange face unexpectedly evokes shame, the infant is quite likely to appear fearful as well, dreading further shame. But shame is the principal affect governing the scene, and fear is actually secondary.

Another way to think about how shame becomes triggered is the *interpersonal bridge* that forms between any two individuals in a relationship.[26] This bridge is the emotional bond that links infant and parent, two siblings, even two friends. That bond emerges out of shared experiences of trust. It is the mutuality of shared interest and openly expressed enjoyment for each other that creates this bridge. Whenever that interpersonal bridge becomes severed, however, shame is invariably activated because of the sudden barrier to further communion. When two friends have a falling out because of a serious misunderstanding, an affront, or betrayal of any kind, disappointment and anger will also be felt, along with sadness and even hurt. But anger and sadness are actually responses to shame in this instance; they follow quickly in the wake of shame. *Disappointment* is simply another name we give to certain experiences of shame that occur when our expectations have been dashed, just as *hurt* is the name we give to shame when we feel wounded inside.

Whenever we're in a relationship in which we need or expect something vital from the other person, any rupture of that interpersonal bridge will activate shame.

> *Weeks before Valentine's Day last year, I began looking for just the* right *gift for him. I felt so happy, so in love. All I could think about was how to celebrate us. He was coming over for dinner that evening and I had everything ready—flowers, candles, wine. I couldn't wait for him to arrive. But it all turned sour when*

*he got there! It was no big deal to him—he hadn't planned any-
thing to make this day special—to make me feel special to him. I
felt like he didn't care about me—even though I'd never told him
how important Valentine's Day was.*

Disparagement, blame, and criticism, however well intentioned, are
other actions that typically sever the interpersonal bridge. Breaking the interpersonal bridge in any significant relationship is the *interpersonal activator* of shame.

In the earliest childhood years, prior to language development, shame
is a wordless affective experience; only considerably later does it take on the
distinctive quality of negative self-evaluation, judging ourselves harshly.
When a preverbal child is shamed by a parent or sibling, the child's experience of shame is obviously wordless. All the child might display is lowering
the eyes or hanging the head. Even a five- or six-year-old child is not necessarily evaluating himself or herself during a shame experience—the child
may cringe inside in a wordless pang of shame, feeling momentarily frozen
in time, blank. Shame scenes are typically relived internally when we later
replay the scene over and over. But the experience can still be a wordless
one, depending on the unique aspects of any given encounter with shame.
Much later, self-judgment and self-condemnation are added to these gradually accumulating scenes of shame and may even be superimposed on previous shame experiences that were essentially wordless at the time they occurred.

The affect of shame actually precedes language or cognition and is
therefore primary over them. It is the later development of our finely honed
ability to use symbolic language that ultimately yields the capacity for evaluating ourselves negatively, but that is not the same thing as experiencing
acute shame in a particular situation. Language and affect remain distinctly
different, though definitely interacting, processes.

*I idolized her, but my older sister didn't pay that much atten-
tion to me when I was a little kid. So when she said she had tickets
for a Broadway show for us, I was incredibly excited. For weeks I
daydreamed about it, imagining every minute. Sometimes I
thought I would burst before the day ever got here. Then I heard
her telling our parents about the show, and that she was going*

with her best friend Judy. I felt horrible, like I was nobody, nothing.

In the initial moment of shame, our experience is essentially wordless, but our shame later deepens as it is relived. This is when language is added to shame. Everything we counted on has been exposed as wrong, a lie, inconsequential to the person we valued so much. Our shame, unspoken and unacknowledged, now grows like a barrier between the two of us.

Sources of Shame

Unique sources of shame exist at every stage of the life cycle. Young children desire to be like anyone they deeply admire, whether a parent, older sibling, or an older friend. But as children, we are always susceptible to shame precisely because we cannot match our elders in either skill or accomplishment. That failure guarantees a universal vulnerability to shame in the earliest years. A young girl who wishes to emulate her older sister will experience shame when she cannot equal her sister's athletic skill; she's simply too young. Childhood is not inherently more shameful than subsequent stages in life, but it is a time when our capacity to both tolerate shame and overcome its sources is most limited.

Adolescence is another epoch of particular vulnerability. The inevitable bodily changes experienced by the girl or boy caught in the grips of transformation into an adult call inescapable attention to the adolescent self, exposing it to view. The body's ancestral journey of transformation itself is unexpectedly a source of exposure.

Hitting adolescence in my family was a nightmare. When my older sister started to need a bra, Dad just wouldn't shut up about it. "You're only thirteen, you're not a real woman yet." And the more uncomfortable and upset she got, the more he seemed to like it. It wasn't any better for me as a boy. When my voice began changing, he called me "Squeaky." Mom just laughed when he made fun of us.

Adulthood has its own distinctive sources of shame, most notably failure either in work or in relationships. Any life event that thwarts our ability to predict and control, to experience power, renders us powerless; powerlessness, in turn, is a trigger of negative affect. We can respond to powerlessness with any negative affect or combination of negative affects. The condition of powerlessness itself is a source of shame throughout life, particularly so during the great portion of life we call adulthood.

In old age, we are far less able to care for ourselves, and all too painfully aware of bodily and sometimes mental decline. Thus, old age can return us to that state of powerlessness into which we are thrust at birth, thereby generating new shame.

Cultural Shame

An additional source of shame throughout the life cycle is the culture in which we live. Every culture has distinctive rules governing the expression of affect. Cultural scripts are the equivalent of cultural rules for governing various types of affect-laden scenes. One particular set of cultural scripts develops in response to shame scenes; these scripts function to control the experience of shame at the wider cultural level.

Different cultures organize shame differently; each culture has its own unique sources as well as specific targets of shame. What is acutely shameful in one culture is not necessarily so in another. While cultures vary in how openly shame operates—for example, Mediterranean cultures are organized openly around shame and honor—one culture does not necessarily shame more than another. Cultures also have quite different rules governing the return from shame to honor. In traditional Japanese culture, for example, the experience of shame itself is intergenerational: bringing shame upon yourself also means bringing shame upon your family as well as ancestors. Historically, the culturally prescribed route back to honor was *hara-kiri*, ritual suicide.

Previous attempts to classify cultures as either guilt or shame cultures are, from the perspective of affect theory, obsolete and misguided.[27] Why? Because shame is a dynamic observed in all cultures, and the distinction between shame and guilt is simply not important. The relevant distinctions concern each culture's unique sources of shame, targets of shame, and pre-scribed remedies for shame—in short, its cultural scripts.

Contemporary American culture generates three prominent cultural scripts: to compete for success, to be independent and self-sufficient, and to be popular and conform.[28] These three scripts function to prescribe certain culturally approved behaviors and to proscribe others that are negatively sanctioned. In response to the success script, failure is inherently shameful; failing at anything becomes a source of shame. In response to the independence and self-sufficiency script, needing becomes shameful. Emotional needing is a potent source of shame, but to need even assistance or help is seen by many people as a sign of inherent deficiency, of being flawed.

> *I dreaded taking family trips because my father wasn't a very good driver and my mother often got confused reading maps. We almost never arrived anywhere on time and without an argument. We'd usually get lost and Dad refused to turn into a gas station and ask for directions. No matter what my mother said, he just kept driving, his jaw set, his hands turning white on the steering wheel.*

Finally, in response to the popularity and conformity script, being either different or alone becomes shameful. To be less social than others is a mark of shame in any culture prizing popularity, just as being seen as differ-ent is shameful in a conformist culture.

These three cultural scripts influence the development of personality by using shame to negatively sanction undesirable behavior like failure, needing help, or being too different from others. These scripts are cultural rules for action, decision, and interpretation within particular life contexts. They shape the contours of identity within this culture by placing a distinctive American stamp upon personality. A similar analysis of other cultures, for example, Anglo-Saxon, Mediterranean, or Asian, would reveal an analo-gous set of cultural scripts.

Internalization of Shame

Shame becomes internalized through its interconnections with other affects, with interpersonal needs, with the physiological drives of sexuality and hunger, and with future-oriented scenes of purpose. That internalized linkage with shame is created through sufficient repetitions of shaming the expression of targeted affects, drives, and needs. When shame is in the process of being internalized, the various affects and needs that are shamed actually become *bound* by shame. This means that shame is now permanently linked with a particular affect or need, for example with anger or distress. These shame binds are the pathways along which shame becomes internalized.

What is the result of these various *shame binds?* The subsequent activation of shame-bound affects, drives, or needs will in turn spontaneously activate shame, thereby inhibiting their expression. Just *experiencing* these affects, drives, or needs becomes shameful. A boy who has been sufficiently shamed for crying will eventually spontaneously experience shame whenever sadness (distress affect) is activated, as when someone dies or a relationship fails. No one has to shame him for crying anymore because his crying now indirectly triggers shame: the two affects have become tightly bound. Similarly, a girl who has been repeatedly shamed for expressing anger or excitement will eventually experience shame spontaneously whenever either of those particular affects enters her awareness. Her internalized shame binds will control all expression of her anger and excitement.

Likewise, when the expression of interpersonal needs and drives is shamed, the result is two additional sets of shame binds. This is how the need for touching and holding, for example, comes under control in any culture. In many cultures the sexual drive is a primary target of shaming, causing sex to become bound by shame. Because shame is spontaneously triggered either by sexual acts, sexual feelings, or sexual thoughts, images, and fantasies, this particular shame bind results in the inhibition or disruption of sexuality.

Through the creation of these specific or multiple shame binds, shame exercises a powerful, indirect control over behavior, eventually constricting personality. Through these developing interconnections, shame binds accumulate and become the pathways along which shame actually develops, ultimately crystallizing a distinctive *shame profile* for each individual. Each person's shame profile comprises that individual's unique set of shame binds. For instance, some people are ashamed of their shyness, their lack of active participation in social settings. Others may feel shame about their own exuberance or volubility, feeling they talk too much. For the first group, the expression of shame—in the form of shyness—has itself been shamed. They may have been consistently mocked and criticized at home, in school, or by peers: *Why are you so quiet?* Such questions call excessive attention to this supposed "failing," generating even more shame. Such questions can also be judgmental, either in intent or impact, prompting shame. For the second group, in contrast, being excited and talkative might have been similarly stomped on by parents, teachers, or peers: *Aren't you ever quiet? Can't you stop talking so much?*

Scenes of Shame

Shame binds become stored in memory in the form of scenes. There are four distinct clusters of shame scenes that become organized around the different motives: *affect, drive, need,* and *purpose.* Each set of scenes governs the further expression of whatever had been previously bound by shame. These scenes next become directly fused, forming a tightly linked cluster of related scenes.

It is this critical interconnection of various and often unrelated shame scenes that defines the process of *psychological magnification.* Scenes organized around affect expression, like anger, fear, or distress, become fused with other scenes organized around interpersonal need expression, for example touching and holding or identification. Scenes organized around drive expression, whether sex or hunger, become fused with scenes governing either affect or need expression. The linkages with shame are now multiple. A boy, for example, who is repeatedly shamed for crying (distress affect) and for needing to be physically touched or held (interpersonal need) begins to fuse those two particular sets of scenes together with additional scenes of explicit shaming around masturbation (sex drive), thereby binding all of them securely together. While he experienced some of the scenes directly, he merely observed other scenes that happened to his sister or brother. We also construct scenes from images of things or events anticipated in the future.

Through this process of psychological magnification, a family of related scenes emerges. Dozens upon dozens of isolated shame events now become interconnected and permanently linked to one another. Any single event can now reactivate the entire family of scenes, and any single characteristic of even just one scene can prompt the reactivation of all scenes that have been interconnected.

> *I wish my parents hadn't named me Grace, because that name was a curse. I was a rambunctious little girl, but they were always reminding me that I was supposed to be just like my name —trying to force me into this mold. It didn't stop with playing rough with my friends out in the backyard. They hated it when I joined the girl's basketball team because it wasn't ladylike, and being good at it didn't make a difference. They'd also criticize me if I'd be yelling about a great school report, or cheering for my team at a soccer game, or even if I was too loud saying how much I liked my spaghetti!*

A girl consistently shamed for expressing excitement affect in such different ways may come to feel acutely ashamed of her body because all of her shame binds involve enjoying her physicality, whether performing well, eating, or engaging in sports. Later, simply having her body seen and openly appreciated by another woman can bring back her entire catalogue of shame scenes, however unrelated they had first been.

The experience of shame itself is thereby greatly magnified. In this way, events that occurred only once are relived over and over, with the resulting affect both deepened and extended over time. Upon each reliving, other scenes, even neutral ones, become added to the growing family of shame scenes, fused directly into the accumulating cluster. Similarly, entirely new affect is also added. We can actually generate completely fresh affect upon each subsequent review of a family of scenes. This new affect was not present during the original event or scene but was added afterward.

Imagine you've been deeply humiliated at the hands of a bully after school. At the time, all you experienced was shame and fear. Later, you relive that scene over and over, and upon each reliving, your shame becomes more deeply entrenched, inflamed. Your fear may diminish, but something entirely new appears that you had not felt during the actual scene: rage and, along with it, contempt for your humiliator. You fantasize revenge. Now this fresh affect about the scene ignites the rapid intrusion into consciousness of numerous prior shame scenes, occurring in vastly different contexts and at the hands of quite different people—your father, an older sister, even a teacher. All of these isolated scenes are now immediately fused into one single blaze of shame and rage and contempt. All those different humiliators now are one. And if seeking revenge captures control of you, then it can dictate the future course of your life.

Magnification entirely changes the resulting experience of shame. This affect becomes deepened, prolonged over time, and increasingly spread to many different people, events, and aspects of ourselves. The experience of shame is now total, not partial—and permanent, no longer temporary.

> *Lying in bed at night when I was fifteen, I felt trapped by my own memories, tied down and helpless, watching a parade of terrible things that happened to me. Like the ways my father always put me down, and kids in gym class made fun of me because I couldn't climb the rope, when my favorite teacher laughed at me because she said I was using words that were "too big" for my age and the whole class broke out laughing, when I was ganged up on behind the school and robbed. I couldn't stop the parade—the memories kept coming and coming, and they jumped out to catch me just when I was most relaxed and almost falling asleep. It made me sick and pissed me off that I was such a weakling, such a shmuck, that everyone made fun of me, and I couldn't even go to bed without feeling miserable. It even happened when I wasn't in bed. I'd be walking to the bus stop and I felt like people were staring at me, like my clothes were dirty or torn and I couldn't see it. They must've thought I was a jerk.*

Through magnification, a family of shame scenes begins to grow and gradually takes on a life of its own. After magnification, shame becomes something vastly different from an affect that merely amplifies our experience. With each new episode of magnification, shame progressively captures and begins to dominate our personality, growing like an emotional cancer within us.

Next, particular scripts arise to govern this growing family of shame scenes. They fall into two distinct classes: *defending scripts* and *self-shaming scripts.* Neither type of script eliminates shame; the first tries to avoid it, while the second reproduces it.

Defending Against Shame

Defending scripts are rules for responding to shame scenes that have not yet happened but that we anticipate. These scripts are not just future-oriented but externally directed. They aim at protection against shame largely at the hands of others. Some eight general scripts can be observed to protect us from encounters with shame: rage, contempt, striving for perfection, striving for power, transfer of blame, internal withdrawal, humor, and denial. They become expressed in unique and varied ways, with several scripts often functioning together.

Rage becomes directed against anyone who approaches. It insulates the self and creates a protective shield: *I hate you! Stay away from me!*

Contempt elevates us above others whom now we look down on as inferiors. Since contempt always partitions the superior from the inferior in any group, this affect blend is the source of conceit, arrogance, and superiority over others as well as of prejudice and discrimination: *I'm better than you are, and you're nothing. I can't be bothered with someone as low as you.*

The *striving for perfection* is essentially a strategy designed to erase every blemish of the self by excelling in an ever-widening circle of activities. Only becoming perfect in every way imaginable will protect you from shame: *No matter what I do, it's never good enough. I have to do better.*

The *striving for power* is a dominating strategy for avoiding shame by amassing power. Its aim is to capture absolute control, whenever and wherever possible: *It's going to be* my *way. I'm the one in charge.*

The *transfer of blame* recruits anger but directs it in an accusatory manner, fingering someone else for whatever mishap has occurred. This transfer of blame is on a deeper level a transfer of shame away from the self: *You did it—it's your fault. You should've known better. I had nothing to do with it.*

Internal withdrawal causes us to hide deeper inside in order to escape from shame. We become shut in as a person: *Quick—hide—cover up.*

Humor scripts reduce shame by recruiting enjoyment affect (smiling, laughter) to promote mutuality and communion: *That's your first mistake of the day—and you get three more!* When humor combines with contempt, however, then we have sarcasm, mockery, and teasing: *You think you're so smart? Clumsy's your middle name.*

Denial is the final strategy. If every attempt to escape from or avoid shame is defeated, the final defense is denial—it simply didn't happen, it doesn't exist: *I don't feel any shame. No way. I've never felt it.*

Self-Shaming Scripts

Self-shaming scripts are turned inward: they invade the self and become the means of reproducing shame from within. Three principal self-shaming scripts can be widely observed: *self-blame, comparison making,* and *self-contempt.* Each of these scripts is rooted in governing scenes of shame experienced earlier in life, usually at the hands of a parent.

A girl growing up in a blaming family will experience blame for mishaps and mistakes. The parent's angry accusation directed at the girl in turn generates shame within her. She will first learn to blame others when things go wrong, much as her parent does. But she will also internalize images of the blaming parent and later direct that same blaming activity inward against herself. Self-blame evolves directly from experiences with blaming parents or others who are significant to us. When we engage in this self-blaming script, we turn the accusatory finger of blame inward against ourselves: *I'm a jerk, I never do anything right. What a moron. Why didn't I see what was going to happen? It's all my fault—how could I do that! I should've known better!* By angrily accusing ourselves when things go wrong, we directly reproduce shame within ourselves. Listen to the things people say when they've goofed or blundered: their exclamations often reveal pervasive self-blame.

The comparison-making script develops and functions similarly. First parents compare us to our siblings and other kids. Then teachers compare us. Next our friends do it—comparing themselves to us and us to them. Comparison making always begins with the awareness of a difference between ourselves and someone else. Instead of valuing that difference, we feel obliged to stamp it out. The awareness of difference is immediately translated into a comparison of good versus bad, better versus worse, and so on. Once the comparison is made, we devalue ourselves. It can happen, for example, when we notice someone who's more popular than we are: *He has lots of friends; I hardly have any. What's wrong with me?* We can compare ourselves to others about every conceivable characteristic: size, strength, appearance, popularity, success, achievement, performance, status, or whatever else becomes salient to us. Invariably, what such comparison making yields is further shame.

Self-contempt is simply contempt turned inward against the self. Instead of feeling contempt for others—whom we look down upon, consider beneath us, and judge to be inferior—we now direct that same contempt inward. In this case, one part of the self becomes the judge and another part becomes the offender. The judging self becomes increasingly vicious and brutal toward the offending self: *You're so disgusting. You're ugly and fat, and filthy too. And you always need to cry on somebody's shoulder. Nobody could ever love such a weakling. You're too stupid to live—out of my sight! Everyone would be better off if you were dead.* In such moments of shame, part of us is judged abhorrent and worthless. No reprieve is possible, and no pardon.

When you think of contempt for yourself or others, picture a lynching. Certainly an extreme image, it nonetheless captures the essence of contempt: to simultaneously punish and permanently distance the offender, whether it's yourself or someone else.

Contempt is an affect blend that combines punitive anger with distancing dissmell. When we observe the face of a person expressing contempt, we notice two things at once: one side of the face looks angry while the other side of the face displays the upper lip raised in dissmell—producing the facial sneer that is so characteristic of contempt. The self-contempt script is simply one more means of reproducing shame. As such, self-contempt can become the source of enduring self-loathing and self-hatred.

Disowning of Self

The three self-shaming scripts are the principal means by which shame becomes entrenched within the personality. For the great majority of individuals, any one of these scripts or a combination of them eventually takes root. But not all people become shame-based in the same way or to the same degree. What makes shame all-consuming and crippling is the further magnification unleashed by the continuing operation of any of these self-shaming scripts.

A border is crossed when the increased level of magnification in turn initiates the process of *disowning*. One part of the self then begins to renounce other parts of the self. It is a much more active process of disavowal than denial is; disowning is an action performed by the contemptuous and blaming self against the shameful self. Now the shameful self must be permanently cast adrift, utterly disconnected. This is how the *needing* or *feeling* part of us becomes completely disowned. Similarly, the *child self* and *adolescent self*—prior phases everyone develops through—can become equally targeted for disowning and disconnection. Disowning results directly from the additional magnification produced by self-shaming scripts.

> *I can't stand it when I whine like a little kid. I just hate it. I feel so lousy that people are seeing me like this. I want to lock up that part of me in a steel box so it can never come out again.*

Splitting of the Self

Unfortunately, the process does not end there for everyone. While for many people only self-shaming scripts develop, for some the level of magnification jumps, initiating disowning. For others, this process of inner strife waged relentlessly against disowned parts of the self culminates in the actual *splitting of the self*. The whole self now fractures into two or more partial selves or even caricatures of a self. Splitting is the final stage of magnification, and contempt turned against the self, the most virulent of the self-shaming scripts, is the principal means by which splitting occurs.

Mary experienced so much shame whenever she felt any degree of need for others that she punished herself mercilessly. It began in childhood when her parents reacted with disgust when Mary was scared, lonesome, or needed their attention. She would repeat to herself night after night, "I will never need anyone ever again." That litany came to govern her life. As an adult, she showed the world a stiff and distant exterior to hide the messy, noisy, angry, and fearful little girl who still clamored for the love she had never received. Mary loathed that part of herself, and whenever she felt scared or needy, she hit herself or beat her head against a wall as if trying to drown out and destroy the insistent voice of her own hunger.

All pathological distortions have their origin in this magnification process. Childhood physical and sexual abuse, for example, are likely to rapidly propel anyone along this magnification continuum. Disowning and splitting also generate the greatest potential for psychic pain and for the most severe psychological disorders.

Shame-Based Identity

Identity is the conscious experience of the self. Identity is also a relational pattern: the active, living relationship that the self comes to have with the self. Just as the self becomes organized around scenes, identity becomes organized around scripts.

Self-shaming scripts eventually produce a *shame-based identity,* a way of being that deepens and spreads shame ever further. Our essential identity now becomes based on shame. Defending scripts alone do not create a shame-based identity; they are mainly avoidance or escape strategies and do not crystallize a shame-based identity until self-shaming scripts also evolve. A shame-based identity is a distinctive pattern of relating to oneself that continuously absorbs, maintains, and spreads shame. The essential core of who we are now is so completely infused with shame that the possibilities for reexperiencing shame become endless. Everything that happens to us is reinterpreted so that defeats, failures, and rejections don't have to be real, only *perceived* that way. Our inner self feels permanently flawed, and the ways we behave toward ourselves only reconfirm our defectiveness. We have become hopelessly mired in the quicksand of shame.

SHAME AND GENDER

Shame has historically functioned as the principal agent of social control by partitioning the acceptable from the unacceptable. Moreover, the experience of shame is also central to the process of gender socialization in any culture. The way in which shame influences the gender experience of women in contrast to men is through the different shaming patterns to which they are exposed. Different shame binds develop for men and for women. The affects and interpersonal needs, in particular, that are specifically targeted for shaming diverge sharply according to gender.

Gender Shaming Patterns

When the expression of certain affects, drives, interpersonal needs, or future scenes of purpose are targeted for shaming, they become bound by shame and suppressed. Whatever facets of our being become shamed are no longer felt as acceptable, either to others or to ourselves. The entire range of affects and interpersonal needs, for example, can from that point forward be partitioned into those we judge acceptable and those we don't. It is this profoundly important shaming process that determines how we actually feel about our affects and needs as well as which ones we accept, which we disavow. Affects, drives, interpersonal needs, and future purposes are differently shamed for women than they are for men, thereby producing the *appearance* of quite different psychologies, of different developmental paths. The differences often noted between men and women are like the differences observed between different cultures. Just as the affects are the same in people living in all cultures, while their *expression* is culturally determined, all of the affects are present in both men and women, but their expression is determined by gender shaming patterns.

Let's first look at how affect is socialized. The specific affects targeted for shaming differ for women and for men, but this pattern is likely to remain stable within a given culture at a particular historical period. When we look across different cultures, we'll likely find some variations in the pattern of targeted affects for each gender.

Expressions of two affects in particular, *anger* and *excitement,* have been traditionally shamed for women in America, whereas expressions of *fear, distress* (crying), and *shame* have received parallel shaming for American men. Through shaming from an early age, men are actively dissuaded from crying openly, being visibly afraid, and lowering their eyes or head in shame—which is why men experience these particular affects as a sign of weakness. What becomes particularly shameful and taboo for women to express, on the other hand, is anger. Angry women, like angry girls, are viewed pejoratively: *She's being irrational, hysterical.* Women are also shamed for expressing excitement, and it is this pernicious shaming that is the source of the cultural disparagement of the "tomboy"—the girl who openly expresses excitement or seeks out excitement-producing activities.

The expression of interpersonal needs has also been differently shamed for men and for women: *power* and *differentiation* needs are culturally shamed for women, while for men to acknowledge *touching/holding, identification,* and *affirmation* needs remains largely taboo. Women have been severely shamed into relinquishing their natural and rightful half of the power in relation to others, particularly men. The exercise of power by women directly invites shaming from men and the wider culture. Women are never supposed to assert their power or be powerful: the powerful woman is invariably disparaged as domineering.

Women's natural need to differentiate, to separate from others while placing their own needs ahead of others' needs, has been equally suppressed through widespread shaming.

> *Momma always told me that because I was a girl it was my duty, my privilege, to take care of the men in my life. It was my job to see they were happy, and if I neglected that I was being selfish and sinful. Every time I heard those two words from her I shuddered.*

From an early age, women are supposed to look after other people's feelings and needs, to nurture others first and foremost. For many women, being called selfish is a profound insult, a way to silence self-assertion. Related to their striving to separate and to assert their own needs over those of others is the parallel striving to gain mastery and competence. Together, these are twin expressions of the fundamental human need to define themselves as different from others, unique. For women, to be powerful is shameful, and to be different and separate from others is equally shameful.

The shaming pattern experienced by men is different, but no less pronounced. Expression of the natural interpersonal need for touching and holding has largely been denied to men because of its widespread association with shame. For men, the need to touch, and even more so the need to be held, have become poignantly bound by shame. Touching other men is almost always taboo. The shame about touching that men experience has an additional association with homosexuality; here is one way in which being gay becomes shameful.

Similarly, men have been shamed for expressing the need to identify, to merge or fuse with others, especially with other men. Identification is a universal human need that can be observed from birth onward among both females and males. Though identification is allowed in infancy and early childhood, it is the later experience of shame about continued facial gazing that begins to inhibit this important need and ultimately constricts and taboos its expression.

Men are also shamed for expressing the need for affirmation, to be openly valued, recognized, directly admired. Whenever boys invite admiration from others, they usually do so through their actions. They either show off or signal "Look at me." At that moment they open themselves to being shamed, in the family by father or older brothers or in the peer group by older boys.

Because of shaming, the only culturally acceptable avenue remaining open to men for expressing the three interpersonal needs is through adversarial contests. Wars, fights, and sports provide a culturally approved arena in which the open expression of these needs can occur without shame. When engaged in adversarial contests, men can touch each other and openly embrace. As players or spectators, men can also identify with each other and feel *one*, and they can directly admire one another. Even men watching a football game—whether in the stadium or on television—can slap, grab, and hug each other in triumph. Only as real or imagined adversaries locked in contest can men openly express these otherwise forbidden needs.

The result of such differential shaming on identity is striking: women are left to seek their identity through relatedness and identification, whereas men must continually seek their identity through power and differentiation. These are the principal avenues for each gender that remain free from shame. This pattern of differential shaming, while culture-specific, is nevertheless reasonably stable.

Recent conceptions of women's development, such as the work of Carol Gilligan,[29] have argued that there is a different developmental path for women than for men. When viewed from the perspective of affect theory, such differences in gender experience become readily attributable to gender shaming patterns. What is shaped in this way is affect and need expression.

The differential shaming that women receive in comparison to men, along with the resulting partitioning of affects and interpersonal needs along gender lines, produces the apparent differences in their development. The fact that women have been targeted for shaming specifically in connection with their power and differentiation needs, as well as anger and excitement affects, has contributed in turn to the gender shame that women have historically experienced. Such a pattern guarantees inferior status of the gender, regardless of what individual females accomplish.

SHAME AND INTERPERSONAL RELATIONS

Two distinct, additional scripts emerge in response to the different patterns of gender shaming experienced by women and by men: a *feminine gender script* and a *masculine gender script*. These scripts partition personality by gender, with affects and interpersonal needs divided into those acceptable for women and those acceptable for men. Developing over a period of time, these gender scripts become dominant over many other types of scripts and increasingly determine the various scenes that will be sought after, celebrated, or avoided. Gender scripts govern the continuing evolution of gender components of identity by defining the principal pathways along which identity must now develop. They also stratify and shape interpersonal relations. These scripts operate as directives and therefore appear as *shoulds,* revealing how shame-producing they can be.

In the feminine gender script, women *should* express the affects of enjoyment, distress, fear, and shame. Women *should* also express the need for relationship, the need for touching/holding, the need to identify, and the need to nurture others. Women *should* therefore search for identity primarily through relationships to other persons, particularly men. Women *should* also be popular and conform, adhering to one of the predominant scripts in American culture.

By contrast, in the masculine gender script, men *should* express the affects of surprise, excitement, anger, dissmell, disgust, and contempt. Men *should* express the power need and the differentiation need in particular. Men *should* therefore search for identity principally through differentiation and through power. Men *should* also compete for success and be independent and self-sufficient, thus adhering to the other two principal cultural scripts that dominate American society. In addition, men *should* engage in adversarial contests.

From Gender Scripts to Gender Ideologies

For centuries these scripted roles for women and for men have been the predominant ones in American culture, and to varying degrees in other cultures as well. These scripts have so dominated contemporary culture that they have evolved into *gender ideologies,* which are a type of ideological script.

The defining characteristics of all ideological scripts are orientation, evaluation, and sanctions. Ideological scripts define our general orientation in the universe, in our society, and in our relationship to others. They give us a sense of "place"; we know where we belong. Second, ideological scripts embody values and injunctions by evaluating what is good and what is bad. These scripts dictate how to conduct our life in a given culture so that we continue to receive approval; for example, premarital sex is bad—just say no. Finally, ideological scripts also embody positive sanctions for the fulfillment of central values and negative sanctions for their violation. Abstinence is rewarded, for example, and premarital sex punished. The principal negative sanctions employed are shame, dissmell, disgust, contempt, and anger for any perceived deviation from how we are supposed to behave. In these ways, gender scripts evolve into more systematic and expansive gender ideologies.

According to Tomkins, ideological scripts are the most important class of scripts because they "endow fact with value and affect."[30] They are the primary agents of bonding and division among people because they give us something to live for, and something to die for.

The impact of these gender scripts and gender ideologies on interpersonal relations has been enormous: they have constricted possibilities and produced shame for anyone attempting to create new patterns for their lives.

In relationships between men, the gender ideology disallows everything but competition. Any expression of identification or touching between males —except when engaged in adversarial contest—is equated with being feminine and unmanly. Because of this entrenched ideological gender script, the homosexual male is inevitably viewed as an inferior male, or even as a female. Homophobia is not simply fear, but a complex of affects that certainly often includes fear, as well as shame, disgust, and contempt for any sign of masculine inferiority. The consequences are revulsion, hatred, and vicious contempt directed toward anyone who is gay or merely perceived to be gay. That same loathing is turned inward against the self if a man is gay but unable to accept his sexual orientation.

The gender ideology in relationships between women and men is based on power as control: men *should* exercise power, but women *should not*. A second feature is dominance/submission: men *should* dominate, women *should* be submissive. Another critical feature of this ideology is nurturing: women *should* nurture men. Because women are scripted to pursue their identity through a relationship with a man, that relationship becomes the defining characteristic of their place in the cosmos. The "successful" woman has a secure relationship with a man whom she supports and nurtures, while the "successful" man has attained power and prestige through competition and advancement in a career.

In relationships between and among women, the elevation of the identification need allows for a greater degree of fusion and merging experiences to occur. Women are scripted to identify with one another and are freer to openly express other interpersonal needs as well, particularly their needs for touching/holding, nurturing, and being in a relationship. At the same time, women are also scripted to compete among themselves for men since relationships with men have been their primary path toward identity. Identification versus competition with other women therefore becomes a conflicting subscript within the feminine gender ideology.

The stratification of any society into distinct social classes—upper versus lower, middle versus working—and the continuing invidious gender stratification both originated from the same source. Tomkins argues that "social stratification rests upon the affect stratification inherent in adversarial contests."[31] During the early evolution of civilization, according to Tomkins, the perception of scarcity, together with the reliance on violence to reduce such scarcity, ultimately generated contests in which there were victors and losers, with the spoils belonging to the victors. Violence was directed first against big game animals and next against human beings for the purpose of allocating scarce resources to the victors. As a result, the full spectrum of the innate affects eventually became partitioned into two distinct sets: the warrior affects versus the loser affects.

The affects of surprise, excitement, anger, dissmell, and disgust were designated for the victors in adversarial contests, for successful warriors, while the remaining affects of enjoyment, fear, distress, and shame were designated for the losers. The warrior "is excited, ready for surprise, angry and proud, contemptuous and fearless. The loser has given up and is relaxed in dubious enjoyment, crying in distress, terrified and humble and ashamed."[32] By elevating disgust, dissmell, and contempt above hanging his head in shame, the warrior is proud more than anything else. Since women were easily defeated by men in physical combat, the next step was to designate these demeaned affects for all women, and from there to "regard children as little slaves and women and to regard lower classes in the same way."[33]

We argue that a parallel partitioning and stratification of the innate primary interpersonal needs into two distinct sets has also taken place: the needs for power and differentiation were assigned to men, while the remaining needs for relationship, touching/holding, identification, affirmation, and nurturing others were assigned to women.

It is only in the last two decades that these powerful scripts have been shaken loose. The women's movement began to reverse this stratification with a new ideology. Women began to reclaim the affects previously denied them: surprise, excitement, anger, dissmell, and disgust. Women are now more validated in both their experience and expression of the full range of the innate affects. Like men, they *should* become angry, or disgusted, express distancing dissmell, or become contemptuous, or become openly excited either during sports or during sex. Also like men, women *should* express their power needs and search for identity equally through differentiation and identification. This has played out culturally with more women now working and entering male-dominated professions. Since as humans we inherit all the affects and needs, expressing just the select few that are culturally approved produces only a partial identity, an incomplete self.

The affects now available to women also fuel differentiation. For women, the need to differentiate was once shamed into suppression, but the renewed cultural pressure for self-definition has thrown into turmoil what had previously remained in silence and shadow. Conflict is inherent between the old warrior/loser script that once clearly and completely defined the place of both women and men in their culture and the new egalitarian script that is replacing it.

While reclaiming the lost affects and interpersonal needs long denied them, women have also been rewriting the script for men, generating a new ideology to place both women and men differently in the universe. Now men *should* express distress, fear, enjoyment, and shame. Men are allowed, indeed encouraged, to cry, to become vulnerable, to expose their shame. Like women, men *should* also express openly their needs for affirmation, for touching/holding, and for identification with other men without the requirement of being locked in adversarial contest. Herein lie the roots of the current flourishing of the men's movement. For men, as for women, power is *shared* in a relationship that evolves between respected equals. Yet the reigning result seems to be confusion and miscommunication as men and women find themselves caught between scripts, conflicted about their roles, faced with mixed gender signals, and thus exhausted!

Identity, interpersonal relations, even imagination—once the prisoners of deeply entrenched gender scripts and ideologies—are now evolving. What has been termed the masculine self and feminine self within each person, we view as the product of the prior partitioning of affects and needs. Reversing that stratification has been one of the principal outcomes of the women's movement, providing fresh fuel for the development of a new vision of integrated identity.

BREAKING FREE

Imagination has been set free from the shackles of older scripts, with each gender reclaiming and redeeming what had been previously disallowed. Rigid distinctions between men's work and women's work no longer hold. Marriage and children are no longer the only culturally approved paths they once were. And there is more equal participation by men and women in the tasks of both parenting and work. These changes are unsettling. But each gender is moving toward a more complete expression of the full range of affects and interpersonal needs—not separate ones for men and women.

The dissolution of affect-shame binds and need-shame binds, which have been patterned differently for women and for men, is crucial to the full realization of what it means to be human. Dissolving the binding effects of shame, along with actively embracing and openly validating all affects and needs, is essential to the attainment of wholeness and the full integration of the self.

That quest is even more crucial for lesbians and gay men because shame is central in our lives in unique ways.

CHAPTER TWO

ༀ

Haunted by Shame

In recent years, scholars in the newly emerging field of lesbian and gay studies have been documenting the history of gay people throughout the centuries and in different cultures. It's as if some great treasure trove has been lifted from the ocean's depths to yield its secrets. Sexual relations between persons of the same sex, particularly between two males, were indeed culturally accepted during certain historical periods besides classical Greece: in seventeenth-century Japan, in China until the end of the seventeenth century, and among the Native peoples of the Americas prior to the arrival of the Europeans. The history of homosexuality is much more various than had been previously supposed. Evidence of patterns of sexual expression between men and between women continues to accumulate, and this places the contemporary lesbian or gay man in an important historical context.

While a relatively greater degree of acceptance of sexual relations between two persons of the same sex actually existed during certain epochs, such times typically gave way to times of stricter taboo. Examining the history of homosexuality reveals the ebb and flow of that taboo. Homosexuality has been variously conceived and characterized as immorality, as against nature, as gender disturbance, and as mental illness. Though declassified as a psychiatric disorder by the American Psychiatric Association some twenty years ago, homosexuality nevertheless remains heavily stigmatized.[1] Because of that stigma, gay and lesbian identities are the last to be fully understood and tolerated. Whereas anti-Semitism and racism have largely become culturally unacceptable, homophobia still remains unchallenged and even widely accepted.

SHAME AND MINORITIES

Because gays are a definable minority, they develop a distinctive identity as a group, just as all minorities do. Shame impacts that process in ways that are uniform across all minorities and in ways that are also unique for each minority. To understand gay shame, we need to start with minority experience in general.

The development of identity is rooted in both positive and negative *identifications*. The need to identify is the need for rootedness, connectedness, and belonging; it is a need to feel identified with and connected to a particular individual or to belong to a group. Individuals identify in order to emulate those they admire, to feel *at-oneness* or belonging, and to enhance their own sense of inner power. Experiences of identification provide strength and healing for us. The need to belong to something larger than oneself is a principal source of identity, and shame is another source of identity because this affect lies at the root of all negative self-images. Internalized negative cultural images have to be consciously confronted and defused in the search for a secure, positive identity, and that can only be based on a sense of pride in self precisely *because of* belonging to one's group. For groups in American society like African Americans, Native Americans, Asian Pacific Islanders, Hispanics, Jews, and lesbians and gay men, their need to create a positive, self-affirming identity specifically as a member of their group becomes the defining feature of their identity.

Identity Development in the Context of Conflicting Identifications

The positive and negative identifications from which identity evolves reflect experiences that are both individually and group based. Anyone who plays a central role in our lives, anyone we admire, becomes someone we identify with and wish to emulate. The child's deepest wish is to be like the loved or needed parent, and that yearning extends to siblings, peers, teachers, and ultimately groups. Just as a uniquely personal identity arises, so does an identity that is racial, ethnic, or religious, but also one based on gender and one based on sexual orientation as well. These are our multiple identities. Individuals develop within changing social milieus, a family, peer group, an ethnic or religious community, and a wider culture. The need to identify presses for expression in each of these settings. Developmentally, we experience connectedness through feeling identified with parents and peers, with members of our own sex, with a particular ethnic, racial, or religious group, and with the wider culture. These are overlapping connections. A sense of belonging grows only through *positive* identification with others. Any specific minority group—ethnic, racial, or sexual—will inevitably be confronted by negative cultural images that, once internalized, obstruct the development of a coherent minority identity.

The process is analogous whether the focus is ethnic or religious, racial or sexual identity. An African American man or woman struggling to reach a positive identification with other African Americans in a predominantly white racist culture will experience a process that is analogous to that of a gay man or lesbian grappling with identification with other gays or lesbians within a predominantly non-gay, heterosexist, and homophobic culture. In varying ways, each has felt like a stranger, each has to deal with historical patterns of oppression, hatred, and persecution, and each is journeying from being an outsider to belonging somewhere.

The striving to experience a positive identification with our particular cultural minority group inevitably brings us into collision. To illustrate the complexity involved, consider the dilemma for a young man who is both gay and a devout Catholic yet refuses to sacrifice either identification. On certain levels, since the Catholic Church condemns homosexuality, each identification conflicts with the other, and his search for a coherent identity dissolves into a struggle to resolve contradictions that appear irresolvable. Internalized negative cultural images about his own cultural group will have to be directly confronted, neutralized, and integrated in the quest for a coherent self, a positive identification with that group, an equally positive self-image, and a secure identity. We'll explore how to accomplish that transformation in later chapters.

Belonging to any minority group within a larger, dominant culture creates an inherent conflict of identification. Members of minority groups inevitably experience conflicting identifications—on the one hand, pressures to embrace their particular group, on the other, pressures to assimilate into the wider culture. For individuals living in contemporary American society, this conflict is further fueled by the three cultural scripts we have described as sources of shame: compete for success, be independent and self-sufficient, be popular and conform. The awareness of being a member of a minority inevitably translates into being different, and therefore potentially inferior, in a culture prizing social conformity. Insofar as an individual's minority identification is predominantly positive, one solution to the inner conflict is to react with contempt toward the dominant culture, rejecting assimilation. However, insofar as your minority identification is predominantly negative, assimilation into the dominant culture is aided by contempt for your own minority group. Rejecting minority group identification is the consequence of that particular solution. You cannot simultaneously belong to a minority group and the wider culture without some measure of conflict. It is that conflict which must be confronted directly if it is to be eventually transformed.

Scenes of Shame

For any minority group, negative identity is invariably rooted in scenes of shame. In a culture that generally neither recognizes nor values individual differences, the awareness of difference between yourself and others almost inevitably translates into an invidious comparison. The awareness of being a member of a minority calls attention to the self, exposing it to view. For that reason, minorities experience themselves as lesser in comparison to the majority culture. Inferiority is always rooted in shame. Members of minorities are made poignantly aware of being different from others in a cultural context. In every case there is a lasting impression of their essential difference, a difference that translates immediately into deficiency and shame.

To illustrate the nature and operation of shame scenes on the cultural level, consider the experience of various minorities living in contemporary America. For Jewish children, absence from school for Jewish holidays is one critical scene that contributes to early awareness of being different. Going to synagogue is another critical scene involving early awareness of difference. Seeing a Hasidic Jew on the street, on television, or in a film is a third critical scene. Here, one is faced with perhaps the starkest contrast between being a Christian American and being a Jew. Christmas programs in school and that holiday's pervasive presence in this culture confront the Jewish child with a celebratory pageant she or he is not part of. Finally, knowledge of the Holocaust, when it first dawns, may caution against identification with people who have been tragic victims. These are a few of the critical scenes involving the early awareness of being different through which one's earliest feelings of shame about being Jewish can evolve. Jews living in other cultures, whether Anglo-Saxon, northern European, or Latin, are just as likely to experience parallel scenes that set them apart as different from the dominant culture.

Knowledge of the Holocaust can produce for a Jewish child what knowledge of slavery does for an African American child, and what knowledge of the Indian wars accomplishes for a Native American child: warning against identification with a repudiated people. Other critical shame scenes for African Americans include those less remote than slavery: having to sit at the rear of buses, attending separate schools, living in separate neighborhoods, being beaten in civil rights demonstrations, watching black youths arrested for crimes on television. Scenes of segregation were commonplace in the United States only thirty years ago. They were, and still remain, poignant scenes of humiliation, lasting reminders for any African American.

For women generally, rape and domestic violence are governing scenes that magnify their powerlessness and consequent humiliation, universal symbols of the violence that women have suffered at the hands of men. The scene of rape is both immediate and historical, for women have always been vulnerable to rape, which remains a terrible and pervasive reality today. In the Yugoslav civil war, for example, it has been a deliberate weapon of terror and humiliation used against Bosnian women.

It is the scene of rape that in part fuels the rage some women now express toward men and also toward the dominant male culture in America. Scenes form around events in the past that become retold in the present, just as they crystallize around interpersonal events experienced more immediately. We have only to recall the Anita Hill–Clarence Thomas hearings before the U.S. Senate Judicial Committee that were televised in 1991. Those were graphic scenes, burned into memory for all who watched the proceedings.

Gay men and lesbians experience countless scenes of derision, ridicule, and often vicious contempt. These shame scenes occur prior to, during, and after adolescence. Peers generally have been relentless in persecuting anyone suspected of being gay or lesbian, and scenes of disparagement are universal for homosexuals. Youngsters learn at a very early age to avoid doing anything that will earn them the slur "faggot." Even when they do not understand the meaning of that particular insult, they know to avoid it. Words like "sissy," "queer," "homo," and "dyke" are wielded as weapons to humiliate others. Being seen by one's peers as gay or lesbian, whether accurate or not, is equivalent to being a leper who is dreaded and shunned. Even for other gays, simply seeing a "queeny" gay man, for example, on the street or television may accomplish the identical thing that seeing a Hasid does for a Jew: confrontation with a jarring image of difference, an image steeped in shame. Both people remind us of our vulnerability.[2] The phenomenon of gay bashing that has become even further magnified in response to the AIDS crisis is not unlike lynchings for African Americans and pogroms for Jews who lived in Eastern Europe. These are all magnified expressions of contempt for those who are outcasts.

Self-Shaming Scripts

Both attitudes and images of particular minorities widely held by the dominant culture become internalized directly through these scenes of shame, following which particular scripts generate and profoundly shape minority identity. By reproducing shame, these scripts become the source of the pervasive self-hatred attached to being a member of any minority group.

The predominant self-shaming scripts that reproduce shame for minorities are the same ones we considered earlier: self-blame, comparison making, and self-contempt. Originating in governing scenes of shame, each script becomes directly targeted to minority status. These scripts ultimately produce a shame-based minority identity.

A *self-blame* script reproduces shame by fixing blame directly on oneself for perceived failings or defects. A self-blame script recruits the affect of anger but directs it in a self-accusatory manner: the self accuses the self. Continuing with our example of the gay man, the target of his self-blame is now his inescapable awareness of being gay and he repetitively blames himself for being deficient in this regard: *If only I didn't have these feelings. Why can't I be like other men—normal! It's all my fault—I'm not trying hard enough to change!* The self now angrily accuses and blames the self. Such a script is extremely self-punitive because he is blaming himself for a fundamental aspect of his essential being.

In contrast, a *comparison-making* script evolves directly from the awareness of difference between self and other. For example, a gay man may look at heterosexual men, become aware of any perceived difference between himself and them, and then translate that difference into a comparison. An adolescent boy who feels different from the other boys around him begins searching for what it means: *Other guys are more manly than I am. Everybody looks up to them. What's wrong with me?* Later, his awareness expands to include erotic desire: *Why do I want to touch other guys, look at them, feel their bodies all over? Why am I so different?* Still later, he scrutinizes himself more closely still: *Why don't I think about girls? Why don't they turn me on? All the other guys can't stop drooling over them. I must be a freak.* Invidious comparisons will cause any boy or man to feel lesser, deficient, precisely because he is gay.

Self-contempt is a third prominent script for reproducing shame among minorities. Contempt is both a punitive and distancing affect blend; it aims to eradicate whatever is perceived as intolerably offensive. When contempt is turned directly against the self, the equivalent of psychic surgery results, in Tomkins's view; the self becomes fractured and one part of the self brutally torments another.[3] The judging self actively, mercilessly persecutes the offending self. For the gay man we've been using as an illustration, being gay itself is now something to be abhorred and spurned—in effect, permanently distanced from his "purer" self: *You're disgusting. No, I'm not. Oh yeah, there's something wrong with you—all you want are men 'cause you're not good enough. Stop it—leave me alone. You'll get what you deserve—they'll fire you when they find out. You're not even a man! I promise I'll stop— really! It'll never happen again. I promise! Sissy! No queer like you deserves to live!* Because of the bifurcation created by contempt, any inner voices usually appear in this characteristic form: one part of the self brutally tormenting another as if a dialogue were occurring between two different individuals. This is the source of his self-loathing and self-hatred, and one way it plays out is through his remaining deeply closeted. For him there is no escape. He must continually wall off his desires for other men from everyone, especially himself.

These self-shaming scripts reactivate governing scenes of shame and thereby continuously reproduce shame. In so doing, these scripts become the source of all forms of internalized self-hatred connected to group status—whether in the form of internalized anti-Semitism, racism, sexism, misogyny, or homophobia.

Contempt: A Strategy of the Powerless

Just as scenes of shame become reproduced through various self-shaming scripts, attitudes of contempt also develop as a means to ward off shame. Historically, African Americans, Native Americans, Jews, and gay men and lesbians have been persecuted, discriminated against, and disenfranchised in both overt and subtle ways. That has been true not only in America, but also across other cultures. For example, becoming publicly known as gay has almost always put people at risk, if not in direct jeopardy of violence.

Whenever people are relegated to an inferior status within a wider culture, they begin to doubt themselves and also to question the worth of the group to which they belong. Whenever people are rejected because of belonging to a particular group, shame becomes radically magnified into inferiority. Whenever African Americans, Jews living in Eastern Europe, Gypsies in Romania, Turks in Germany, or homosexuals living in any culture are persecuted, humiliation is imposed with a reign of terror.

In such a context, a persecuted or disenfranchised minority can insulate itself against humiliation by responding with contempt toward the dominant cultural group. One example is the dismissive term "breeders" used by some gays for heterosexuals, which reduces their humanity by focusing on their status as animals. However, when the barriers to assimilation are gradually removed, even partially, then the pressure to assimilate and identify with the dominant culture intensifies, and contempt magnifies further, turning more fiercely against one's own group, even against one's own self.

Violence and Hatred: Reactions to Powerlessness and Shame

Not only does shame fuel the development of particular attitudes of contempt, it also fuels the hatred and violence that play out directly between different groups of people. Hatred is invariably fueled by shame, by feeling oneself wronged in some way, feeling violated by others or taken advantage of. Humiliation is always a fertile breeding ground for vengeance. But it is aided, and doubly magnified, by powerlessness. Whenever a group of individuals feels persecuted, neglected, disenfranchised, or otherwise looked down upon, the resulting shame and powerlessness inevitably become fused. Eventually, shame turns to rage and contempt for our perceived humiliators —those who oppress us. Powerlessness and humiliation, separately but especially together, are the principal sources of violence.

As a case in point, consider the riots in Los Angeles, California, that were sparked by the first jury verdict in the Rodney King police brutality case. The verdict that the police were not guilty seemed like a final slap in the face, an unbearable insult, a new level of shame that was intolerable, and it ignited an explosion of rage. But it was a blind rage, a powerless rage, a fury born of helplessness and shame, much like that of a child knocked off a playground see-saw who, feeling the agony of shame, now returns with a stick to beat the humiliator—only magnified a thousandfold.

People who belong to different ethnic, religious, and racial groups, and who feel outcast or lesser because of it, live lives of unrelenting exposure to shame, just as people who live in poverty suffer the certain shame of being poor. Surrounded by affluence in this country, they are reminded daily—by television if nothing else—of all they do not have that others so obviously possess. Theirs is a daily diet of shame. That shame, growing day by day, breeds only more resentment, an ever-deepening hatred. When that pent-up rage is finally unleashed, violence invariably ensues.

In addition, when that rage becomes further magnified by contempt for one's perceived humiliators, they cease being fellow human beings deserving respect, but instead become meaningless objects to be squashed and destroyed. Only when we feel such unrelenting contempt for others can we treat them with brutality.

We will not stop the recurring cycle of hatred and violence that plays out repeatedly between different minority groups in so many countries, or between one minority and the majority group, until we understand the cycle of shame and rage that fuels it. Nor will we comprehend that cycle until we come face to face with shame.

SOURCES OF GAY SHAME

Shame fuels hatred toward ourselves, just as it fuels hatred toward others. Shame is the affect from which all stigmas and taboos spring. Anyone who is publicly shamed is immediately stigmatized. And anything which is shamed, provided that shame also becomes widely shared, must then be avoided precisely in order to avoid shame. To dissolve the taboo surrounding homosexuality we must examine the sources of shame for lesbians and gay men. Unexamined shame is always an impediment to further growth, an obstacle in the lives of individuals, groups, and cultures.

Family

Shame about men loving men and women loving women is communicated directly through the family. When children either misbehave or violate their parents' expectations in other ways, parents will often become alarmed, criticizing and punishing the undesirable behavior, thereby shaming the children. These "transgressions" can be anything from fibbing, neglecting homework, associating with kids the parents don't like, all the way to violence and crime. Obviously, different parents have different degrees of tolerance.

When the behavior provoking alarm deviates from culturally approved patterns of gender-appropriate behavior (like "tomboy" behavior in girls or "sissy" behavior in boys), the conditions are set for associating shame with essential aspects of identity and sexuality. The young boy who asks for a doll to play with or the young girl who rejects so-called feminine interests invites shaming from parents. Judgments about what is acceptable or unacceptable become indictments and eventually are internalized as rules governing behavior to ward off shame.

Sexuality itself is targeted for at least some degree of shaming in almost all cultures; it is virtually impossible to grow up without learning that sexuality is in some way inherently shameful. For many cultures, only the blessing of marriage legitimizes sexuality, which has certainly been the legacy for Catholics and southern Baptists, for instance. But the requirement that sexual delight must occur only within marriage has also been deeply embedded in American culture from its Puritan beginnings.[4] An important extension of this article of faith is that love must be added to raw sexuality to elevate it from the animal to the human plane, with marriage deemed the sublimest form of love.

If marriage alone makes sex of any kind legitimate, and if only people of different sexes are allowed to marry, then gay and lesbian sexuality is placed irrevocably outside the bounds of the acceptable. This is compounded when heterosexual siblings are held up to the gay child as the standard of perfection. Children learn by what they see; when they observe that no "nontraditional" family patterns are prized, they inevitably learn shame. This has been the case for children born out of wedlock and therefore "illegitimate." The illegitimate child, the bastard, is a child born in shame—the product of a shameful union (Dorothy Allison's powerful *Bastard out of Carolina* is all about shame). The adulteress or adulterer is similarly condemned to shame. The individual man or woman who departs from received patterns of intimacy by daring to love someone of the same sex is likewise branded. The very nature of the family as an institution, as it has existed into this century, has been a source of shame about any form of love other than heterosexuality.

Peer Group

We find numerous sources of shame in the peer group. Peers are merciless in persecuting anyone they even suspect of homosexuality. A boy who shies away from competitive sports may be exposed to his peers in the same way as a girl who is too aggressive—each becomes targeted. Mockery, sarcasm, ridicule, and teasing are all weapons that are wielded by peers in their war with one another and in defense of their own honor and dignity.

The peer group subculture of early adolescence is the arena in which the ravages of shame reach their peak. The dynamics of the peer group are invariably the dynamics of shame. First of all, the peer group plays a key role in effecting eventual separation from the family by offering an alternative source of identification. By replacing parents with peers as identification figures, the adolescent gradually shifts allegiance, thereby aiding his or her development as an individual. Think of how important your friends became to you in your early adolescence, how vital it was to spend time with them (even on the phone), to be respected by them. Their importance makes the peer group a new source of shame and a powerful socializing force. What the peer group enforces is compulsory heterosexuality.

The period of early adolescence, which begins when girls and boys reach the age of eleven or twelve, is a universal time of heightened susceptibility to shame, principally because of the inevitable bodily changes that take place. But it is also the time when any outward expressions of affection for anyone of your own sex, particularly in the form of touching and holding, become directly targeted for additional shaming. This is the case in America as well as in Anglo-Saxon and northern European countries; other cultures display varying patterns.

I was at a museum in Paris last summer and this bunch of cute Italian boys on a tour blew my mind. They would stand in front of paintings with their arms around each other's shoulders, leaning on each other the way I would do only with a lover—and definitely not in a museum! I was envious of how free they were to touch each other. If I'd done that back in high school I would have been crucified.

Examples of the slurs used by peers to shame and humiliate each other are "faggot," "lesbo," "queer," and "homo." These terms make their appearance well before the onset of adolescence. The negative affect buoying those insults begins the association of homosexuality with shame, often well before any awareness of homosexuality has even developed. We learn that homosexuality is shameful before we learn that those words are about *us*. To call someone "gay," "queer," or "faggot" in this manner is to publicly shame them, and children and adolescents learn very quickly how to avoid being seen in these ways.

Even when the perception of gayness is utterly inaccurate in adolescence, the equation between gayness and shame has been indelibly made in everyone's mind. A boy or girl called "queer" must now disprove that charge or be forever branded because the peer group has lent its moral authority to the accuser who, in effect, now speaks for the group. Sometimes boys can be goaded into foolish risk taking or even violence, such as beating up someone else, just to prove they're "real men" and not "sissies." When the detection of gayness *is* accurate, peers will be relentless in persecuting that individual.

In either case, the lesson is clear: being gay is shameful, an inherent flaw. To be *seen* as gay opens us to ridicule and disparagement. So we hide and remain closeted in order to avoid shame, but that's illusory—secrecy only reinforces rather than releases shame.

Religion

Throughout recorded history, the major religions of the world have all been the basis for censuring and suppressing homosexuality in particular cultures and nations. In every case, homosexuality is viewed as against both God and Nature. Not only do religions themselves condemn us, but even nonreligious people use religion against us.

What most religions consider natural is heterosexual marriage; anything else is judged unnatural. If we are unnatural, we are unworthy of belonging. If we are unnatural, we oppose Nature's way and Nature's God. To be unnatural, therefore, is to be abhorrent and shameful, completely outside the natural world and the divine order of things.

As two men who are Jewish, we both vividly recall the first time in synagogue when that telling passage in Leviticus detailing the list of abominable acts was actually recited during the religious service. Could that passage, read in many congregations during the High Holy Days, actually be referring to us? We felt branded, and we anxiously looked around—feeling acutely exposed, self-conscious, shamed—wondering if others could see inside of us and know the secret truth lurking within us. The hunger to touch and hold another man had a horrifying name: *abomination*.

The great religions have openly decried homosexuality on theological grounds, though in some instances they have remained essentially silent. But in no case do our great contemporary religions espouse tolerance—let alone acceptance of homosexuality as morally equivalent to heterosexuality. Individual, enlightened clergy may urge acceptance, but religious doctrine and theological belief generally remain closed to that idea. That a man could love another man and be sexual with him, that a woman could embrace another woman sexually and lovingly—these are judged to be unholy according to accepted religious doctrine.

While religion has been generally viewed as offering relief from the burden of shame (sin), religion in fact has more often been the cause of *further* shame, generating shame precisely in the interests of furthering social control. Religious views about sexuality illustrate the point. To varying degrees, all societies have suppressed the free and open expression of sexuality because it is so contagious, invariably evoking sexual desire in others. By judging certain forms or occasions of sexual expression to be immoral or sinful from a religious perspective, religion directly fosters the increased social control required of any organized society.

Civilizations remain intact, stable, and continue to evolve only so long as order prevails, and the order that is asked for or demanded from the members of any society must be anchored somewhere. It is invariably anchored in the order attributed to Nature. By appealing to Nature or God as the foremost principle of order, never to be questioned, religion actually blurs the distinction between what is truly natural and what is merely necessary for achieving social control. The ordering of social behavior is therefore the prime business of religion.

Homosexuality became shameful in certain societies because it challenged the order inherent not in Nature, but in approved gender roles and, therefore, social relations. When no threat was perceived—as between male citizens and lower-status males or adolescent boys in classical Greece, for example, in a manner judged acceptable for the culture—then it was allowed to occur, but only in a restricted form that was governed by clearly prescribed rules.

But homosexuality was condemned, even when it had been previously tolerated or accepted, precisely when it became a threat to the creation or preservation of social order. It became illicit, sinful, when the practice of sexual relations between people of the same sex threatened to undermine the need for increased social control. This was certainly the case for the early Israelites when they were gripped by the task of fashioning a coherent identity as a people distinct from others, just as it was for Spain at the end of the fifteenth century when unification created a Catholic state, for the Spanish Conquistadors upon their arrival in the Americas where they sought to impose Catholic hegemony on the Native peoples, and for China at the end of the seventeenth century when the new Manchu rulers determined that social order had to be greatly strengthened.[5]

Consider the situation existing in Spain at the end of the fifteenth century, when that country became unified under Catholic rule. In the effort to create one Catholic country, the necessary subjugation of both Jews and Moors required the repudiation of the *offending other*—anyone seen as different. Jews were expelled or forced to convert. Targeting homosexuality for condemnation became a tool for achieving cultural superiority of Catholicism over Islam, whose attitude toward same-sex relations was more relaxed at the time. The condemnation of homosexuality spread throughout Spain, and it was carried to the New World when the Conquistadors encountered the *berdache*.[6]

Both Jews and Moors were certainly equated with shame, as was homosexuality. But shame was not the only affect operating. The affect of dissmell, with its active repudiation and distancing of anything that is foul-smelling, was radically magnified and powerfully brought to bear on the task of forging a distinctive identity for Catholic Spain. Because dissmell forever distances the impure in our midst, dissmell is the guardian of purity. Whatever arouses shame is an impurity that must be rooted out completely. Condemnation and prohibition reveal the operation of shame as a force governing social order because violating prohibitions always invites shame.

This historical example illustrates the use of shame to force people to conform to a prescribed pattern of social relations. Rigidly prescribed gender behavior and gender roles serve the purpose of furthering social control by suppressing certain affects and needs while encouraging others. The suppression of homosexuality, when it occurs, also serves the purpose of strengthening social control. There is a deep cultural dread of same-sex relations. The foundation of civilization *appears* to rest on the regulation of desire, sexual and otherwise.

Until the last decades of this century, certain conditions held true: in order for any society to endure, its members were required to marry and procreate. The preservation of the family became a social good because it had survival value from an evolutionary perspective. In order for the culture to expand, children had to thrive. The only ordering of social relations that eventually monopolized a given society was one that guaranteed protection to children and therefore ensured the survival of the family. As long as marriage and procreation dominated a given culture, homosexuality remained a potential threat that either had to be contained through certain restrictions (for example, adult males must marry and procreate while only taking the dominant role in sex with adolescent boys) or else made illicit. The biblical edict "Be fruitful and multiply" was indeed an evolutionary imperative—but the current projected rate of population growth on a global scale renders that imperative obsolete.

The very concept of the family itself has been heavily determined by religion, but the nature of the family as a coherent social form has undergone radical transformation. Whereas extended families used to be much more common in the United States, we have moved not only beyond them but beyond the nuclear family. The American family no longer solely comprises two married parents of different sexes plus their biological children. Single-parent families are more numerous, and new family forms are evolving at an accelerating pace: foster families, step-families, along with gay and lesbian families. We are witnessing the emergence of increased numbers of women who choose to have children not only without marriage, but also without men, through sperm donors. The very concept of "family" itself is undergoing profound transformation, and we are only at its initial stage.

These changes in family structure are so profound, so deeply disturbing to the ordering of social relations, that former Vice President Dan Quayle was moved to publicly chastise *Murphy Brown*, a popular television sitcom, for presenting a career woman's decision to raise her unplanned child entirely on her own as one viable alternative. What was the point of his attack? The necessity of upholding "family values" as he had inherited them, unchanged. What he asked publicly was this: "Where is the father in this scenario? Aren't fathers necessary to the family any longer?" In his attack, Quayle was addressing not just the scenario of a career woman faced with an unplanned pregnancy, but the deeper, more revolutionary change actually at work in our concept of the family itself: the very idea of a family without a father. Women choosing to have children without men is a real threat to the established social order and also challenges the previous dominance of men, just as the insistence of gays and lesbians to be treated equally challenges the status quo.

We are witnessing the emergence of an ideological dispute about the full inclusion of gay men and lesbians in society, as evidenced by the recent Oregon and Colorado state ballot initiatives designed to limit civil liberties for lesbians, bisexuals, and gay men. This dispute will likely rival the one now raging about abortion. With the lifting of our culture's long-standing, strict taboo on shame, those subjects previously hidden by shame are now given the spotlight. Homosexuality has entered the arena of public discourse and inquiry, so both the social and natural sciences have at long last turned to examine, more or less objectively, the once "abominable sin." But the very openness of discussion is seen by many in the religious right as one more sign of social breakdown and chaos. Homosexuality itself is seen as the harbinger of disaster.

The claims made to Nature and particularly to Christian morality for the preservation of natural order by those opposed to the full inclusion of gays are fundamentally no different from the claims made over a century ago in defense of slavery and, when that institution fell, in defense of segregation. Slavery was once justified by Christian doctrine, and even ministers and priests referred to biblical texts to support their arguments.[7] Nature and morality are once again being invoked against the full inclusion of gays, but now the claim is made in defense of "family values," as though last century's family form is the only true one.

The people who are ideologically opposed to the inclusion of gays in society on religious grounds tend to be the same people who are opposed to abortion and the right to die—also on those same moral grounds. If all individuals were allowed freedom of choice regarding abortion, suicide, procreation, sexuality in all its forms including homosexuality, as well as marital and family patterns, these people fear the collapse of the social order we have inherited.

What lies at the heart of all such religious ideologies is the claim of *moral infallibility:*[8] one God, one morality, one interpretation that holds true for all people and that can never be questioned. There can be no reasoned debate, therefore, nor any alternative view that is judged morally equivalent. The contemporary dispute about homosexuality is ideological, not dispassionate. Homosexuality has rarely been a subject for open inquiry, free of bias. We can no more convince many contemporary theologians that homosexuality is natural than Galileo could convince the scholars and theologians of his day that the earth revolved about the sun. Even science is not immune to ideology, yet the heresy of one age eventually becomes the truth of another.

But why now? Why precisely at this moment in history, in the final years of the twentieth century, and none other? Because civilization is in transition and the forms that have carried social relations into this century will not be the forms that carry us beyond it. Whether we as a species survive on this planet beyond this century will depend on our collective ability to create new enduring forms for social and political relations that will, in turn, ensure greater harmony than we have so far been able to sustain.

Culture

In American culture, as in most others, there is a lack of cultural validation for gay relationships. Every culture influences the development of its members through the set of scripts offered for living the good life. The prevailing cultural expectation has been that everyone would marry, and there is only one form of relationship permissible for marriage. To marry and procreate has been a dominant cultural script in all cultures.

Cultural models for living a life outside of this modal pattern have been lacking. We have not been shown images of men who love men and women loving women, especially not in our schools or in our history lessons. Until recently, even our books and films failed to include images of gay and lesbian persons or their relationships. Schools and the arts are important instruments of every culture through which both values and taboos are transmitted. We learn from what we are shown, from what we actually observe. But we also learn from what we do not see. Despite some changes, images of gays and lesbians as normal everyday people in loving and lasting relationships with each other are glaringly absent in our culture. What we are exposed to instead is relentless heterosexuality in pop music, billboard and magazine ads, movies, and television. Is it any wonder that gays and lesbians can seem so alien when their images are still mostly invisible to the wider culture? This nonstop drumbeat of heterosexual indoctrination is the very air we breathe. Only occasionally do we become aware of its power to shape how we think and feel about ourselves.

> *When my son entered middle school, everything changed. He put up a* Sports Illustrated *swimsuit calendar in his room and stared at it daily. He became preoccupied with his appearance in ways he had never been before, spending hours in front of the mirror preening and grooming himself. Even his taste in clothes changed. All he talked about was girls and sex, and he was so smug about it—at eleven! To me he seemed like he was taking on a role of some kind, like he was in a play and was completely lost in the part. Whenever I asked about any of it, he said it was because of the kids at school.*

The failure to openly recognize and value different patterns of intimate relations unavoidably communicates that these different forms of love are deficient and unworthy, hopelessly flawed, inherently shameful.

Heterosexism

Heterosexism can be defined as the widespread cultural assumption that all people actually are or would want to be heterosexual. This assumption is not a matter of fact but of value—a presumption held to be true regardless of the evidence. It is a stance that is ideologically fixed. Holding that assumption is what heterosexism is all about. Heterosexism establishes heterosexuality as a universal good for all individuals and measures individual lives according to that blind standard. If heterosexuality is *the* preeminent developmental pattern, anything else is judged to be lesser in comparison. If heterosexuality is the *only* normal developmental path, all others are by definition abnormal. If everyone really *would* be heterosexual if they only could, there must be something fundamentally wrong with gays and lesbians the way they are.

Heterosexism is a profound source of shame for lesbians and gay men, and it functions to shame anyone who is different and to silence lesbians and gay men in many situations where their heterosexuality is assumed.

Homophobia

The term *homophobia* is a misnomer because it connotes a passive, avoidant response much like that present in true phobias such as the fear of heights or the fear of crowds. Those fears restrict your behavior, making you avoid situations where the fear might be triggered: tall buildings in the first case, subways or football games in the second.

The aversion to homosexuality that has been termed homophobia is in reality a far more toxic, virulent reaction, one that is fueled principally by the affects of shame, dissmell, disgust, and contempt—with *or* without the addition of fear. When it is present, fear can either play a secondary role relative to the other affects or instead be coequal to them. In certain instances of homophobia, for example, fear is of equal intensity to shame.

*My girlfriend likes going to this club because it's really cool
but I hate dancing there because they got all these faggots hanging
out, and I can't handle it when they look at me. I won't even go to
the john in case one of them makes some kind of move on me.*

But in other instances of homophobia, shame and contempt predominate over fear.

*Whenever I see one of those stupid talk shows full of lesbians
I just wish I were there to tell 'em they don't know what they're
missing. I'd like to crush them, make them beg for what I've got,
because there's no way they could've had a real man.*

There are also times when fear can eclipse all of the other affects, though they are likely to be present at least to some degree.

Thus the ambiguous term *homophobia* is used to refer to various combinations or blends of different affects, not one uniform phenomenon. While examining the specific affect combinations that are actually embedded in homophobia certainly makes the phenomenon appear more complex, it nevertheless yields a much more precise understanding of how homophobia is not only generated, but actively maintained. Only by addressing the specific affects involved, and thereby confronting them directly both in others and in ourselves, can we neutralize and ultimately transform them.

How does hatred first develop toward gays? Heterosexual men, for example, learn from a very early age to feel shame about anything even remotely associated with homosexuality, and thereby equate being gay with shame. That evolves directly from peer group ridicule. Next they begin to feel disgust for every perceived sign of homosexuality—as if they were trying to spit those qualities out, whether perceived in themselves or in others, because they had unknowingly allowed something really polluted to get too close to them, to come "inside." Thus, discovering that a close friend is really queer can instantly trigger disgust, just as it does in the movie *The Crying Game* when the protagonist suddenly discovers that the "woman" he just had sex with is really a man—and he vomits. After disgust, heterosexual men next feel dissmell for the homosexual in their midst, in order to permanently distance the now known contaminant and thereby keep themselves pure. Like the leper of years past, the homosexual must be shunned and quarantined. When, however, punitive anger is finally added to dissmell, it produces contempt and gays become directly targeted for verbal assault and for violence—bashing.

As another example of how such affect-laden judgments are generated and perpetuated, let's consider an image that is now being used by people who are actively opposed to gay rights of any kind, opposed to the advancement of equality for lesbians and gay men. In the current debate taking place in the United States on gay issues, whether in the military or in the high school health curriculum, opponents will cleverly connect images of homosexuals with a truly disgusting image. How? By simply proclaiming publicly that *homosexuals ingest feces.* This is a gross exaggeration of rimming, a sexual practice of both non-gays and gays.

What's the result? A graphic image that is guaranteed to universally evoke disgust now becomes connected both with homosexuality in general and with specific individuals who are gay or lesbian—and that connection has been indelibly made. The very idea of ingesting feces itself is so beyond the limits of the acceptable—simply imagining it is so acutely revolting—that it must instantly be rejected.

Religious leaders in the United States also trigger disgust about homosexuality by linking it with damnation in the minds of listeners. They quote contemporary translations of certain passages from Scripture: "And the land shall vomit them forth." Embedded in these images are the affects of both shame and disgust.

Through this incendiary rhetoric, the powerful affective response of disgust is *imprinted* directly onto any scenes involving gays and lesbians, regardless of context. The two images are simply fused together. Eventually, the disgust response can then be spontaneously evoked by any images of gays or lesbians, even by any reasoned debate over the advancement of gay rights. Our culture has a whole arsenal of images that create disgust about gays and lesbians. Another prominent one is the charge that gays are child molesters. Bestiality is also linked with gays when opponents ask, "Why not grant rights to people who have sex with animals too?"

This strategy for perpetuating homophobia has appeared in previous centuries and earlier even in this century, but used against Jews rather than gays. Christian laity and clergy publicly and slanderously accused Jews of murdering Christian babies and using their blood to make unleavened bread during the Passover celebration. That idea was as horrific an image then as gays ingesting feces is today. In the case of each image, disgust is directly evoked to produce horror—fueling anti-Semitism in the first instance and homophobia in the second. Disgust is a potent weapon to use against any perceived enemy.

The further addition of contempt to this already powerful equation means that homosexuals should be both punished and expunged from the human community. Earlier, we introduced the concept of a lynching as a special metaphor for contempt. In a lynching, an individual is singled out as a pariah, someone who must be exterminated. By further magnifying shame and disgust, contempt for homosexuality makes the homosexual seem deserving of contempt, thereby validating such extreme, overtly expressed sentiments as "Death to Fags" or "God Hates Homosexuals" and such extreme actions as gay bashing. The rhetoric of hatred readily becomes the violence of hatred.[9]

Homophobia expresses the shame perceived to be inherent to homosexuality, the fear and dread of homosexuals as though they were alien beings, the deep disgust and revulsion for all things homosexual, and the punitive distancing of the homosexual discovered in our midst—who deserves to be put to death when found out. Why? Because homosexuality is seen as a disease that will spread to others. Homophobia therefore functions in another important way, as an *anticontamination script:* its purpose is to quarantine the contaminant in order to preserve the pure. Homophobia protects society from contamination; that link is even more insidious in the age of AIDS.

The origins of homophobia are diverse. There are distinct origins in the peer group and school setting, where the use of terms such as "faggot," "queer," and "lesbo" communicates the entire set of affects that govern homophobia. There are additional origins of homophobia in the particular masculine and feminine gender scripts and ideologies that have evolved to govern gender components of identity. Homophobia also has origins in cultural scripts, particularly in the governing cultural script to be popular and to conform. Being different from others or simply being seen as different becomes acutely shameful in response to this cultural script that is so pervasive in contemporary society. Finally, homophobia has also been historically associated with other forms of racial/ethnic prejudice, as John Boswell has shown through exploring historical links between anti-Semitism and homophobia.[10] Hatred against one group walks hand in hand with hatred against others.

On closer inspection, then, homophobia is the direct result of four affects magnified together: shame, disgust, dissmell, and contempt. The aversion to homosexuality is fueled less by fear than by shame, disgust, and dissmell, which are further magnified by contempt. The source of the virulent hatred expressed in homophobia lies principally in the dynamics of contempt. It is this affect that actively punishes while at the same time permanently distancing whatever has aroused that contempt.

These affects can be expressed by the dominant culture and its representatives toward homosexuals, by gays and lesbians toward one another, or instead turned inward against ourselves. In the latter instance, homophobia itself becomes internalized and is experienced directly from the self against the self. Contempt directed outward lynches others, but contempt directed inward lynches the self.

Powerlessness

Human beings appear unable to thrive without experiencing a sufficient degree of inner control over their own lives—*power* in a positive sense. The experience of inner control is the felt experience of power. Whenever we are able to predict events that matter to us or influence their outcome, we experience a measure of power. We are born powerless and also experience the longest period of helplessness in comparison with other species. As we grow up, our abilities gradually unfold—learning to walk, to use language, and eventually to plan our future—thereby shrinking the condition of relative powerlessness and extending our perception of power.

Power and powerlessness are two ends of one continuum. Throughout life we are always moving between more or less power, decreased or increased powerlessness, which are not affects per se, but *activators* of affect. Whenever we experience power, we are also likely to experience the positive affects: surprise—startle, enjoyment—joy, or interest—excitement. Conversely, whenever we are rendered powerless, any of the negative affects will be activated: fear—terror, distress—anguish, anger—rage, shame—humiliation, dissmell, or disgust. Throughout life we are therefore vulnerable to the specific affects that powerlessness unleashes.

Powerlessness is a principal source of shame for all people. Powerlessness occurs in very different circumstances: when someone you love dies, an important relationship fails, your home is vandalized or damaged in a disaster, you lose your job or you're passed over for promotion, your health is threatened by illness, disability, or aging. But powerlessness also occurs whenever we are threatened with violence, have our fundamental rights curtailed, or are discriminated against because of essential aspects of our identity. This has been particularly true for women living in most cultures, for they have been historically devalued, disenfranchised, and disempowered by not being allowed to vote, own property, seek divorce, and in some instances leave the home unsupervised.[11] Such a feeling of powerlessness is equally familiar for gay men and lesbians living in a great majority of cultures—individuals who continue to be persecuted in contemporary society simply because of who they are.

The recent state ballot proposals in Colorado and Oregon, one successful, one not, are frightening examples of institutionalized powerlessness —state-mandated discrimination. As many Jewish groups have wisely pointed out, such laws recall the ways in which Nazi Germany sought to first isolate and then progressively deprive its Jews of all rights by *legal* means, ultimately rendering them powerless and trapped. This historical parallel is an important one. To limit even one set of rights of a certain group of people threatens all of their rights, while to limit the rights of one particular group then paves the way to do so for other groups. That is the lesson of history. The citizen groups backing the ballot initiatives are dishonestly framing the issue as one of not granting "special rights" to gays and lesbians because they already have the same rights as others do. By actually advocating discrimination, these groups are using the perceived difference between gays and non-gays to render gays and lesbians powerless.

We are apt to experience powerlessness with any of the negative affects, or any combination of them. The affective responses to powerlessness are also likely to be experienced at the highest levels of intensity: terror, rage, anguish, and humiliation. As these affects magnify—that is, increase in intensity, duration, and frequency—we simultaneously struggle to contain and suppress them as we have been taught to do from earliest childhood. What this produces is a condition that Tomkins calls *backed-up affect,* a distortion of the innate affect mechanism caused by the chronic suppression of affect.

Whereas the innate affects are brief in duration, suppression paradoxically causes affect to last much longer. When affect backs up, it does so not only on the psychological plane but on the physiological level as well, so affect plays a significant role in both health and illness. Definite endocrine changes accompany the suppression of affect, so a person who chronically suppresses anger may live with a permanent elevation in blood pressure. Not only does affect directly mediate endocrine changes, it also impacts the immune system: positive affect enhances immune functioning while negative affect suppresses it. What we ambiguously refer to as stress is on closer inspection the experience of affect and backed-up affect along with their accompanying endocrine changes.

> *When I'm working too hard and suddenly realize I'm chain-smoking,* that's *when I know something's going on. I have to slow down and ask myself: Okay, what are you covering up? What are you upset about? Because that's always at the bottom of things.*

When we feel ourselves under stress or feel overstressed, we are experiencing the consequences of affect, typically at the highest levels of intensity. In turn, as one of the most important activators of the various negative affects, powerlessness is one of the most significant sources of stress in our lives.

The affect dynamics of powerlessness are experienced by the unemployed, the poor, and the homeless every bit as much as by persons with AIDS, members of minority groups, and the aged. In every case, we can observe a distinctive *powerlessness-affect-stress cycle*. Powerlessness first activates any of the negative affects, either singly or in combination, and those affects in turn result in what we ambiguously call stress. It is this cycle that can have such devastating impact on individual lives.

AIDS

Our responses to the contemporary AIDS epidemic reveal the role of affect in general and shame in particular on both a personal and a wider, societal level. AIDS activates incredible powerlessness coupled with uncertainty. Actually receiving an AIDS diagnosis or merely imagining yourself becoming HIV positive is an invitation to either real or imagined catastrophe, since AIDS can be neither completely controlled nor predicted. We still do not know enough to determine its precise transmission, necessary precursors, or possible co-factors, to accurately predict its course, or to produce its cure. That life-threatening uncertainty renders all of us potentially powerless. Whenever we experience powerlessness in a significant sphere of life, as we have seen earlier, this returns us to the original primary scene of infant helplessness.

People living with AIDS will experience powerlessness with any combination of negative affects: fear, distress, anger, dissmell, disgust, or shame. The most toxic combination is fear and shame. Since AIDS is perceived as a stigma, an HIV diagnosis itself is both a sign of shame and a cause of further humiliation due to public revulsion, much as leprosy was a dreaded stigma in previous centuries.

Diseases like AIDS also bring on various physical debilities, like incontinence, which are inherently shame-inducing. Visible signs of disease like KS brand the body with shame and disgust.

Further, many people experience an HIV diagnosis as a "death sentence." A person with AIDS is faced with terror and shame, both activated by AIDS. But those affects are further magnified by the fear, humiliation, dissmell, disgust, and rage that are generated by society's response. Our culture's first response was silence and denial, then dread of contamination.

The cultural shame and disgust about homosexuality have been displaced onto AIDS and thus transferred directly to people with AIDS. But the reverse is also happening: the shame, dissmell, and disgust about AIDS contamination have been displaced onto gays. Because of these two factors, being gay unfortunately equals having AIDS in the minds of many people. By perceiving AIDS as a "gay disease," our culture equally repudiates gays and people with AIDS via dissmell and contempt. In the particular case of AIDS, the affects of shame, dissmell, and disgust are further magnified by terror.

A gay man who is HIV negative faces the question of whether to become involved, sexually as well as intimately, with someone who is HIV positive. Mixed HIV status couples present difficult choices and unique challenges. Each may feel shame, but for different reasons. One already feels contaminated, the other risks contamination. A positive HIV status is only a harbinger of stigma to come, while continuing to be HIV negative can provoke shame about *not* being HIV positive.

A potential dilemma exists for some people who are AIDS survivors, as well as those who continue to test negative for the HIV virus, while numerous friends succumb to it: *survivor shame.* It's not guilt for having transgressed, but shame, a feeling of unworthiness. Anyone who survives a catastrophe or disaster is certain to experience shame at having survived when so many others did not. This is akin to the survivor shame experienced by soldiers returning from battle or veterans after discharge, all of whom are only too keenly aware of their fallen comrades who have not survived. Likewise, many survivors of the Holocaust feel shame for having lived when people they think were far more deserving of life did not.

Mitchell had lost two lovers to AIDS and found himself feeling intense shame: *Why them and not me? What makes me more worthy of survival?* This shame sent him into a tailspin and for a few years he avoided making any deep connections with other men and avoided sex completely. The thought of discussing HIV status with another potential lover was shadowed by feeling that he didn't deserve to be alive. This shame sends other men in the opposite direction, into unsafe sex because they don't care about the risk after having lost so many friends and lovers: *We're all going to die anyway.*

In the case of AIDS, the resolution of shame is made even more complicated because the source of shame itself, either AIDS or a positive HIV status, cannot be eradicated. We have to learn how to effectively tolerate this shame, to counteract it by creating new scenes of enjoyment and excitement, and to have a dream—something to live for—that will carry us into the future, however uncertain it appears. Doing all that in the face of AIDS means applying the various principles and strategies for healing shame that we will consider in the next chapter and focusing them for this unique challenge.

Silence

Silence breeds shame every bit as much as shame breeds further silence. The two are locked in an endless cycle of mutual reactivation. Silence first of all communicates shame because whenever there is a subject that cannot be spoken about openly, we invariably feel shame. Children learn this very early in their families, when parents respond with embarrassment or shock to their questions like "Where do babies come from?" "How come Jeffy's parents sleep in one bed and you and Mommy don't?" "Why doesn't my sister have a penis, too?" Much shame, in fact, is produced that way. A child who asks about a forbidden topic like sexuality and is greeted with silence learns not to trespass on that subject again. What cannot be spoken of openly must be too shameful to approach—in a word, taboo. Shame bars the tongue, silencing speech, rendering whatever has been shamed now more hidden, unalterably secret.

When silence is systematically imposed on a broad societal plane, it becomes a more powerful form of oppression than is experienced in the family. The tyranny of silence has been the special form of societal oppression directed at gay men and lesbians, just as segregation and apartheid have been forms of societal oppression targeted at other groups. Silence utilizes shame on a broad scale to keep a group of people hidden—prisoners within their own society. Shame is that powerful a weapon: it can have devastating impact on an entire group of people. The Stonewall Rebellion in New York City in June 1969 therefore marked a turning point: a dramatic public refusal by gay men and lesbians to continue to remain silent. That event marked the breaking of the deeply held cultural taboo on homosexuality, the beginning of the journey from silence into openness, from shame toward pride.

THE METAPHOR OF THE CLOSET:
COMING OUT OF SHAME

The declaration of our sexual orientation and sexual identity, however we define these to ourselves, is an open expression of our positive identification as gay or lesbian. To come out of the closet in this way is to not only identify ourselves as gay or lesbian, but to identify *with* other gays and lesbians—to feel positively identified with them as a group. Deeply embedded in this process is first and foremost an encounter with shame. It is shame that bars positive identification with other gays as well as self-identification as gay. Being in the closet means being in the closet of shame, still in hiding, cloaked in secrecy. The shame embedded in coming out, and also conveyed in the metaphor of the closet, is certainly well mixed with fear; historically, humiliation has been imposed on gays and lesbians with a reign of terror.[12] There was in the past, and continues to be, real danger in being openly known as gay, but it is shame that keeps so many still in the closet even when the possibilities of actual danger have markedly lessened.

By coming out of the closet we have been in, however we may experience it, we are embarking on a deeply personal journey out of shame. We are coming out of shame, out of hiding, and coming not only into openness but into our own. This process called *coming out,* which is so deeply rooted in contemporary gay life, occurs gradually over time, not just on one day in one single moment of self-revelation. The process is continuous, not instantaneous, though it may be marked by dramatic moments or events. Coming out demands a continual engagement with the dynamics of shame, not just with fear.

Coming out is essentially a process of identity transformation that partially involves redefining the self within us. But at the heart of the process is a struggle with shame, and this is what makes coming out so deeply ambivalent for many of us. One of the factors that inhibits coming out is the inevitable loss of identity we will experience. To come out means fundamentally giving up our old identity as a presumed heterosexual.

> *It was harder telling old friends I was gay than people who didn't know me that well. A lot of my friends were upset, wondering why I waited so long. Didn't I trust them? They seemed almost suspicious, like I'd been some kind of spy suddenly revealing who he really was. I wondered that myself—I spent so many years pretending to be straight, who was I?*

Our parents and families also must inevitably struggle with shame when we finally come out to them: Will they tell their friends? How will they deal with their own shame? With feeling disappointed in us or in themselves? *Their* struggle has often just begun whereas ours has abated if only enough to allow us to come out. Shame leaves us all ambivalent because it divides us from others, but we also feel deeply divided within ourselves. To come out of the closet, and therefore out of shame, is to begin resolving the shame we have carried for so long about being gay. But coming out involves something else as well—a conscious, deliberate act of will.

We perceive essential aspects of the self within us, struggle with them for years, but then we actively participate in organizing and rearranging that unfolding experience of ourselves. We are reinventing ourselves in the very process of coming out, shedding our former selves like a snake shedding its outworn skin. We have at last burst free of our older, constricting self. This transformative process is an encounter with ourselves and an encounter with shame at the very core of our being. Through consciously confronting shame we transform it, and in so doing we transform ourselves.

In addition to conscious choice and an act of will, coming out also signifies regaining power over information. Instead of continuing to dread exposure, we are taking direct control over when, how, and whom to inform. In this way we are taking back the power over a fundamental aspect of our own lives. Of course, there are always potential risks and even real dangers in coming out: loss of family or peer support, loss of job, public ridicule, violence. Nevertheless, the decision to come out itself is self-empowering. Both the transformation of shame and regaining control over information together enhance our personal power—not over others but fundamentally over our own lives. This is the essence of empowerment. Coming out is, therefore, not only an individual act of identity transformation, expressed in action, but a political act as well.

Even the phenomenon of *outing* is illuminated by the dynamics of shame. It's no accident that gay people, who for centuries have dreaded being exposed or outed, have now reversed roles and instead are prepared to out other closeted gays, primarily those they perceive as obstructing progress on gay rights. By reversing roles and threatening to out other gays, individuals in the gay community are now unfortunately using the dynamics of shame as a means of intimidation. But that is far from the only way to regain power.

Gay men and lesbians are no longer numbered among the powerless; instead they are actively taking back their power. In switching roles from being powerless to being powerful, gays are actually *recasting* the scene and rewriting the script that had dominated their lives—public exposure, a threat they had always been forced to live under. The journey from shame to pride is mirrored in the journey from powerlessness to power.

The process of evolving a gay or lesbian identity is not experienced identically by all men and women. Though it always involves—even to very different degrees—resolving the deeply felt struggle to fundamentally *be* who we are, the process is unique for each of us. Some are aware of an erotic attraction to others of our own sex from an early age, while others become aware only much later in life. Some bury that awareness, others act on it, even in childhood or early adolescence. Some enter heterosexual relationships or marriages, some never do. For some, coming out is turbulent or sudden, for others it is more quiet or gradual. Some do it all by themselves, others find assistance along the way or even have it done for them. Gay men and lesbians are fascinated with each other's coming out stories, as different as they are, because through these stories we are able to identify with others who have lived parallel lives and thereby see more deeply into ourselves. As Paul Monette writes, "I still shiver with a kind of astonished delight when a gay brother or sister tells of that narrow escape from the coffin world of the closet."[13]

I know I was always attracted to other boys, from as early as I can remember. I was curious about them, wanted to look at them, be with them, touch them. I got really excited whenever I saw a boy who interested me. Somehow I knew this was wrong. When my parents caught me on top of other boys, pretending to be wrestling, they yelled at me and I got punished. Once, when I ran outside to show the bigger boys in the neighborhood the nail polish on my fingernails that I asked my older sister to put on, they all jeered and mocked me, calling me "Sissy." I was only five years old at the time. I went back home and wouldn't talk to anyone about what had happened. I learned I was different from everyone else, and I felt like I didn't belong, anywhere.

Whenever I tried to be close to other boys, I felt brushed aside. But one day an older boy asked if I wanted to jerk off with him. I was twelve and he was fourteen and my initiation into sex between males had begun. I hadn't even heard the word "homosexual." Of course, I had heard the word "faggot" being shouted by other boys, but I barely knew what it meant. I wasn't queer. All I knew was that I wasn't like the other boys, at least not like most of them. Two years later the secret got out in school. One day I was cornered at school, in the gym locker room, by another boy who taunted me, "Faggot! Here, suck this!" And there, in front of everyone I went to school with, he whipped out his penis and pushed it toward my mouth. I had been sitting on a bench at the time. Suddenly, I felt sick. The mockery was endless. The only place to hide was in my head—so I did. I disappeared like a rabbit down a hole.

Years later, I was riding the subway home late one Friday night. A group of four young guys, all outlandishly dressed, came aboard the car I was on and stood nearby. They were laughing, joking, their eyes darting quickly around the subway car—at last becoming fixed on me. I felt drawn to them somehow, fascinated by each one of them. I kept staring at them, laughing at their jokes, amused by their mannerisms. Perhaps I had read somewhere about queeny men, but I had never seen any before, certainly not this close. I wasn't put off—not even a little. They seemed to sense my interest, my curiosity, perhaps even my hidden desire. They kept looking at me, but I had only half-conscious thoughts at the time. I still lived my life as if lost in a fog. Suddenly, the subway train came to another stop, the doors opened with a jolt, and in unison they all turned toward me, gesturing, smiling, at last calling, "Goodbye!" They pointed toward me with their arms outstretched, their wrists waving, as if in a grand gesture of farewell. And I, smiling too, called back, "Goodbye." Then in unison again they turned, laughing loudly, and instantly jumped off the subway car before the doors closed. They were still laughing, looking back in my direction and pointing, as they walked off. What might have been a moment of self-consciousness instead became a moment of self-awareness. In one blinding flash of recognition, the thought came into my mind: Take me with you, please. But I just stood there frozen, unable to move, and then the subway doors closed. We were off, and they were gone.

After that I withdrew even more, until years later when I went into therapy to get cured. Naturally, it didn't work. Oh, I did grow more self-assured and more confident, but these "feelings" for men didn't go away. Still, I had always expected marriage and children in my future—not a life with men. I had always yearned to be a father with children of my own from almost as far back as I could remember, certainly from as far back as I desired to touch and be close to other boys my own age. I still remember imagining the distant day when I would finally become a father.

Therapy ended, successfully I thought, and later I got married. Children eventually came along, but these "feelings" for men never quite left me. They might subside for a time, but they always recurred. At the time I had no other way to understand them except as a sign of sickness. So I continued to suppress them—for several more years. Then I met an out gay man I had an affair with, and those suppressed emotions and desires were finally out in the open. Though my hunger was satisfied for a time, my life was thrown into impossible turmoil. After all, I had a family and I wasn't prepared to give that up. How did I come to terms with it all? Once again I suppressed what now became for the first time much more clearly recognized as a "need" for a man in my life.

This time the suppression of essential aspects of my nature lasted even longer. I had even thought I could live without ever again satisfying those "other" desires of mine. How else was I to reconcile my need for a man with being married and having children? So the years slowly ticked past, and I learned how to live an incomplete life.

Unexpectedly, one day I met another man who was to change my life forever. Our relationship began quietly enough, as co-workers. But it gradually deepened, reaching a level of emotional intimacy that I scarcely had ever experienced before. Each of us felt deeply drawn to the other—profoundly so, inexplicably. When our intimacy at long last embraced the forbidden, the erotic, this time I was prepared. I knew that—this time—I would give myself to him. I would not again shrink back out of shame and fear. I had to give myself to this new experience in order to become whole, for my life finally to be complete.

For months I wrestled with myself until finally I resolved to follow a different path than the one I had been walking up until then. The inner conflict was agony. I even heard myself saying to this brave new man in my life, "One day, I want to live with you." Though my choice to have the complete relationship with a man I always longed for was a conscious one, it still remained secret, entirely hidden from everyone.

But secrets have a way of surfacing, and this secret was no different. Its revelation prompted as great a crisis as any I had ever experienced. Conflict and ambivalence raged within me. I had to find a way to navigate this new turbulence. Then it came. It was early one morning, well before dawn. I began to write down all of the conflict within me: what to do, how to proceed, how to live my life from this point forward. Right then and there I turned to face my shame. I turned toward an uncertain future, guided by the hope that one day I would make this *dream a reality.*

SIGNIFICANCE OF SHAME FOR SELF-ESTEEM, IDENTITY, AND INTIMACY

Coming out of shame is a journey toward wholeness and self-respect. These are the fundamental building blocks of what we somewhat ambiguously refer to as *self-acceptance.* In order to become whole, we must embrace all of the facets of our being—including those parts we have disavowed or cast away. We can never become whole by disowning essential aspects of our nature. Wholeness is never attained by splintering the self further, only by uniting and integrating it more completely. We transform shame, and in so doing become whole, by actively reowning all of those rejected orphans within us. That is the path of healing, the path that ultimately leads toward realizing inner worth and securing self-esteem. If shame is the source of low self-esteem, dignity and pride in self are the source of high self-esteem. Not only must we develop an inner source of valuing and pride in self, we must also acknowledge shame and thereby redeem it.

Self-esteem rises and falls along with the vicissitudes of shame. For self-esteem to remain securely anchored within us, we must learn to tolerate recurrences of shame, know how to release shame without internalizing it further, and develop tools for effectively counteracting the sources of shame throughout the life cycle. For women who love women and men who love men, that is an enormous challenge, particularly when society conspires against us. But self-esteem is not alone in foundering in the storm of shame. Identity becomes equally captured in its relentless grip.

What we mean by identity is larger than the myriad of coalescing beliefs, attitudes, and perceptions that we invariably hold about ourselves.

Identity is not just the cumulative answers to those ageless questions "Who am I?" "Where do I belong?"

Identity is the conscious experience of the unique and unfolding self within each and every individual, coupled with a distinctive inner relationship that actually evolves inside of us. In part we *detect* who we are, the very self unfolding within us, and in part we *invent* who we are. The process we engage in when we give shape to our individual identity is historical, creative, and active—however subliminal it may be. Identity unites who we were in the past with who we have become in the present, but also shapes our future self. The inner experience of ourselves over time is both continuous and discontinuous; in important ways we are still very much the person we always were, but we are also distinctly different now in other, vital ways. We never remain altogether static and unchanging.

Our inner relationship includes the characteristic ways we treat ourselves in every major circumstance, from triumphs to defeats, and in every minor one as well. It's ongoing and constant, whether we're tuned in to it or not. It's the ways we speak to ourselves, the thoughts and feelings we have about ourselves, but it's also actions—the ways we behave toward ourselves.

Identity also embraces characteristic and patterned expressions of affect from ourselves to ourselves, just as we express particular affects toward countless others. All of our relationships with other people are actually governed by affect. Those relationships are simply more visible, more easily observable, whereas the inner relationship with ourselves is invisible. Our various and changing relationships with others form the unfolding tapestry of our lives as we live them out over time, but this other, hidden, inner relationship with ourselves forms the often inexplicable core of our being. Identity is fundamentally a relational pattern within the self, one that is distinctive and active, however subliminal.

By shaping this emergent inner relationship that we come to have with ourselves, shame places a distinctive stamp on identity, thereby exercising a powerful role in directing, distorting, and even crippling identity. In the lives of lesbians, gay men, and others who experience themselves as bisexual, the struggle to attain a secure, coherent identity—one that gives dignity to self and meaning to life—is made profoundly difficult.

Self-esteem and identity are precious to us all, but especially urgent in the lives of gays and lesbians. Intimacy is equally so. Our capacity for intimacy can be damaged by the ravages of shame. In order to experience intimacy, we must be able to approach others and also be willing to be approached by them. We must convey our interest openly (none of us do all that well at mind reading). We must allow ourselves to communicate the excitement we feel in discovering new friends. We must also enjoy communality with others. In that process, we open ourselves to each other and become deliberately vulnerable.

Vulnerability is an opening of the self in union with another. In order for vulnerability to occur in safety, without shame, it must be followed by the other person also becoming vulnerable. That is what completes the experience for both and leads to deepened intimacy. But hasn't vulnerability been precarious in the lives of lesbians and gay men? For us the hope of safety has too often been eclipsed by the shadow of danger. Tomkins notes that when two individuals are able and willing to *mutually* unburden themselves of shame, this shared experience can produce a tie that binds the two forever. However, when shame remains impermeable, unexpressed and unshared, then intimacy is altogether prevented. Shame will bar the gates to intimacy like no other affect can. It is the foremost obstacle in the pursuit of intimate relations between all individuals, regardless of sexual orientation.

Because shame can reach so deeply and widely into our individual and collective lives, it is an affect that is quite capable of capturing and dominating us. For this reason alone, women who love women and men who love men become people who are haunted by shame.

REVEALING ONESELF AND ENCOUNTERING SHAME

Just as shame has numerous sources, both historical and current, it also plays out in everyday life in various ways. Once its characteristic signs are known, you can readily observe shame in several contexts particular to gay life. Though different in certain respects, each of these contexts involves interactions with other people, even casual ones, coupled with a certain measure of self-revelation. Because shame always reveals the inner self by exposing it to immediate view, any circumstance that directly invites us to reveal ourselves further, particularly while we are encountering others, has greater potential to evoke shame. When we encounter others, we invariably do so in the shadow of shame.

Self-Disclosure

Whenever gay people are faced with situations in their daily lives that involve self-disclosure or invite self-identification as gay or lesbian, they are immediately thrown into a scene fraught with the potential for shame. It happens when someone asks you if you live alone, or who you're bringing to an office party, or what you did over the holidays, or where you've gone on a vacation. Our first impulse is often to lie or deflect the question if we're not out at work or to certain friends.

Societally imposed silence, coupled with accumulated scenes of ridicule connected to being gay, has reinforced the behavior of continued hiding and secrecy. Historically, hiding has been necessary for survival. The gradual lifting of the societal taboo on homosexuality in recent years has increasingly called into question the decision to remain hidden. But whether we self-disclose being lesbian or gay to family, friends, co-workers, or even acquaintances continues to be problematic even now when the risks of exposure seem less severe. If we work in a city with an antidiscrimination policy, our fears may be lessened, but the majority of gays and lesbians don't live with such protections. More to the point, even legal "protection" doesn't guarantee that the climate at our workplace is open and supportive.

Self-disclosure is an inherent source of shame, however and whenever it occurs, because it invariably means exposing your inner self directly to the gaze of another person. Self-disclosure of any kind is actually a form of *self-exposure,* so that whenever we reveal ourselves, we risk shame. The risks will vary depending on exactly what we reveal. It's one thing to tell someone you're interested in them and be rejected. Coming out to someone who doesn't know you're gay or lesbian risks not only rejection, but disgust, contempt, and possibly the loss of the relationship.

Even people who are completely "out" may unexpectedly find themselves tongue-tied and embarrassed about being gay in a new setting, or with new people in a familiar setting. The acute self-consciousness and awkwardness we feel, the anticipation of censure, condemnation, or judgment, the dread of rejection, even the worry that self-identifying as gay will evoke shame on the face of the other person—these are all ways in which shame dynamics operate in this context, making it so highly charged. How will the other person respond? Shock, outrage, disgust, silence, denial?

Anyone whose inherent differentness is hidden must struggle with whether or not to reveal it, how and when to self-disclose. This is equally true for African Americans, for example, who can "pass" as Caucasian. But the dynamics of self-disclosure and self-exposure reach a heightened level for gay people, since to self-identify as lesbian or gay opens you not only to ridicule and judgment but to the severest of all social sanctions, ostracism and violence. To identify yourself as gay means publicly connecting yourself to what is judged as unnatural or diseased in the minds of others, especially for gay men now, because they are branded with the additional stigma of AIDS.

> It was strange when I came out to my family. Almost every-
> body asked right away, "Are you okay?" Meaning, did I have
> AIDS? And even though I was glad they cared, it really bothered
> me that they saw a disease first, and me second. They didn't ask if
> I was dating anyone, if I was happy, they asked if I was sick.

Facial Gazing

There is another context in which self-exposure operates, this time with other people who are also gay or lesbian. One of the most potent shame scenes occurs whenever two individuals look directly into each other's eyes. This is not *inherently* a shame scene, but it has become so through socialization. Looking directly into someone's eyes, regardless of their sex, is the most intense form of intimacy that human beings experience. It is through the eyes that we are able to experientially enter one another and, in so doing, feel merged as *one*. The eyes are not only the principal vehicle for accomplishing this identification, but they also are a prime organ for the expression and communication of affect. Tomkins says that the power of this connection and the need for societies to control it result in the universal taboo on the eye-to-eye scene expressed in the so-called evil eye.

Even in Sophocles's great tragedy *Oedipus Rex*, the real crime that Oedipus actually committed was not sleeping with his mother, but having uncovered and *seen* her nakedness—and his punishment was not castration, but *blindness*. The punishment, according to Tomkins, is not a sexual metaphor; the visual offense was judged the greater crime. When psychoanalysis later adopted the Oedipus myth to interpret the family romance of mother-

father-child, the meaning of that myth was subverted: the greater importance of the eye-to-eye scene was buried and its significance therefore lost.

Think of earliest infancy and one of the most universal scenes: mother
or father cradling their infant during breast or bottle feeding. During feeding, infant and parent smile into each other's face and gaze into each other's
eyes, locked in a facial embrace. Through their eyes they enter one another
and experientially become *one*. That facial embrace, in which infant and
parent gaze fixedly into each other's eyes and smile lovingly into each other's
face, continues well past the moment hunger is satiated. That is fusion,
merging—the felt experience of identification—the source of that oceanic
sense of basic security.

That primary scene of mutual facial gazing is what we recapture later
in adulthood whenever we encounter another person with whom we are able
to once again surrender to that facial embrace without shame. When we
have truly found such a person, we invariably label what we are feeling as
"falling in love." We even recognize two lovers by the simple observation
that they are able to gaze endlessly into each other's eyes wherever they are
—on the beach, in a restaurant, on a bus, even on the checkout line at the
grocery.

Our capacity to look directly into someone's eyes and hold that mutual
gaze is rendered taboo in all cultures by shaming children in two different
ways: *What's the matter with you? Don't be so shy—come out from there
and show your face.* But children just as often hear the opposite: *Stop
staring! Don't be so rude!* When children are thus doubly shamed, for being
shy *and* for staring, they invariably learn to inhibit the facial gaze. By adulthood, when we meet the eyes of another person, particularly a stranger's, we
invariably look away. The eye-to-eye scene, which in infancy was filled with
enjoyment and serenity, now has become a shame scene of enormous power.

But there is another side to this question. We're also taught in business
and professional settings to look directly into people's eyes when shaking
hands or speaking, and in those instances *not* making eye contact can give
the message that we've got something to hide, that we're untrustworthy.

That scene of looking directly into the eyes of the stranger is, for gay
men and lesbians, a highly charged interpersonal moment, known in the gay
world as *cruising*. Our eyes communicate affect of all kinds, not just explicitly sexual interest. When we look at the face of a particular person
who interests us, we directly convey our interest. We are captured by the

stranger's face and wish to explore it with our eyes. When our eyes meet the stranger's, we bid one another enter. It is affect and identification at work here, not sexuality specifically or even necessarily. The eyes may indeed convey sexual interest, but that is a special case of a much broader phenomenon.

We look at the stranger's face because it interests us and we wish to explore it visually. We look to explore, to convey interest, and to admire. We look into the stranger's eyes in order to experience mutuality, oneness—to merge. Also, we look so that we might register our sexual interest, our attraction to the stranger, even our availability. Cruising between gay men or between lesbians comprises all of these various dimensions, not just sexual desire. Because mutual facial gazing has already become a shame scene for all people anyway, it is much more so for gay people in this particular context. Not only do we run the risk of identifying ourselves as gay in a situation of unknown danger, but the very act of signaling interest to a stranger, sexual or otherwise, opens us to shame when our interest is not returned.

> *I was walking my dog in the park, thinking about some problems at work. Then I felt someone was staring at me. I looked up, saw her, then looked away. I felt uncomfortable because there were all these people around, mothers with their kids, you know. But I was fascinated, and surprised, curious. I looked back. Now she was looking away, and I felt embarrassed. Was I wrong thinking she was interested in me? I felt stupid. Maybe she was looking at my dog—I mean, Doris is beautiful! Then she looked up, and neither of us broke the contact. Incredible deep eyes; I just dived right into them. The embarrassment melted away and there was nobody there but us.*

Body Exposure

Cruising in the gay world becomes a highly charged shame scene because, like self-disclosure, it is invariably a time of heightened self-exposure. Since cruising goes beyond the eyes to involve the whole body, there's a third form in which self-exposure may be observed: body exposure. Here, the body itself is exposed to view and becomes a source of further shame. First of all, every individual growing up in an appearance-oriented culture like ours will internalize some degree of body shame. This is a culture that holds some very specific images of what we should look like: women should be slim, men should be tall.

How pervasive and long-lasting that shame will be varies widely, of course, but no one escapes. There are particular arenas for body exposure, and therefore body shame, in gay life that cannot be discounted: the bar scene, discos, the beach with varying degrees of nudity, restaurants, movies and concerts, music festivals, and of course the gym. In each of these situations, gay men and lesbians expose their bodies to one another—or *feel* as if they do—and they immediately begin to compare their own body to someone else's: God—*look at those pecs! I could work out a million years and never look like that!* When we make these comparisons, we can become immersed in shame. Invidiously comparing ourselves to others on any characteristic, the body included, usually ends in a reversal: we devalue ourselves for the comparison. In these various situations involving body exposure, it is the body itself that is compared, found lacking, and judged to be deficient. The beach scene, in particular, reawakens earlier shame directly connected to nudity because the body is on public display with the least allowable covering. All of the prior experiences of adolescent shame about our bodies being seen (in gym class, at school, in summer camp) now become focused, concentrated in this single moment.

The human body has been a source of shame for some time, especially in American culture, but also in other countries. Uncovering parts of the body is a potent source of shame in particular cultures around the globe; many Islamic women, for instance, cover their hair and some parts of their faces. The degree to which the body becomes directly associated with shame varies from culture to culture and has also changed over the centuries. That shame has multiple sources; the image by which we're shamed is often cultural, yet the transmission of shame occurs through the family and the peer group. In the family, parents and siblings directly shame children about their bodies. Families also have their own particular targets for shaming, targets that sometimes contradict cultural norms.

My mother was always saying I was too skinny, who did I think I was, a model? But I wasn't trying to be anybody, just me. That was my body type—long legs, no hips, an Italian Twiggy. So

*there she was making fun of my dress size and nagging me about
how little I ate at dinner, in front of the family, even in front of my
friends! I was mortified when she'd call me "Beanpole."*

Body shame is also transmitted by peers, who can be unbelievably
cruel in ridiculing others who are too tall or too short, too skinny or too fat,
girls who develop breasts well ahead of their peers or instead lag behind
them or have breasts that are too large or breasts that are too small, boys
who mature either very quickly or very slowly or have penises that are too
big or penises that are too small, and any child who shows a disability of any
kind. Body shame also stems from the epoch of adolescence itself. Adolescence is a time of universal vulnerability to shame because the uncontrolla-
ble ways our bodies are changing expose us to unwanted attention.

Body shame also comes directly from the culture in which we live. In a
culture that overvalues youth and prizes bodily appearance, the body becomes an inescapable source of shame. All of us invariably age, and the
humiliation that accrues from aging is not mitigated in American culture by
enhanced respect for our elders. Instead we cast them aside. In cultures that
have historically prized and esteemed their aged members, China and Japan
for example, the potential shame of growing old is markedly lessened—
though Japan is now becoming more like American culture in its response to
its aged. American culture's fascination with appearance becomes an additional source of shame about the particular body we have inherited. We are
continually shown images of the ideal man or woman through the media,
and all of us fall hopelessly short of the ideal, whether it's Marky Mark or
Cindy Crawford. We do not enjoy our body and do not admire it because we
are not encouraged to do so. Instead we criticize and hate it and seek ways to
disguise or alter the body we have. Because they've learned to be hypercritical of their appearance, women suffer more shame about their bodies than
men, and we see its signs in the diet industry, cosmetic surgery, and the
spread of eating disorders.

For gays, body shame is even further magnified since gay relationships,
particularly for men, have for so long been moored to youthfulness and
attractiveness—to certain images of the body itself. With the body being the
principal focus of attraction and, paradoxically, also the source of shame,
the very process of encountering others is made deeply ambivalent for all
people, especially problematic for many, and altogether impossible for

some. Situations that promise encounters with nameless strangers, the bar and the gym in particular, invariably become scenes of heightened shame. Whenever rejection is even anticipated, the potential for shame intensifies.

The female body has been an object for admiration in many cultures for quite some time, unfortunately contributing to women being viewed solely as sex objects. That has certainly fueled exploitation. But admiration does not have to be exploitative. The situation for men is different because the male body has not been an equal object for admiration. Openly expressed admiration for the body has generally been reserved only for women —except perhaps in classical Greece—although that is now changing to also include the male body. We can see widespread evidence of that change occurring in American culture in print and television ads for cologne, underwear, and soap.

To some extent, the male body continues to be a source of shame, not of admiration, with the mutual expression of admiration between men equally bound by shame. Men do not freely admire each other, thereby meeting each other's need for affirmation. Nor do they openly admire each other's bodies. While that is almost universally the case for men, it is less true for women. Women are certainly more able to admire one another openly, thereby affirming each other, because the expression of this particular interpersonal need has not become bound by shame for women in the way that it has for men.

GAY ATTITUDE:
A DEFENSE AGAINST SHAME

There is a particular defending script that gay men and lesbians use against shame: attitude. What does this actually refer to? In places like a bar or even the gym, for instance, gay men will act or appear "superior" to others by, in effect, elevating their noses and thereby looking more or less disdainful. There's a caustic line that sums it up perfectly: "Honey, he doesn't have attitude, he has *altitude*."

> *One night at the bar, I spent the evening just observing people's faces and not really listening to what they were saying. It was like watching TV and turning the volume way down, you*

know? What I did was just look for the emotions I saw on every-one's face, and I was amazed. There was all this shame: guys with their eyes down, heads down, avoiding each other's eyes, some even blushing. It wasn't even for very long, kind of in flashes, but I did see it. I also saw all this other negative stuff: people sneering, or looking like they wanted to spit, or looking angry. I especially noticed guys with their noses in the air, acting like their shit didn't stink.

Contempt is the source of conceit, arrogance, and superiority, of judgmental, fault-finding, or condescending attitudes toward others. The message conveyed by the look of contempt is a strident one: I am better than you, cuter than you, more sophisticated, my body is superior to yours, so don't bother approaching because I'll look down my nose at you. Gay attitude is rooted in contempt as a defense against experiencing further shame. Contempt for others is an attempt to protect ourselves against shame by *transferring* it to someone else. Unfortunately, despised minorities often target other minorities or particular members of their own group for shaming in an attempt to transfer shame. It's not surprising, then, that we direct against our gay sisters and brothers the opprobrium we receive from the wider culture. In the gay world, we're currently seeing a great deal of contempt for drag queens and leather queens, expressed in the desire that they not be included in Gay Pride parades because they're spoiling it for "normal" gays. Here gay men are being criticized and looked down on for not fitting in enough with the straight world. We hear something opposite among lesbians who attack "lipstick lesbians"—gay women who dress and wear makeup in ways that are stereotypically feminine in our culture. These women are accused of not being "real" lesbians.

These are just two examples of contempt directed at certain gays and lesbians by other gays and lesbians. Think of all the times you've heard gay friends or acquaintances disparage each other in some way, specifically in a gay context. By criticizing other lesbians and gays for not being hip enough, political enough, young enough, mature enough, out enough—or whatever failing we choose as a deadly one—we divide our community.

Shaming other gays and lesbians may give us a false sense of safety by making us feel superior, but it can never create real inner security. It is a response to shame that doesn't truly transform it. Contempt is *not* pride, it's arrogance. Contempt also distorts our relationships with others, in this case other gays and lesbians. Contempt always divides us into the worthy and the unworthy.

> *You know what I enjoy most about going to P-town? Every-*
> *one seems so relaxed. Men and women talk to each other, go to*
> *each other's bars. Even better, there's this feel about the place,*
> *that people can smile at each other, compliment each other and*
> *it's not a come-on. It's just enjoying the scene. Why can't it be like*
> *that back home?*

It is our powerlessness and shame that breed contempt, and gay atti-tude is how our contempt manifests itself. But attitude is a waste of the real power we possess, and contempt yields only a false sense of empowerment. Feeling better than others, feeling superior even to other gays, is only a mask disguising how we secretly feel.

CHAPTER THREE

From Gay Shame to Gay Pride

The 1996 presidential election is moving into full swing in the United States, and with it has come the emergence of gay/lesbian rights as a subject for national debate. Lesbian and gay issues have moved center stage both in the media and in national politics beginning with the last national election. That was a time of hope. But how much has *really* changed since 1992?

The Colorado ballot proposition opposing gay rights was overturned in the state courts, yet the final word has not been heard. New municipal and state ballot initiatives threaten us, promising continued confrontation with intolerance at all levels of society. The ban on gays serving openly in the military became a focus for intense ideological dispute early in Bill Clinton's presidency. Though fiercely debated in the media and in televised congressional committee hearings, the ban still stands despite some cosmetic changes.

Even members of Congress are not exempt from intolerance. In 1995, Representative Barney Frank was actually referred to as "Barney Fag" by the House Republican majority leader, Representative Dick Armey, during an interview with radio broadcasters. Armey made the unbelievable claim that it was merely a slip of the tongue and not at all a revelation of his true feelings. That this occurred after the Republican sweep to power in the 1994 midterm elections signals a return to a climate of meanness and bigotry. We now face a hostile Congress and a diffident White House.[1]

The 1992 Republican Party convention is not so distant—but it will be forever seared in memory as a poignant image, an extraordinary display of shaming voices attached to familiar faces—prime-time faces—that were also angry, disgusted, and contemptuous while they were speaking to the nation. Who was their hatred and contempt directed at? Toward the *offending other* in their midst—the homosexual. Gay rights have no place "in a nation we still call God's country," proclaimed Pat Buchanan. All of the speakers evoked images of moral decay, as though homosexuals were likely to bring about complete social ruin just by being alive.

The AIDS crisis has made our opponents' metaphors of illness and decay even more damning. Those hateful faces and accusatory voices at the Republican convention focused their attacks on the "homosexual lifestyle" as a contaminant that must be expunged from the human community. But homosexuality is no more a lifestyle than heterosexuality is: the lesbian or gay experience is a way of *being*, not a "style."

All of these attacks were justified by appeals to Christian religious values, much as slavery in the United States was once justified by Scripture. After all, we face a religious war for the soul of America, according to Pat Buchanan at the 1992 Republican convention. Because they are the offending other, gays and lesbians are not under God and not part of America. This religious war is once again sanctioned by the highest religious authority. Even Pope John Paul II has approved such rhetorical attacks against gays and lesbians—much as the non-Christian world had been subjugated in previous centuries and Native peoples murdered and destroyed "in the name of God." If gays and lesbians are this decade's prime target, who will be next?

In one sense, the shaming that is being directed at gays has progressed from a private and more personal level, involving mainly family and religion, to a public and national one where it now plays out openly in the arena of politics and culture.

When political leaders in the United States publicly single out gays and lesbians, marking them as a pollutant, they are doing what has been done for centuries—placing gays and lesbians completely outside society. Even more, they are trying to do what Hitler and the Nazis did so effectively sixty years ago to the Jews—mobilizing public contempt toward a particular group judged to be a cancer destroying the nation from within. Whenever a particular group of people becomes the approved object of contempt by the wider society, anything becomes possible. *Any* action may be taken against them, even murder, because contempt invariably makes its target less than human.

What television accomplished during the 1992 Republican Party convention was to facilitate the rapid magnification of the affects of shame and contempt along with the accompanying ideology of contempt-based group hatred. That spectacle sent a resounding message to the American people: lesbians and gay men live the wrong kind of life; they are sick, evil, sinners, hated by God, in a word, an abomination; they are not like the rest of us; they are alien. All of religious authority seemed on their side, for where were authoritative dissenting voices?

No one of equal authority rose to challenge these harbingers of hate. As a community, gays and lesbians are too enmeshed in shame to respond adequately and without shame. Besides, there was no opportunity for anyone to respond to these attacks at the time—no equal airtime. We were, in effect, silenced.

Such a message, steeped in graphic visual and auditory images, served only to reconfirm the prejudices of the wider society toward gays and lesbians as well as the negative attitudes of lesbians and gays toward themselves. Those vivid televised speeches, accompanied by applause and cheering from the assembled Republican Party delegates, actually telescoped the process by which shame becomes internalized and then magnified. Anyone watching those proceedings could immediately enter the televised scene and thereby experience the intended feelings and perceptions: being lesbian or gay is absolutely shameful, disgusting, and the only proper response toward gays is contempt.

Gays and lesbians watching had their own shame and self-contempt reawakened, however subliminally, however brief or lasting. Once again we were graphically shown the contemptuous faces we had known in earlier years. Once again we heard the accusatory voices we had repeatedly heard in scene after scene throughout childhood and adolescence.

These are the shaming faces that haunt us, and their shaming voices unfortunately become installed as inner voices within us, which we then mistake as our own.

SHAME SCENES CONNECTED
TO BEING GAY OR LESBIAN

Think back to childhood for a moment. Remember when your friends would gather and suddenly start taunting and jeering? Someone would be singled out, targeted for shaming by the group. Usually it would start with just one or two individuals, but it would quickly gather steam as others joined in—while everyone else cringed in silence. No one stood up to them. "You wimp," they would say. "Sissy." "You homo." "You faggot, you queer." The taunting would have been different if you were a girl: "You boy!" "You act like a boy!" "Are you a lesbo?"

One seven-year-old boy recently told us that he was called "gay" for wearing a yellow slicker to school and thereafter refused to ever wear a raincoat again. Another was called "homo" just for playfully patting another boy's back on the soccer field, and you can bet he never did that again. Even when the action being shamed isn't specifically gay, as in these examples, that label is used because it's the worst imaginable slur, the most hated. Whether or not the action prompting the insult is actually connected with homosexuality, the connection between shame and homosexuality is indelibly made. Such a moment is a scene of ridicule and humiliation. You've been shamed in front of everyone that you have to look in the face, live with, play with, study with.

In that singular moment when such an insult is hurled at a particular child, time becomes frozen. The moment burns itself into memory for the individual who is targeted and also for others standing around watching.

The child who already senses being different from other same-sex friends can only feel incredibly exposed and deficient in response. This awareness of gender difference is often the earliest conscious perception of what will much later unfold as homosexuality.

I don't fit in. I don't like playing the same games the other boys do. I don't even like playing with them at all 'cause they don't seem to like me.

That scene of public group shaming is even more pernicious for the boy or girl who is suspected of actually being queer—he or she may be forced to live with incessant ridicule. The girl who feels drawn to other girls and the boy who feels drawn to other boys have now been taught to hide, to deny, to pretend, because their survival depends on it. Everyone present during the scene, even as bystanders, has learned—and continues to learn whenever that scene is reenacted—that attachments to our own sex make us suspect because they are shameful. Why else would we have been targeted for ridicule in the first place? Shame is inherently self-validating: to be shamed makes us feel deserving of shame. Such shame is like an exile from which there can be no way back. Secrecy, avoidance, and denial then become vital means of protection against further shame.

This peer group shaming scene via name calling is universal throughout childhood, occurring in many cultures, and it is the earliest typical scene of shame directly connected to being gay or lesbian. Through its reenactment, homosexuality and shame become tightly bound together for every individual, gay and non-gay alike. Later in adulthood, whenever someone cracks a disparaging "gay joke" or makes a derogatory antigay remark in your presence, whether or not you're gay yourself, you can be instantly transported back into those earliest shame scenes from childhood.

If you *are* gay and hear an insulting gay joke, then it's your own shame that is reactivated. If you're not gay, you fall silent anyway because you react much as you did in that original peer group scene: distancing yourself from the target of shame by tacit agreement. In either case, you feel initially startled during these equally offensive adult situations because you're still controlled by those older scenes of peer group ridicule. If you feel momentarily paralyzed in the present circumstance—wondering what to do, questioning whether or not to object, even doubting your perception of what you heard—it's because you're simultaneously reliving the original scene at that very instant.

We are once again gripped by shame—the shame we had first experienced during that original scene even if we had only been spectators at the time. As spectators in the original childhood scene, we experienced shame vicariously, through identification with the person actually targeted for shaming. This can happen in different ways. A gay child who escapes notice and therefore shaming nevertheless witnesses (and maybe even participates in) such scenes, just as a non-gay child who is caught up as a bystander in the group shaming scene is also a witness. Both the gay and non-gay child who are witnesses will initially feel shame, and either child may later come to identify with the shamer and so lose awareness of shame.

The same dynamic occurs when we unexpectedly hear viciously racist, anti-Semitic, or misogynist jokes or comments, become frozen in the moment, and then feel like kicking ourselves afterward for not having objected or challenged the speaker. At that moment, we are simultaneously gripped by the power of old scenes.

Public name calling and other forms of ridicule during childhood constitute one class of scenes in which shame and homosexuality become inextricably bound together. Another occurs during early adolescence, during the junior high or middle school years, ages twelve to fourteen. This is the period when the peer group subculture coalesces into a socializing force that now rivals the family, at least in the United States. Because all adolescents yearn to belong to their group, peers at this time are able to exercise even greater power to shame one another.

Family life teachers are reporting that many young teenage boys are ashamed of masturbating.[2] They now equate it with being gay and therefore with losing their manhood. What we see operating here in the peer group in a new way is our widespread cultural taboo on masturbation. That taboo was behind the controversy over former Surgeon General Joycelyn Elders's suggestion that schools discuss masturbation in sex education programs. But that taboo reveals the power of shame, and the power of homophobia in our culture.

Vulnerability to shame becomes especially heightened as a result of the bodily changes taking place in early adolescence. Further, images of maleness and femaleness are forming, as are gender components of identity. We're shown particular images in the media of men and women to admire— sports figures, celebrities, film, rock, and rap stars, military heroes. We're taught to emulate these images, but we also learn to compare ourselves to them, often feeling lacking as a result. Rarely do we live up to the images we're handed by our culture. The process of discovering what it means to be a man or a woman is thus partly cultural and partly personal.

To be publicly shamed by our peers for being queer at this particular time, for even looking or acting queer, unfortunately contaminates our emerging identity with judgments of being lesser. The homosexual male is invariably judged to be an inferior male, or equated with being a woman in a society that denigrates women. He is weak, not strong like men should be. He's also fearful, when true men are courageous. Similarly, the homosexual woman is judged to be an incomplete woman; lacking a man to be sexual with, she is simply not a real woman at all. She is hard, not soft, forceful instead of yielding. During adolescence, avoiding such indictments becomes paramount.

KEY DIMENSIONS OF SEXUAL ORIENTATION

To understand the dynamics of gay shame, we first have to reconsider the nature of sexual orientation itself. But sexual orientation has unfortunately been presumed to have only an erotic basis. Gay people are seen as gay because of who they have sex with, not because of who they *are*. But non-gays would hardly limit heterosexuality to its obvious erotic basis.

The erotic is one important dimension of what we generally refer to as sexual orientation. This sexual, specifically erotic dimension manifests in overtly expressed action, but, more important, it originates and appears initially in the form of *scenes* that are entirely internal. It is these imagined *erotic* scenes that become directed toward our own sex, the other sex, or both sexes. Operating first in our imagination, these explicitly sexual scenes form the erotic basis of sexual orientation, however it is directed.

There is a second dimension to sexual orientation that is not specifically erotic at all. Quite the contrary, these scenes involve imagined *touching/holding,* a physical closeness. These are explicit scenes involving touching another person or being held, but they are not inherently sexual or even romantic. Here, touching expresses affection and tenderness, communicates protection and security, and is the foundation for trust—whether for infants, children, adolescents, or adults. Again, these touching and holding scenes occur entirely in imagination, however subliminally, and they become directed toward our own sex, the other sex, or both sexes. These two classes of scenes, erotic/sexual and touching/holding, both begin in imagination, but then may carry through into action, eventually culminating in overt expression. First you imagine hugging another boy, then you actually embrace him; first you imagine sexual acts like oral sex, then you do it. Sexual orientation refers to the predominant or recurring *direction* of these different types of scenes.

There is one final dimension to sexual orientation which, like the others, originates in another class of scenes; these particular scenes, however, are neither erotic nor physical. Instead, these are *identification* scenes. What is imagined here are scenes of merging and fusion with another individual. We imagine the deepest union with someone we yearn to be close to, the intimacy of being fused as *one;* we desire both to possess and to be like the other. This fusion through gazing continuously into each other's eyes is as fundamental a dimension of sexual orientation as the purely erotic is.

Erotic/sexual scenes, touching/holding scenes, and *identification/facial gazing scenes* constitute what is generally referred to, rather ambiguously, as *sexual orientation.* There's no hierarchy of scenes intended here. One type of scene is not superior to another; they're merely different, but each is nevertheless crucial to what we call sexual orientation. Similarly, we are not creating a separation between erotic/sexual desire and love/intimacy. All three types of scenes are vitally important. Ideally, all three become interconnected in our significant relationships, so that sex, affection, and intimacy become securely blended and freely expressed. These scenes can also vary independently in their direction. Children, for example, usually identify first with their mothers and then their fathers, but identification scenes can later accumulate primarily around one sex or the other. When fusion is desired with both sexes, erotic/sexual scenes may be directed exclusively toward one sex. Even when all three types of scenes are directed toward both sexes equally, this can occur simultaneously or else alternate over time, first toward one sex and then the other.

In order for our sexual orientation to develop positively, each of these three types of scenes must also become fused with, and thereby amplified by, positive affect. In the case of erotic/sexual scenes, the critical affect that must be fused with the scene is first excitement, followed by enjoyment; in the absence of fusion with excitement affect (the source of sexual arousal) the sexual drive simply ceases to function. At the first sign of fear, shame, or disgust, the drive is entirely disrupted, demonstrating the primacy of affect over the drives. Touching/holding scenes must become fused primarily with enjoyment affect, leading to the experience of mutual enjoyment when two individuals touch or hold each other; at certain times excitement affect may also become added to the experience, for example when the anticipation of a long-awaited embrace initially kindles excitement, later followed by enjoyment. Finally, identification scenes become amplified principally by enjoyment affect and produce the mutual enjoyment of facial gazing, the communion with another person that is felt by both people as union, *oneness*. For all three classes of scenes, the impact of shame is disruptive. The internalization of shame around these core scenes will distort their expression, crippling personality.

Erotic/sexual scenes, touching/holding scenes, and identification/facial gazing scenes accumulate in some women only around images of other women, just as they accumulate in particular men only around images of other men. The direction of these scenes—toward men, women, or both—results from a complex interaction of various factors. They include our genetic inheritance, prenatal influences, environment, culture, and the decisions we make in conducting our life. Even though there's an innate component to a same-sex sexual orientation, we still have to act on it; we have to decide to give it expression. And based on the accumulating evidence from both the natural and social sciences, homosexuality ought to be viewed as normal.

Sexual orientation *is* complex and only a complex theory will adequately capture and explain its nuances. We are arguing for a richer, more complete language to describe sexual orientation, to keep it from being moored to its more obvious erotic basis. We need to begin to define for ourselves what being gay and lesbian means, not remain silenced by the forces that shame us. So many of us know that there is much more to sexual orientation than sex, just as we know that the categories we have inherited for describing sexual orientation are more constricting than liberating.

SHAME BINDS: THE PROCESS OF SHAME INTERNALIZATION

Shame becomes internalized when connections are created between shame and other affects, between shame and any of our interpersonal needs, and also between shame and the physiological drives. The consistent or sufficient fusion of shame with other affects, drives, and needs is the key to its internalization. When a child is shamed for crying, those two affects become tightly bound. The identical thing happens when a child is shamed for expressing anger or even enjoyment. When it is an interpersonal need like touching/holding or a drive like sexuality that is responded to by shaming, the identical linkage between them develops because they happen simultaneously. With sufficient repetitions, the sequence of affect, interpersonal need, or drive followed by shame creates distinct *shame binds*. These shame binds then function to control the further expression of whatever has now become permanently linked with shame. Following the creation of a shame bind, just experiencing a particular shame-bound affect, drive, or need will itself spontaneously activate shame. No one else has to shame us again. Now shame is able to exercise a powerful, indirect control over our behavior.

Whenever she voiced anger toward her parents as a child, Karen was lectured and chastised repeatedly and in a demeaning way: *Don't you dare yell at me! How can you be so disrespectful! Nobody in our family has ever behaved like you! I can't believe you're our daughter! You're a disgrace!* Her parents' shaming behavior silenced her completely. Later as an adult, she found herself becoming frozen whenever she felt the least bit angry toward anyone. It could be in response to not getting a birthday card from someone she hoped would write to her, or even something minor like being in a rush and getting stuck in traffic behind a slow driver. Anger would start to mount inside of her, threaten to break free, but then she would feel inexplicably speechless, paralyzed. Invariably she would hang her head, feeling worthless for feeling angry in the first place. Being angry was shameful to Karen. Her natural feelings of anger spontaneously triggered shame because those two affects had become bound together. That shame bind now permanently controlled *any* future expression of anger. It could equally silence even her inner experience of anger.

While any of the affects, drives, or interpersonal needs can be readily targeted for shaming, a particular pattern of shame binds governs the gay and lesbian experience. Feeling lesser precisely because we are lesbian or gay is the specific consequence of this group of shame binds. When any of the classes of scenes that make up our sexual orientation (touching/holding scenes, identification/facial gazing scenes, and erotic/sexual scenes) are directed toward or focused around our own sex, and when these scenes also become fused with shame instead of the positive affects of excitement and enjoyment, then the stage is set for the development of specifically gay or lesbian shame.

Shaming the Need for Touching/Holding

Shame becomes bound to touching/holding scenes when boys are ridiculed, laughed at, or mocked for touching one another. That shaming occurs in the family when boys are greeted with handshakes instead of with hugs by their fathers, older brothers, or other male relatives because they're judged to be "too old" for hugs. For girls, shame around touching or embracing other girls is not as intense or widespread, but shaming still occurs in the adolescent peer group if girls are too affectionate in public.

These shaming interactions can also occur when mothers shame their sons or fathers shame their daughters. For example, fathers will often shame their adolescent daughters for wanting to continue sitting on their laps as they had always done before. Parents, siblings, or relatives of either sex can be the source of shaming targeted to same-sex touching. For example, one boy was repeatedly shamed by his older sister whenever he reached to embrace or kiss his older brother.

Often, the mere look of shame on the face of either parent, in direct response to physical contact, can itself be enough to generate shame in the young girl or boy. Even when shaming the need for touching/holding does not occur directly within the family, it will definitely happen outside the family. Peers are brutal in shaming anyone they observe to openly express physical affection for another, especially during early adolescence. This general shame bind translates into a specifically gay or lesbian shame bind when the principal or exclusive focus of touching and holding becomes, however subliminally, your own sex. Then the shame that has been bound to the need for touching/holding renders such contact forbidden.

Boys don't hug or kiss other boys, or touch each other gently, with affection. Girls may walk arm in arm or dance together, but they don't embrace with their whole bodies. Children do all of these, but not boys becoming men, not girls becoming women—unless it's with the *other* sex. Just to imagine scenes of touching or holding someone of your own sex in any of these ways can spontaneously activate shame: *There's something really wrong with me.* This self-judgment begins in adolescence and continues well into adulthood.

What does remain an acceptable form of physical expression for both boys and men, however, is hitting or punching each other. Only that form of touching between males remains free of shame. How does this come about? The pattern of gender shaming in contemporary society is revealing: boys are heavily shamed for expressing the affects of fear, distress, and shame itself and also for expressing the need for touching/holding. But they are equally encouraged to express anger while also asserting their need for power—these are culturally approved. The result of this differential shaming pattern is that touching between males can still occur, but only when it serves the expression of anger or the expression of the need for power, as in dominance. The only form of male-to-male touching that remains entirely free of shaming, then, is aggressive or combative touching—boys actively hitting or punching each other, during roughhousing or sports. Boys are shamed for embracing but are expected to be physically aggressive; girls are shamed for being "unfeminine," aggressive and violent.

The inherent human need to touch, hold, or be held becomes severely suppressed, eventually constricted, and actually altered through such shaming. Though variously experienced as a need just for bodily contact at certain times, and at other times as a need to give or receive physical affection, shaming produces constriction and inhibition of that need. But since holding also communicates protection and safety, which is the basis for trust and security, shaming the need for holding prevents restoration of security. The shame that has become bound to the need prevents its outward expression and may even silence it internally as well. In effect, touching has become taboo.

When this need is directed toward a person of the same sex, either in adolescence or in adulthood, then the more general taboo on touching created through shaming takes on new, more insidious meaning. To desire to touch or hold another woman, or another man, is not merely shameful but abhorrent because it now additionally signifies both our inherent deficiency and aberrant nature as a woman or man, respectively. The girl who craves the touch of another girl is a mockery of a real woman, unfit to belong, someone who will defile the pure and lead them astray. The adolescent boy who desires to affectionately hold other boys or explore their bodies by touch makes "real" men uncomfortable by seeming to be a predator, a misfit, someone who must be distanced from other men because he is loathsome.

Touching and holding is a need that requires fusion with enjoyment to be fully integrated within our personality. When that need instead becomes fused with shame, it is eventually disconnected. That is why we can encounter gay men and lesbians who not only don't freely touch, hug, or kiss each other in public, but feel uncomfortable doing so even in private. In a sense, they have no privacy because they feel judged by *watching* critical eyes even when they are alone.

Shaming the Need for Identification/Facial Gazing

The second pathway into gay shame involves the need for identification. This is a need to feel *one* with another, and that merging occurs principally through the eyes. Holding someone's gaze for an extended period of time—with each person looking willingly and directly into the other's eyes—permits direct and full communication of *all* affect, not just sexual interest. Always interpreting the facial gaze as sexual unfortunately limits our understanding of this phenomenon because such an interpretation restricts the full range of expression to a decidedly narrow bandwidth—the specifically sexual. By gazing into each other's eyes over time, we momentarily surrender our separate selves and experientially become one. It is the deepest form of intimacy that human beings ever experience; it is also incredibly difficult for almost everyone to look continuously and comfortably into another's eyes.

The taboo on facial gazing is first of all a taboo on intimacy. What is being restricted and suppressed is the free and open expression of intimacy between any two individuals. But the taboo also limits the unconstrained expression of affect, whether involving intimacy or not. Affects are highly contagious. The expression of any affect by one person will trigger similar affect in another, just as we often "catch" someone else's joy or misery. Affects also escalate; the expression of anger can intensify that feeling in us all by itself. The facial embrace magnifies both of these consequences.

Because the mutual facial gazing of the eye-to-eye scene has a unique capacity to foster the expression, communication, contagion, and escalation of affect—as well as the reduced control over affect—the taboo on facial gazing becomes necessary in all societies.[3] Since cultures place additional taboos on the free expression of sexuality, mutual facial gazing also comes under taboo, according to Tomkins, because facial gazing is a vital part of sexual exploration, the communication of sexual interest or desire, and therefore a form of sexual "contagion."[4] Two people looking into each other's eyes will communicate as well as heighten their sexual desire—which gay people recognize as cruising and non-gays refer to as "scoping."

What begins as a scene of identification/facial gazing between infant and parent later becomes heavily infused with shame, deeply conflicted and ambivalently longed for, overlaid with complex meaning and taboos. Instead of only providing identification, looking into the eyes of another person while that person also looks deeply into our own eyes now communicates affect of all kinds (from interest to anger or fear); immerses both in an experience of unparalleled mutuality by profoundly deepening their shared intimacy; and also heightens sexual desire when it is present.

Facial gazing is crucial to the fundamental interpersonal need for identification. When that need becomes primarily or exclusively directed toward your own sex, then a second source of specifically lesbian and gay shame emerges. The dawning awareness that you desire to commune with other women, or with other men, by gazing into their faces, by looking deeply into their eyes—like when you can't stop staring at the new girl in your neighborhood or the new boy in class—magnetizes all of the taboos surrounding the eye-to-eye scene and then focuses them into one single taboo: *This must mean I'm queer.*

Mutual facial gazing between men or between women becomes not only a sign of shame, but, equally important, a source of further shame as well. Only *queers* do that—only inferior men, only incomplete women. In effect, the facial gaze loses its wider meaning of fusion, merging, and instead becomes reduced to only its sexual meaning. Not all looks are sexual, but some looks definitely are. Eventually, all looks become interpreted as sexual, in both intent and impact, even when they are not. By constricting the need for identification, as it becomes expressed through facial gazing, we unfortunately also limit our capacity for intimacy.

What happens? Men and women who dimly sense their essential difference, their attraction to their own sex, now hide their looking at other men or other women because it has become shameful to look—and even more shameful to be seen looking. To be *caught,* exposed, makes them vulnerable. When others become aware of it, they will point the finger, thereby shaming the looker. So we must look furtively, if at all. Or better still, just avoid the eyes of others entirely. One man told us that he was terrified of betraying himself as a teenager, so he made sure that he only looked at men who were with women. That way, he hoped if someone saw him staring, they'd think he was looking at the woman in the couple, not the man.

Generally taboo, facial gazing is also now specifically taboo because it is a sign of inherent defect as a man or woman, of our aberrant nature. The general shame already bound to the need becomes additionally overlaid with shame specific to its same-sex focus. A further complication growing out of the interpretation of facial gazing as exclusively sexual is the myth that two gay men or two lesbians can't be friends without eventually having sex—our intimacy is always associated with the sexual.

Shaming the Sexual Drive

The third principal manifestation of gay and lesbian shame develops through another class of shame binds. Here the sexual drive becomes fused with shame instead of excitement affect or in addition to it. While it's only one dimension of sexual orientation, the erotic is nonetheless significant to both gays and non-gays alike.

In virtually all cultures, the sexual drive becomes bound by shame to varying degrees, beginning in earliest infancy when the infant first "discovers" its genitals. Whereas the infant's prior discovery of its fingers or toes was greeted with smiling and obvious joy by the parent, the equally natural discovery of its genitals is instead greeted quite differently by any or all of the following responses: a sudden slap on the wrist; a look of disgust on the parent's face; an angry verbal outburst; forceful removal of the infant's hand each time it returns; a look of obvious embarrassment on the parent's face; the upper lip of the parent raised in dissmell as though the child had become foul-smelling and now must be kept at a distance; the upper lip curled up but only on one side of the parent's face in a sneer of contempt that both punishes and distances the evil child. These are not reasoned responses.

When such a response happens, the parent is governed by scenes of shame, rooted in the parent's childhood experiences that parallel the infant's. It is the parent's own shame scenes that become reactivated by the infant's behavior, and those parental scenes now become imported into adult consciousness, compelling their reenactment. The parent simultaneously relives scenes from childhood at that very moment when the infant's discovery of its genitals triggers the parent's sudden, unexpected reaction.

Parental shame scenes mediate the reenactment, thereby recycling shame from one generation to the next. The consequence of such reenactments is that the infant's initial curiosity about and interest in touching its genitals now has become linked with shame and can eventually become completely bound by it.

This is only the first of many linkages between the sexual drive and shame for a person of any sexual orientation. Nudity, curiosity about the parent's body, masturbatory activities, and childhood sex play are additional pathways along which shame and sexuality become fused. Nudity on the part of children, particularly when unexpected or inappropriate in the parent's view, may prompt the sudden reactivation of parental scenes, resulting in the parent shaming the child. The intensity of the parent's reaction is usually governed by the parent's own scenes, not the child's actual offense. When children become curious about and desire to see and touch their parent's body, even the parent's genitals, this curiosity will reactivate any analogous shame scenes embedded in the parent's memory.

The child's behavior need not be identical to the parent's in the parent's original scene, simply analogous. New situations only have to be *sufficiently* similar to governing scenes in order to reactivate them and cause them to intrude into present-day adult consciousness. According to Tomkins, we are always responding to the similarities between old scenes and new situations.[5] The parent detects a similarity, however subliminally, between the child's current behavior and the parent's governing scene, prompting its reactivation and return. That scene then intrudes into consciousness and the parent becomes lost in the scene, reenacting it while also recasting it: now the parent plays the part of his or her own parent in the original scene.

Similarly, children's masturbatory activities typically remind parents of their own childhood, which now governs how they respond. If the parent had been brutally shamed for masturbating, the parent is likely to repeat the pattern in at least an analogous fashion. Affects like disgust and shame that the parent now experiences and that become engendered in the child are likely to be identical to those embedded in the parent's original scene. These reactions are also apt to be more intense than the responses to an infant discovering its genitals since masturbation is judged more severely.

Touching becomes erotic and curiosity leads to behavior. When children are discovered engaging in natural exploration of each other's bodies or in actual sex play with one another, the current situation acts like a magnet: analogous scenes from the parent's childhood quickly capture the parent in an affect storm. Parents in this situation may also be responding to the imagined judgment and condemnation they expect from the other child's parents: *They'll think I can't control my own children! They'll think I'm a bad parent and my child's a pervert!*

Shame about sexuality is passed from parent to child along any of these pathways. Such shame scenes accumulate around the earliest expressions of what will later emerge as the adult sexual drive. The common denominator running through all of these varied scenes is sexual curiosity, sexual interest, and sexual touch. Because all of these scenes have certain similarities, they eventually become interconnected.

Adolescence brings on new sources of shame due to the onset of bodily changes. But it also brings on changing encounters with sexuality, and therefore new sources of shame directly connected with sexuality.

> *I thought I would die of embarrassment the day I got a hard-on in the showers after gym class in eighth grade. I couldn't help it —and I couldn't make it go away. Everybody saw! They laughed at me, and even told some of the girls. I couldn't tell my parents why I was so miserable.*

Maturation of the sexual drive heightens and varies its expression: masturbatory activities to orgasm, erotic fantasies, erotic dreams during sleep, wet dreams, sexual activities with friends of the same sex, sexual activities with friends of the other sex. At the same time, various parental, cultural, and religious injunctions prohibiting sexual activity become mobilized; they also function as additional sources of shame directly connected to the free expression of the sexual drive. Often, the cultural injunction that sex before marriage is taboo generates intense *immorality shame* for many people.

> *As soon as I started dating, my parents went nuts. Only sluts had sex, they'd say, only whores. It was evil and wrong even if I let a boy touch me anywhere. I felt suffocated—convicted before I had done anything.*

That shame does not automatically dissolve, even for non-gays follow-ing marriage, but can remain a continuing barrier to sexual fulfillment. Some women, for instance, feel repugnance for sex even when they're married: *It's dirty. I hate it.* Those feelings will inhibit excitement and enjoyment. Some men may not be able to ask their wives to perform certain acts because they feel too ashamed to even mention them.

The analogous injunction that only love makes sex worthy or valid by elevating sex above its baser nature is another source of considerable shame about sexuality. In certain cultures, including the United States, this injunc-tion is a direct residue of a Puritan past.

These general taboos surrounding sexuality are further compounded by still more specific taboos surrounding same-sex attraction. Earlier we examined a number of different sources of shame embedded in the gay/lesbian experience, including family, peer group, religion, culture, heterosex-ism, homophobia, powerlessness, AIDS, and generations of silence about all matters homosexual. These are the principal sources of the taboo on sex between males and between females, whether operating during childhood, adolescence, or adulthood.

That taboo is at once the product and the source of shame. The shame about engaging in specifically sexual activities with someone of your own sex paralyzes its outward expression, but shame may also spread inward to silence even the perceived awareness of such a desire. By adolescence, a direct linkage between shame and gay sex has emerged. This shame bind governing sexuality can make us feel either that all sexuality is shameful or just that sexual feelings for our own sex are shameful.

The resulting sex shame bind now governs sexual desire. In the case of a same-sex sexual orientation, erotic/sexual scenes have become fused with shame instead of with the excitement affect that is required for the sexual drive to function effectively. Such desires mark you as defective, and acting on them makes you abhorrent. The developing awareness of yourself as gay or lesbian becomes inextricably infused with shame, and you will inevitably feel lesser because you are attracted to your own sex.

In addition to fusion with shame, the sexual drive is also likely to become fused with dissmell or disgust. That's because dissmell and disgust are so often utilized as a means of generating shame about sexuality. When-ever the expression of sexuality or the content of sexual fantasy contains such associations as "dirty" or "smelly," this is a clear sign that fusion with dissmell or disgust has occurred in addition to fusion with shame.

> *My lover, Brad, is always bugging me to blow him and I absolutely refuse. It grosses me out so much to even think of it, I won't even let him give me a blow job. Jerking off together is the only thing that feels clean to me.*

The Magnification of Shame Scenes

Through these accumulating shame binds, shame becomes internalized and subsequently magnified. The mere experience of whatever has become bound by shame is now sufficient to indirectly and spontaneously activate shame. In effect, shame has become autonomous, operating entirely with a life of its own. The various scenes in which these shame binds become stored are like nuclei of shame lodged within us. But scenes do not remain isolated and disconnected, for they are not static events. Shame scenes become interconnected, thereby fusing with one another and greatly magnifying one another. This is *psychological magnification*, the process of connecting one affect-laden scene with another.

Consider what happens for a young man who has isolated experiences over time of finding himself looking longingly at other men, at their bodies, directly into their faces, sometimes catching their gaze. Instantly he looks away, but he knows he *has* looked. On other occasions he fantasizes embracing another man, affectionately, tenderly, or simply running his fingers over the other's face, arms, chest—touching, exploring. The moment comes and goes. Perhaps he has a close friend and they sometimes hug, feeling enjoyment mixed with embarrassment. Whenever he spies an attractive man walking toward him, he feels a sudden quickening of breath; sometimes he even allows himself to imagine them locked in an explicitly erotic embrace, but the image is fleeting. Restless at night, he relives these scenes over and over (either with masturbation or without), causing explicitly erotic scenes to become interconnected with scenes of facial gazing and other scenes of simply touching or holding a man.

But he has other scenes as well, scenes of shame and fear, even scenes of contempt experienced at the hands of peers. He remembers the ridicule meted out to another boy on the playground by a group of kids mercilessly taunting him with "faggot" as he tried unsuccessfully to get away. Now he cringes at the memory: *That could have been me.* But there were times when it *was* him. Suddenly, he remembers that other scene at the library when he had been too playful with a classmate, and this tougher boy looked at him funny and suddenly said too loudly, "What are you, a homo?" Everyone in earshot turned to stare. How his face burned in shame. Now he cringes even more when reliving that once distant memory. His shame burns hotter. *Got to hide this,* he whispers in his mind. Everywhere he looks, people are making fun of queers and fags. He knows schoolmates who beat up fags for fun. He listens to lectures from clergymen about this sin of pollution. Even his own father sometimes voices disgust: *Those people are sick.*

With each reenactment of these unrelated scenes—either in his actual experience or only in his own imagination—they become increasingly fused and interconnected, thereby magnifying one another. For this young man, shame is becoming deeply embedded in his accumulating experiences of how he responds to other men. Even his dawning awareness of himself as gay is being directly molded by shame, leaving him feeling lesser precisely because he is not like other men he knows but is instead a man who desires to be intimate and sexual with men.

DEFENDING SCRIPTS SPECIFIC TO GAY/LESBIAN SHAME

How does the individual woman or man whose emerging awareness of being lesbian or gay has become infused with shame now adapt both to that emergent awareness of difference and to that growing sense of deficiency? Strategies develop to protect us from further encounters with the alienating affect. The accumulating family of shame scenes, in turn, generates specific rules that are designed to govern those scenes. These rules or strategies are the scripts that enable us to avoid or escape from shame. *Defending scripts* predict future occurrences of shame, attempt to control them or compensate for them, interpret their meaning for us, and otherwise guard the boundary between ourselves and other people.

Earlier we considered the principal defending scripts that develop in response to shame (rage, contempt, perfectionism, striving for power, transferring blame, internal withdrawal, humor, denial). There are defending scripts specific to gay or lesbian shame, and they fall into two sets: scripts that attempt to control only the experience of gay shame itself and scripts that become additionally directed against other gays or lesbians as a means of transferring shame.

Shame connected to being gay or lesbian is principally defended against by three particular scripts, which can occur in varying combinations. The first is *striving for perfection,* a general strategy that aims at erasing every blemish of the self, driving a person to always excel or outdo others. Being perfect becomes the way of compensating for the inner deficiency that internalized shame creates. When that shame becomes rooted in our sexual orientation or sexual identity, it can feel as if only the endless quest after perfecting ourselves can erase the stain.

As one illustration of the perfectionism strategy, let's consider the appeal of military life for gays and lesbians. A lot of gays wonder why anyone would want to join a group that loathes them, a group in which silence— Don't Ask, Don't Tell—governs the expression of homosexuality. With an understanding of shame, you can see how some gay men and lesbians may actually become drawn to life in the military in order to perfect themselves and thereby better control or defend against their own shame or compensate for it—particularly the shame about being gay.

What we are offering here is only a hypothesis about why some lesbians and gays may, in fact, *desire* to live in such a tightly structured world like the military. There can be many reasons for deliberately selecting a regimented life, one that requires giving up so much personal freedom. But keep in mind that at least in the United States, joining the military makes you an integral part of a highly esteemed group whose purpose is defending the safety and honor of the country. Soldiers are the ultimate patriots.

This country maintains a widely shared cultural ethic that those individuals who are willing to serve their country in uniform, who are therefore also prepared to die for their country, are the noblest Americans. They, above all others, are deserving of honor and esteem. This is one of the highest cultural ideals to aspire to in this country, the essence of the *perfect* American. By joining the military, gays and lesbians immerse themselves in that noblest of images and thereby enhance their own image of themselves— counteracting shame.

Another strategy is *internal withdrawal,* which causes the self to hide more deeply inside. Shame often becomes too agonizing, particularly when intense exposure fears have developed along with shame. The individual then escapes further shame by shutting in his or her authentic self, thereby creating a secret self that may or may not bleed directly into awareness. The natural curtain of privacy that each of us at times draws about ourselves now becomes a permanent shroud of secrecy from which there can be no escape. To venture forth means encountering shame. The self is in retreat, hiding first from others, next from itself. Gay desires become ever more isolated and cut off. Being deeply closeted is one manifestation of this strategy, and some people take more extreme steps to create a double life. Hiding is the hallmark of this particular script.

The final strategy of defense is complete *denial*. The shame attached to your homoerotic feelings has become so intolerable, and the awareness of same-sex attractions so deeply disturbing, that both must be actively denied: *I'm* not *gay. I* don't *feel that way*. The very existence of homoerotic feelings now must be eradicated. That is what denial initiates: denial of shame itself as well as denial of whatever arouses shame. The attraction to your own sex now must be denied at all cost because no other way has been found to effectively control shame. Utilizing this script produces people who may on occasion be sexual with their own sex but who nevertheless stoutly maintain, for whatever reason, that they're *not* homosexual. Denying the presence of homoerotic longings is absolutely essential.

A second set of defending scripts additionally becomes directed at *other* gays and lesbians. The two principal scripts in this group are the *transfer of blame* and *contempt*. The aim in each case is to guard the boundary between ourselves and the outer world. Protection against further shame is aided in these instances either by transferring blame directly onto other lesbians or gay men or by openly displaying contempt for them. The transfer of blame is a strategy that recruits anger but then directs it in an accusatory manner. The person gripped by inner warfare over being gay or lesbian can partially deflect shame by angrily pointing the accusatory finger of blame directly at other gays, thereby transferring shame as well. The transfer of blame onto others masks the deeper transfer of shame away from oneself. Someone gripped by this strategy might constantly make fun of people he accuses of being gay: *Look at that fag!* Or he might even let himself have sex with another man when he's drunk, then accuse the guy of taking advantage of him. That accusation feeds on our cultural stereotype of gays as predators.

The contempt strategy functions somewhat differently. Here, other gays or lesbians are actually looked down upon, judged as inferior, because contempt always elevates us above anyone who is the object of our contempt. We might hear people talk contemptuously about "lipstick lesbians" or say how much they despise "leather queens" or people who are "too out": *They're spoiling it for everyone else.* Contempt is both a punitive and a distancing response. When people in deep turmoil over being gay react to other gays with open contempt, they are attempting to reduce their inner torment by distancing themselves from the perceived source of that torment. If my emergent awareness of being attracted to my own sex causes me acute shame, then distancing and repudiating anyone who behaves or dresses in too blatant a manner—like drag queens—or is gay in a way I have not chosen or accepted—Dykes on Bikes for example—becomes a means of distancing my own shame. In turn, I feel better than them, and therefore less shame, by making myself feel superior. All this is in direct response to my own feelings of inferiority.

Both contempt and transfer of blame scripts can also, in extreme cases, lead to gay-bashing violence. This is particularly true of people whose homoerotic desires are latent and must be warded off at all cost. Any awareness of gay feeling is too agonizing and so must be defended against by the severest action, as though attacking someone else would, in effect, destroy the perceived enemy within.

Distinguishing between these two different sets of defending scripts—those attempting only to control shame and those additionally directed at other gays—is important because they operate quite differently, creating distinctive profiles. Of course, any combination of the scripts in either set can be utilized by the same individual, either at different times or in different circumstances. Some lesbians and gay men are more likely to utilize scripts that are only from one or the other set, while other lesbians and gay men will actually employ particular scripts drawn from both sets.

FROM SELF-SHAMING SCRIPTS TO A SHAME-BASED GAY/LESBIAN IDENTITY

These scripts are never more than partially effective. If they did not work at all, they would not develop. But if they were completely effective at controlling shame, their use would decrease as shame lessened. Paradoxically, then, their use and frequency actually increase as these scripts prove partially *ineffective*. What unfortunately results is the development of yet another set of scripts. Though analogous to defending scripts, these scripts become directed *inward* and become the means of reproducing shame. These are *self-shaming scripts*. What ultimately results is the emergence of a *shame-based identity* as a lesbian or gay man. A shame-based identity means that our entire being has become infused with shame. That is the only way we can see ourselves, hopelessly equated with shame. Which scripts actually develop for any given individual is mainly a function of experience and modeling in the family and peer group.

While defending scripts remain externally directed, self-shaming scripts actually invade the self. Earlier, we identified the three principal self-shaming scripts: *self-blame, comparison making,* and *self-contempt*. In a self-blame script, the angry accusatory finger of blame turns inward against ourselves. We now direct that angry blaming activity in a self-accusatory manner. The self mercilessly accuses the self, as though having been brought before some grand tribunal for being gay, blamed as the clear and obvious reason for our failings in life.

> *It's all my fault. I try to just be friends with a guy, but it never works. I always want to go to bed with him. I always screw things up. I'm hopeless—I don't deserve to live.*

The self metes out swift punishment, angrily blaming the self over and over for being gay. Gayness itself is the target of the self-blame script and, in turn, validates its use over time. Directing blame inward against ourselves, in effect, *proves* our unworthiness as gays and lesbians.

In a comparison-making script, the awareness of difference between yourself and others is immediately converted into a comparison that ends with yourself being devalued for the comparison. Perceived differences between yourself and others are translated into invidious comparisons: *She's so cute—I feel fat and ugly every time I see her.* Comparison making moves on to sexuality. Every gay man and every lesbian at some time begins comparing themselves to other men and women who are not gay. It is that comparison itself which is so insidious. Few differences are as fundamental as our sexual orientation. When we compare ourselves to others who are different from us in essential ways, we do ourselves injury. And that injury arises precisely because the very action of devaluing ourselves for whatever comparison we've made always reproduces shame. In comparing ourselves to another who is more *something*—more masculine, more feminine, more culturally acceptable—we do not elevate ourselves along with the other person, thereby enhancing both. Instead we feel lesser, plunged into the whirlpool of shame.

The final self-shaming script is self-contempt. This particular script recruits contempt and directs it inward in a vicious assault against the self, producing the equivalent of psychic surgery, splitting the self into two parts: a judging self and an offending self. Feeling superior, the judging self towers over the offending self, which responds in turn by feeling inferior. And exactly what part of the self is the offending self? Gayness, of course. That's the aspect of the self that is being judged and found wanting.

> *What's wrong with you? How could you go to that bar again and pick someone up? That's all you ever think about. You're sick, you're disgusting, you're such a sex freak!*

The very heart of the self has been put on trial, and a self-contempt script invariably consumes your inner life. Judgment follows judgment, feebly answered by protestations, followed by still more judgments, until the self is finally convicted of its heinous crime—being gay or lesbian. Unfortunately, the consequence is not mere punishment, as generated by a self-blame script, but worse: *banishment.* Gay desires now must be permanently disavowed.

The specific target in each of these self-shaming scripts is being lesbian or gay—that aspect of our being which is secreted away because it has already become shameful through prior encounters with others. While self-shaming scripts can certainly be directed against virtually any facet of the self, in these instances being gay is their principal focus and the target of unrelenting shaming directed entirely from within. In response to being targeted by any of these self-shaming scripts, gay desires become increasingly embattled, tortured, actively despised and hated. That is the nature of the assault from within. We are at war with our own basic nature, hating or despising our secret longings.

When any one or combination of these self-shaming scripts begin to dominate the personality, they produce a further magnification of shame. The process of *disowning* is a direct consequence of the heightened level of shame that we now must live with. In this process, one part of us actively begins to disown those parts of us perceived as sources of shame. Since gay desires are shameful, they now become progressively disconnected, forced from consciousness—forever placed beyond the bounds of the acceptable. Being gay is no longer even the *bad me,* being gay is now the *not me.*[6] In this process gay desires are not merely denied but actively disavowed, literally pushed out of awareness. They may surface only in dreams or in half-conscious thoughts. Or gay desires may become so cut off that they can be expressed only in hidden and secret ways through leading a double life. Or the agonizing awareness of those incompletely disowned desires may finally climax in suicide because living with them is impossible. Self-annihilation is the ultimate consequence of disowning.

When gay desires are not faced directly and consciously, and thereby integrated, they can only remain disconnected. The extreme fragmentation of the self through splitting, which we considered in Chapter 1, need not actually occur, but actively disowning gay desires will force them to varying degrees out of full awareness. Being completely closeted to others is one inevitable consequence of disowning. The deeply closeted man or woman lives with such inordinate shame that only a coffinlike existence is possible. Even more extreme is the person who cannot admit gay desires to consciousness at all; the merest flicker of gay feeling is simply too intolerable. A man like this, for example, may see gay desire everywhere but in himself. He even looks for it in others, feeling alarm at its presence, wishing to destroy it—so he never has to recognize gay feeling in himself. By continuously attacking gayness in others, the individual who has disowned it in himself can remain temporarily safe.

The developmental progression from self-shaming scripts through the process of disowning finally culminates in the formation of a shame-based identity. The shame-based gay man or lesbian could easily echo the Duke of Bourbon in Shakespeare's *Henry V,* who cries out when the French are defeated at the Battle of Agincourt, "Shame, and eternal shame, nothing but shame!" Now gay identity is permanently riddled with shame, existing in a state of perpetual inner strife waged against the enemy within. A shame-based identity is the true source of what has been referred to as internalized homophobia: self-hatred.

COMING OUT OF SHAME: CREATING A WHOLE SELF

We have explored the process by which shame can capture and dominate gay desires. What, then, are the ways in which to come out of shame and transform gay and lesbian lives? Fundamentally, internalized shame must be returned to its interpersonal origins, to its governing scenes. It is those scenes along with their accompanying scripts that must be directly transformed. We begin by making shame itself more conscious. Shame's hold on us is so very powerful that just being able to consciously *recognize* it, along with having a language that enables us to fully understand its impact, is a deeply significant first step toward resolving shame. The importance of the conscious awareness of shame cannot be emphasized enough. Now we'll explore the critical dimensions of the process of transforming shame scenes and scripts.

Transforming Shame Binds

The various shame binds that constrict the gay/lesbian experience must first be made fully conscious in order to ultimately dissolve them. The three principal shame binds governing gay life are those surrounding the need for touching and holding, the need for identification and facial gazing, and the sexual drive. In each case, the bind itself is made more conscious by recognizing shame whenever it becomes activated.

When we're bound by shame, either experiencing or expressing the needs for touching or identification as well as sex will spontaneously activate shame, thereby constricting their full expression. To reverse their effects, we must first allow ourselves to bring both shame and the shamed need or drive into sharper focus by experiencing both of them for a longer duration of time. That will enable us to better tolerate shame itself. Though it can be very painful, we must learn how to stay with the feeling of shame longer without quickly escaping it.

I was so self-conscious around other lesbians, I usually fled. I couldn't stand feeling exposed and embarrassed. Then I tried something else—at a bar or wherever I'd be—I tried to imagine my favorite aunt was with me, the one who completely accepted me the way my parents couldn't. In my mind, I'd imagine explaining to her how I felt, and I'd hear her loving voice supporting me, helping me, and sometimes just asking kind questions. I got a lot clearer about myself explaining things to my aunt in these circumstances. Eventually, I got better at standing my own shame. I got to understand how lonely I was, how much I needed another woman to hold me.

By not banishing shame, but enduring it, we can more fully experience the associated needs and the drive that had previously become shame-bound. By observing both shame and whatever had previously become bound by shame, each becomes changed by being made more conscious. Observation fundamentally changes the nature of what is being observed. The event observed is no longer occurring quite so automatically as it had before consciousness was focused on it.

The next step involves recovering the actual scenes in which these shame binds are rooted. The shame bind itself is stored in memory as a scene, and it is that scene which is the originating source of the bind. Or it may have been a series of interconnected scenes. Lev remembers two major shame scenes that kept him from reaching out to other boys. When he was six, he and another boy agreed to show each other their penises. Lev stripped, but his friend just pulled his pants away from his waist. Lev felt cheated, fooled. Some years later, hoping to initiate sex, he showed his penis to another friend, who refused to do the same and even reported the incident to other kids at school. Shamed for sexual curiosity with other boys, he held back from making any kind of overtures for years afterward. Even when guys made passes at him, he was so afraid of being further shamed, he either laughed them off or pretended they hadn't occurred. Sometimes, a pass would only register with him much later.

Gershen remembers that as a young adolescent there was one particular teenager several years older whom he often looked at—into his face, directly into his eyes. This went on for weeks whenever they crossed paths in their neighborhood, until one day the guy forced a confrontation: *Why are you always staring at me? You got something against me?* Gershen felt trapped and denied staring; from that day on, he avoided other men's eyes.

By tracing the shame about touching, facial gazing, or sexuality back to its originating scenes, in effect we are reversing the developmental sequence. That reversal is an essential aspect of the transformation process. The shame that we experience spontaneously whenever the particular need or drive is awakened is now becoming both more conscious and less mysterious.

Equally essential to the process of transformation, the need or drive itself must also be directly validated, actively embraced, and owned as an inherent part of us. Brian was deeply conflicted about his desires for other men. He had been suppressing his homosexuality for decades and also had been married for over ten years at the point when his attraction to men finally surfaced consciously. This embroiled him in profound inner turmoil. But he had to find out, he had to know what it was like to have sex with another man. Ambivalently, he began to face himself more honestly by observing his own experience. Never having allowed himself to really *look* at other men, now he began to. He had always had blinders on. Now when he walked down the street, he looked into men's faces, directly into their eyes. And he allowed into consciousness whatever feelings or fantasies spontaneously appeared.

Over time, Brian became aware that certain men attracted him; in their presence or when gazing into their faces, he felt enjoyment and excitement. He yearned to continue looking, to visually explore their faces. At other times, he felt a hunger to reach out and touch one of them, to simply hold someone or be held. Sometimes, his desire was explicitly erotic. Brian was learning to embrace his need for a man. From there, he went on eventually to give expression to his need, at first ambivalently, with shame, with a sense of immorality absorbed from the culture as if by osmosis, but then with increasing conviction about the *rightness* of his desires. Brian was gradually dissolving his various shame binds by openly embracing and validating his need to touch and hold other men, his need to identify with men and experience the intimacy of fusion, and his explicit sexual desires for men and ability to express them with mutual erotic delight. He was actively claiming his gay desire as inherently worthwhile and valid. This transformation gave him the strength to separate from his wife and pursue a fuller life as a gay man.

The need to touch others or be held by others of our own sex itself must be openly validated as an important aspect of our being, as *natural*. Women who yearn to embrace other women fondly and affectionately must claim that need, while men who hunger to touch or hold other men must learn to experience that need as having an inherent place in their lives.

The need to identify with others of our own sex, to gaze freely into each other's faces and eyes and sustain that gaze, must be released from the shackles of shame by affirming its essential value. Men who long to feel *one* with other men must learn to surrender to the facial embrace, to gaze freely and deeply into one another's eyes. Women who desire the deepest fusion possible with other women must similarly open themselves to gazing directly into one another's eyes. The need to fuse or merge, to identify, itself must be actively embraced as vital and innate, otherwise we're leaving out one of the key components of a positive gay identity.

Finally, the sexual drive must be set free by dissolving the constricting effects of shame, as well as affirmed by openly embracing sexuality as natural, as intrinsically good, something to be prized. Men who feel erotic excitement toward other men must learn to express it free of shame, with shared erotic delight. Women who desire other women must savor erotic excitement along with delight. Free sexual expression includes an entire range of possibilities, from anonymous sex, one-night stands, and sex clubs to multiple sex partners, dating, enduring relationships, and monogamy. While some of these forms of sexual expression may be less ultimately satisfying than others, exploring rather than denying our own eroticism can lead to an acceptance of our sexuality as a healthy component of our identity. We have to fully embrace sexual desire, not become sexually anorexic.

We must cultivate ways of celebrating the mutual experience of sexuality, identification, and touching/holding when expressed between two people of the same sex. The expression of these three deeply human traits, when expressed freely between two men or two women, must become occasions for celebration, no longer held prisoner by shame. The positive affects of enjoyment and excitement must be awakened and then fused directly with the touching/holding need, the identification/facial gazing need, and the sexual drive. Enjoyment affect is particularly critical to the need to touch and be held and also to the need to identify, while excitement affect is absolutely essential to the full functioning of the sexual drive. When these two needs along with the sex drive become fused with the positive affects of enjoyment and excitement instead of shame, then shame binds have indeed been transformed. Now we are well on the way toward reclaiming what has been shamed.

Transforming Defending Scripts

The strategies developed to guard against shame connected to being gay cannot be transformed until they are first made fully conscious. The striving for perfection, internal withdrawal, and denial—along with the transfer of blame and contempt that become directed at other gays—first evolve in response to *experienced* shame about being gay or lesbian, but then function to control the *future* experience of shame. Change or growth cannot occur in the absence of conscious awareness. Linking any of these scripted responses to shame with the actual, prior experience of shame is therefore vitally important. We must recognize, for example, that shame causes us to strive endlessly for perfection in the misguided belief that if we can perfect the self then we will be free of shame. Likewise, we must see internal withdrawal as a strategy of escape: we are desperately seeking protection from shame when we shut ourselves in. Denial is only our last resort to protect ourselves; unfortunately, the price we pay is a loss of authenticity. What we lose is our essential wholeness.

The strategies aimed at other gays, transfer of blame and contempt, must also be connected to our prior experience of shame in order to make each defending script more present in awareness. We must see that targeting other gays for blame or contempt actually originates in our own deeply felt experience of shame. Each is a means of reducing the shame we feel so painfully—in the first instance by transferring it directly to other gays through accusatory anger and in the second by distancing ourselves from the perceived source of our shame through looking down on certain gays. That's what may be going on when we hear people harping about how life would be better for most gays and lesbians if drag queens would stop parading on Gay Pride Day or, conversely, that the only thing wrong with gay life today is conservative gays. Constant blaming or disparaging of whole groups of lesbians or gays is not an objective and reasoned analysis of gay life. It's a response to shame.

Once we are able to recognize the operation of any of these defending scripts, they will no longer operate quite so automatically. We have initiated the process of transforming them simply by observing them more consciously. The next step is *naming* these defending scripts accurately so that we are increasingly able to locate them consciously whenever they are operating. We must know that we are aiming for perfecting ourselves, or escaping by withdrawing deeper inside or by means of active denial. We must name transfer of blame scripts accurately as well as contempt scripts in order to know the difference between them, thereby consciously observing them in action. Without an accurate name, we cannot clearly perceive what is happening.

> *Every time I read some article or interview with a conservative lesbian or gay who's supposedly speaking for all of us, I go off the deep end. I call all my friends and rant and rave like it's the end of the world. I've even been blaming conservative gays for all the antigay initiatives that keep cropping up. Recently, in the middle of a tirade, I caught a glimpse of myself in a mirror and was shocked: who was that lunatic? I looked out of control. I shut right up, because I realized how intolerant I'd become. Me, Mr. Live-and-Let-Live, didn't sound any more thoughtful than straight people who blame AIDS on gays.*

The accurate naming of inner events both expands and deepens awareness; it is therefore central to the process of transformation. Naming also enhances the felt experience of power because events are no longer mysteriously happening to us: now we are more fully conscious in the moment. Once conscious, we are able to anticipate and ultimately act upon those events at the time, and occasionally even in advance. That is what allows us to transform scripts, even ones that had been previously automatic and relied upon too rigidly.

In effect, we must learn how to better tolerate the very experience of shame itself. Through being able to endure that most deeply disturbing of affects just a bit longer, we are actually developing the necessary inner resources for tolerating shame with increasing effectiveness. In itself, though important, the ability to better tolerate shame is far from sufficient. We must also develop more effective means for counteracting the sources of shame.

Counteracting the Sources of Shame by Transforming Powerlessness

Since situations of powerlessness are a prime source of shame, let's consider how developing the psychological skills involved in *recognizing powerlessness* furthers the process of transformation. In order to break free of shame, we must learn how to recognize powerlessness and, at the same time, how to strategize realistic ways of regaining power. That is what self-empowerment is all about. The coming out process for gays is one example of moving from a position of relative powerlessness to one of more equal power. We no longer hide behind a mask, a false identity. The process of coming out is fundamentally a process of transformation of self. Living from a position of personal power means that we seek to maintain our rightful half of the power whenever that is possible. In so doing, we are fundamentally transforming our relationships. Political activism on behalf of gay rights is only an extension of self-empowerment to the societal level.

Of course, there are circumstances in which we are in fact powerless, such as death or aging. But simply realizing that we are powerless in a particular circumstance or relationship is actually the first step toward regaining a sense of power. Whenever we are able to identify two or more alternatives for coping differently with a powerless situation, knowing that we have choices available to us in turn brings us back to a position of power. Simply put, seeing choices and making choices both enhance power. This is not power over anyone else, but equal power—power in relation to others. Most important, we also have the power directly over how we feel about ourselves.

Sarah knew that she could not *make* her mother accept her as a lesbian. As much as she wanted her mother's love and approval, Sarah was powerless to make it happen. She could ask, plead, demand—but only her mother had the power to grant or withhold. Realizing this enabled Sarah to finally stop expecting her mother's acceptance. With that she was no longer quite so vulnerable to shame. She decided that she would have to be pleased and proud of herself—enough for both of them. One day Sarah told her mother, who had been cold and aloof ever since Sarah came out to her, that she was going to live her life in the way that was right for her. If her mother desired to be part of it, wonderful. If not, Sarah would live well anyway. In effect, Sarah offered her mother a *choice:* either you can accept me as I am and share my life or you can be left behind. In any event, Sarah would be participating actively in creating her own future—with or without her mother.

While there are real limits to our power, we actually possess far greater personal power than we have usually believed possible. Living from a position of personal power, and thereby maintaining *equal power* in as many situations and relationships as possible, is the most adaptive strategy for effectively counteracting the sources of shame. Contacting and using the personal power we all inherently possess is a vital part of transformation.

Transforming the Experience of Shame by Refocusing Attention

To enable individuals to better tolerate shame whenever it recurs and to develop increased power over the affect of shame itself, we have developed a method designed for the specific purpose of releasing shame at the very moment when it is generating. We know that this strategy can be learned through practice because we incorporated it in the self-esteem curriculum that we developed as an educational course at Michigan State University. While another way to transform the powerful hold shame has on us, this tool will not directly heal the wound caused by internalized shame nor permanently dissolve magnified shame—other processes accomplish that— but it will enable us to let go of shame in many different present-day situations in which the experience of shame has been profoundly disruptive. Just as there are times when we need to surrender to shame, to become immersed in it precisely to understand shame and its sources more completely, there are other times when we need to function effectively. When we're dancing or making love, for example, these are not the times to immerse ourselves further in shame. These are times when we need to *release* shame.

Let's review how shame actually feels on the inside. When we're shamed, our attention immediately turns inward, and we become suddenly impaled under the magnifying gaze of our own eyes. Now we are *watching* ourselves, and we feel excruciatingly exposed, revealed as lesser. This inner scrutiny in turn generates the torment of self-consciousness, causing shame's binding, paralyzing effect on us.

The tool for releasing shame in the moment when it is generating is *refocusing attention*. What we must accomplish, by a sheer effort of will, is actually turning our eyes back outside. By consciously refocusing attention *outside* ourselves, we immediately release shame. This refocusing of attention during the actual experience of shame is best accomplished through becoming immersed in external sensory experience, particularly visual and physical. We can immerse ourselves fully in music or dance, in jogging, swimming, or bicycling, or simply in the sights, sounds, and smells of the out-of-doors. The key is becoming completely immersed in sensory experience that is external, not internal.

Refocusing attention is also very useful for interrupting internal shame spirals. We must first recognize, intervene consciously in, and then terminate these shame spirals. Doing so is not denial or escapism—it is the key to mastering shame in the present. The time to experience shame more fully is *not* when we have to function effectively, whether at work, socially, or intimately. Any attempts to understand the experience while it is spiraling or snowballing only embroil us deeper in shame. Deliberately refocusing all of our attention back outside by becoming visually and physically involved in the sensory world surrounding us actually *breaks* the shame spiral and allows shame feelings and thoughts to subside. In this way, individuals who previously had been held prisoner by shame can now begin to enjoy various activities—from public speaking and dancing to sexual pairing. New scenes of enjoyment are in this way created where before there had only been shame.

> *My brothers and sisters used to make fun of me because I was the tallest and skinniest in the family and I always looked out of place in family pictures. It got worse in junior high with a growth spurt that left me feeling like a freak. It didn't help that my own family called me "Giraffe" and made dumb jokes about nosebleeds and asked "How's the weather up there?" It also didn't help when I began figuring out I was gay. I felt even more geeky and stared at. It got so I hated being outdoors or in a crowd where I felt people were staring at me. As soon as I met someone's eyes I imagined they were mocking me just like my family did, and I'd want to die. Then an assignment in a high school art class started to turn things around. We were supposed to spend a day in a park or some public space sketching things we saw. I was really freaked out about doing it, but I realized that when I was looking at people, dogs, trees, clouds, and trying to get the details down on*

a pad, I wasn't self-conscious at all. Even though I wasn't that good at drawing, I started carrying a pad around with me sometimes, to deal with feeling self-conscious or embarrassed by stopping to sketch things and focus outward, sometimes to just remind myself to do it. After a while, I didn't need the pad.

Many people experience acute shame in very specific settings, from the dance floor to the bedroom. In every case, the inner feeling is one of exposure: everyone's watching, laughing, mocking. In reality, however, the watching eyes belong to us, the mocking voice is our own. Exposure generates self-consciousness, which produces paralysis. If you find yourself feeling self-conscious when dancing or having sex, for example, and feel inhibited or even avoidant in response, there is a way out of the paralyzing effect of shame in these instances. First you must decide you want to overcome the constricting effects of shame; then reenter the shame scene and simply refocus your attention directly onto your partner.

Become immersed in the sights and sounds surrounding you. If you're dancing, listen harder to the music, feel it pulsing from the floor up into your body. Open your eyes wide to take in the flashing lights. Savor your own sweat, the feel of your body captured by the music and magnetized by your partner and the heat of all the people dancing around you. If you find you're talking to yourself, then talk to yourself about what you're experiencing— that is, describe it inside as if you're recording it for future reference. Watch your partner's face and eyes and hair and hands. Bathe in everything you're seeing and feeling. Savor the pleasure your partner is experiencing in your presence. Look into each other's eyes. Enjoyment and excitement are contagious when all attention is turned outward.

Gershen used to feel immobilized by shame on the dance floor until he began practicing refocusing his attention in the manner just described. It took months to disconnect and dissolve the shame that had kept him from enjoying himself when he danced. Applying the tool systematically and consistently eventually worked.

It can require months of actively refocusing attention in order to complete the process of dissolving and disconnecting shame. Initially, self-consciousness will rapidly return, only to be effortfully released each time it returns. With determination and persistence, however, shame will last for increasingly briefer periods, and also return less often, as you continue the process of reentering the scene coupled with refocusing attention—whereas enjoyment and excitement will burn longer and more brightly. Eventually, you will feel only a twinge of shame upon stepping onto the dance floor or into the bedroom, and later in the process only a twinge immediately before doing so. Later on, your anticipatory shame will occur only at the thought of dancing or making love. Eventually, shame will become disconnected from dancing or sex, though of course it can be retriggered. But if it is, you'll have experience in dealing with it. Creating new scenes of positive affect is absolutely critical to this process; enjoyment and excitement must become fused with the specific scenes that previously had been fused with shame.

Refocusing attention is an *affect* tool for releasing shame whenever shame generates. This tool works at the level of affect by combining it with behavior and cognitive responses. Through practicing this tool, we become better able to tolerate shame because we now possess a ready means for releasing it. By using this affect tool, we're learning an alternative means for coping more effectively with shame when it does generate, thereby reducing our reliance on previously learned and less adaptive defending scripts. Developing more adaptive means for dealing with shame breeds confidence.

Transforming Self-Shaming Scripts into Self-Affirming Scripts

As in the case of both shame binds and defending scripts, the three scripts that reproduce shame from within first must be made fully conscious. Only then can they be systematically replaced with new scripts that are inherently self-affirming. Essentially, we transform self-shaming scripts by rescripting them and turning the feeling of shame into feelings of self-love and self-respect. The initial step in this transformation process involves consciously *observing* our inner voices and identifying the ways we behave toward ourselves in particular situations. There are dozens of situations that illuminate how we shame ourselves.

Remember, the inner voice of shame is simply an entrance: it is the conscious residue of the scene. Imagine yourself in each of the following situations, and then try to identify your usual inner voices or ways of behaving.

1. When you get up in the morning and look at yourself in
the mirror, how do you behave toward yourself? What do you say

inside, and how do you feel about yourself, as you first encounter your reflection in the mirror? Do you ever criticize your appearance, denigrate your physical attributes, or compare your body unfavorably to others' bodies? And when you look in the mirror, do you take in your whole body or look only above the neck at your face? How about when you look in the mirror that final time before leaving your home for the day, what happens then? Later in the day, whenever you encounter your reflection, what do you say inside and how do you feel at those times? Whenever you look at yourself in the mirror, how do you really feel about being gay or lesbian? What do you think of yourself truly when you see yourself staring back at you? What are the actual words you whisper to yourself about being gay?

2. When you've blundered, failed, or made a serious mistake of judgment, how do you behave toward yourself? What words do you say to yourself? How do you end up feeling about having failed or blundered? Do you ever blame yourself for mistakes, or hear a voice inside saying, "Well, you should have known better"? When things go wrong or relationships fail, do you ever find yourself blaming yourself for being lesbian or gay?

3. How do you react when you've done well at some venture or actually accomplished something of importance? How do you speak to yourself at these moments, and how do you honestly feel about your accomplishment or success? Do you ever hear a voice inside saying, "It could've been better—it wasn't good enough"? And whenever you begin to feel good about being gay or lesbian, do you ever hear a voice inside whispering doubt?

4. How do you react to your own anger? How do you respond to your having become angry with a friend, parent, or lover? Does becoming angry at someone else cause you to feel guilty or ashamed afterward? Do you feel wrong or bad for having become angry in the first place? Do you ever feel angry about being lesbian or gay? Does that anger make you feel worse?

5. How do you react toward yourself after interacting with someone in a position of authority, like a supervisor at work or a

teacher at school? How do you speak to yourself then? How do you behave toward yourself? Do you worry about what that person actually thinks of you? Does that person suspect you're gay? Does he or she know for certain? Whether or not the person actually knows that you're gay or lesbian, *you* know it—so how do you behave toward yourself? And how does all that influence the ways you perceive your relationship?

6. You've just come away from meeting some new people for the first time. Do you worry about what they thought of you? Do you find fault with how you came across? Do you replay the situation, while also replaying over and over all of the things you could have done better or said differently? Do you criticize yourself? Or do you compare yourself to those strangers, and then feel lesser for the comparison? Do you wonder if they knew you were gay? Do you worry about it? If you came out to them, what do you suppose they really felt about you? If you didn't come out, do you regret not doing so? How do you behave toward yourself in either case? If these people are gay, do you wonder if you're "gay enough"? Butch enough? Political enough? Doing enough to fight AIDS?

7. When you leave the company of non-gay people you know, how do you react inside? How do you behave toward yourself? Are you critical of how you acted, poking holes in yourself? Do your friends know you're gay or lesbian? Are your friends accepting? Neutral? Somewhat critical? How does this shape how you feel about yourself, how you behave toward yourself? Did you hold back talking about yourself as gay in some way, or did you feel you talked about it too much?

8. You've just come away from a visit or phone call with your parents. Are you nurtured by the contact, or disappointed? How do you come away feeling about yourself? Do you behave toward yourself, even subtly, with blame or contempt? How do you feel about being gay after an interaction with your parents? Do you feel confident or in doubt, secure or at war with yourself? Do you come away feeling more self-loving or more self-hating?

9. How about when someone you know pays you a compliment or even says, "I like you." Do you feel unworthy, undeserving, or ashamed? Does the other person know you're gay, and how does that change your response to yourself? Do you ever find yourself whispering inside, "If he *really* knew me, he couldn't possibly feel that way about me"?

10. How do you behave toward yourself when someone you know well actually disappoints you in some way? How do you react to your own feelings of disappointment? Do you reject these feelings or criticize yourself for having them? How does being lesbian or gay influence the way you react toward yourself?

11. When you've disappointed someone special, how do you react inside? Do you angrily accuse yourself over and over, actually blaming yourself for being a disappointment? Or do you criticize yourself mercilessly, loathing yourself, holding yourself in contempt? In the midst of these inner conversations, do you also find yourself attacking, either with blame or contempt, your gayness? Does that seemingly unrelated aspect of yourself nevertheless become drawn into the melee?

12. How do you behave toward yourself when you are suddenly feeling helpless, scared, needy, or insecure? What do you say to yourself in response to your own neediness? Do you feel worse because you're feeling needy? And how do you feel about being gay or lesbian during these particular moments? Are you somehow more uncertain, more uncomfortable, because of being gay? Do you regret being lesbian or gay now, whereas at other times of greater inner security you feel no regret? Do you suddenly hate that part of you, wishing you could somehow pluck it out? How about when you've become unexpectedly jealous, for example because your girlfriend or boyfriend has found a new interest, or a new friend? Even though you know there's no real threat, still you're jealous. What are the words you actually say to yourself in response to your jealousy, and how do you end up feeling about yourself? Do you feel even worse about yourself because you're jealous?

Inner voices emerge all the time, and these twelve universal situations help illuminate them directly. These situations are entrances to observing the moment-to-moment operation of the various inner scripts that reproduce shame.

Go through each of these situations several times in your imagination, trying to identify your typical reactions. Observe your usual inner voices as you picture each situation in succession. When one of these situations next occurs, go through the series of questions related to the situation. Then observe and examine your responses. Pay close attention to how you're actually behaving toward yourself. Continue to monitor your inner voices by observing how you feel and speak to yourself whenever such a situation recurs.

Remember, the words spoken inside, if any, along with the feelings you experience, will reveal the distinctive way you relate to yourself. Making this pattern conscious is crucial to changing it.

The very next step in the process of transforming self-shaming scripts involves *naming* the script precisely. We need to be able to distinguish a self-blame script from a comparison-making script and a self-contempt script in order to begin the process of relinquishing them. Self-blame scripts involve angry self-accusations, whereas comparison-making scripts involve invidious comparisons, and self-contempt scripts demolish the self with character assassination. Are you convicting yourself of some crime, are you ending up depressed because other people are so much better than you, are you finding yourself loathsome, disgusting, and pathetic? In each case, a different script is operating.

Being able to identify and then distinguish one script from another actually enhances conscious awareness of how each of those scripts function.

> One Sunday morning I was channel surfing and I got stopped by this TV preacher who was pointing his finger and shouting. I wasn't listening to his words so much, but looking at him. His face was twisted and angry, and it blew my mind. Because I realized that was me, in a way. That's how I reacted whenever I goofed things up at work or with my lover: "You did it! It's all your fault!" Nobody else was making me feel like that—it was me.

By observing our various self-shaming scripts consistently over time, we bring them ever so gradually into sharper focus. In effect, we're teaching ourselves to become accurate observers of our own inner experience. Naming confers power. We know when we're finding fault with ourselves (self-blame) and when we're feeling inferior to other people (comparison making). By accurately naming the script, we acquire the power to change it because we're making its moment-to-moment operation more conscious.

Once the particular script has been accurately named, we next seek to return that script to its originating scenes. We call this the *recovery of the scene.* In effect, we are attempting a difficult task of memory: actually attaching faces to the accusatory or disparaging voices that we hear continuously speaking inside of us. Remember, even the voice of conscience once belonged to a face that looked angry, disgusted, or disappointed while it was speaking. It will definitely be hard to tell at first which script is operating because they make us end up feeling the same, and, in fact, more than one can be operating at a time, causing us to feel shame on many levels.

> *So I turned off the TV, a little stunned, and asked myself how I got this way. I felt kind of stumped. I mean, my parents didn't talk to me that harshly, at least I didn't think so. I stuck with it, though, letting myself go back into the past, like I was an archaeologist exploring a dig. It took weeks. I thought about the family at holidays, birthdays. Then I remembered one Thanksgiving when there was some kind of disaster in the kitchen, and my mom got really furious at herself. I realized I was being like her— attacking myself. She used to put herself down when things went wrong, and no matter what my dad said, she wouldn't stop. It was so awful to watch that I used to just phase out and ignore it. But I guess it left a mark on me. The next time I spent a weekend home, I watched for it, and, sure enough, she overcooked a roast and you could've thought it was a crime from how she carried on.*

Recovering scenes involves attempting to visualize the auditory voice speaking within us, thereby working toward recapturing the entire scene. Ask yourself *whose* voice is speaking inside: is it your mother's or your father's voice? The voice of an older sibling, or of another relative? Try to *visualize* the voice. Ask yourself when you might have actually heard something similar and try to picture that scene. Over time, specific details of the scene will return.

Next, begin to *observe the voice* consciously, as though you were a neutral or friendly observer. Be curious about the voice that is blaming, contemptuous, or comparing. Don't agree with its pronouncements, don't take issue with them. Attempting to counter, protest against, or challenge our shaming inner voices only serves to strengthen them further. Just continue observing those voices consciously while attempting to put faces to them. The very act of observing your inner voices itself changes them, for they are no longer operating as automatically as before. Conscious observation of inner voices and self-shaming scripts brings them increasingly into fuller awareness. Now you are able to see yourself in action—and, once seen, take action to change.

> *My lover suggested that whenever I started getting down on myself the way I was doing, I should imagine I was watching TV, and instead of a televangelist, that was me on the tube, yelling and pointing my finger. It made me laugh, but it also gave me something concrete to work with. And since I'd discovered something about myself through the TV, it made sense.*

At this point we must actively begin to replace these self-shaming scripts with self-affirming scripts. What this entails is re-creating fundamentally new scripts out of old ones, and thereby actually *rescripting* old scenes into new ones.

Imagine you're a screenwriter and you've just been handed a *bad* screenplay that you must entirely rewrite to make it over into a *good* one, focusing on some specific scenes. First, you'll write new dialogue, so that the characters will have new words to speak. Then you'll change the setting, placing the characters differently on the stage of your imagination, giving them new gestures to enact, new expressions to display, new affects to feel and project. The entire action of the scene has been changed, even the outcome is different. What you have accomplished is deliberately recasting the scene with new actors playing entirely different parts, speaking newly written dialogue, feeling altogether new affects, thereby creating an entirely new result.

The old script has been rewritten, the bad scene has been transformed. Each individual is actually both scriptwriter and director in one, as well as principal actor and ultimate critic.

Three critical processes must be effectively and directly engaged in this rescripting process: language, affect, and imagery. We must have new self-affirming words to say to ourselves to replace the old shaming words, thereby engaging language. Then we must actually experience new feelings of love and respect for our essential self. That step engages affect. Finally, we must actually *create a new scene* by actively visualizing someone else speaking the new words inside of us. It should be someone with whom we currently have a mutually respecting relationship or someone in the past like that. It can be a lover, best friend, teacher, colleague, neighbor, or relative— anyone whom we can rely on now as an inner ally.

The process sometimes works best if the imagined person is older, closer to a parent's age, but feel free to experiment. The same image won't work for everyone. By vividly picturing a person you trust and admire actually speaking inside, you directly engage imagery. When all three processes become actively engaged together in creating these new scripts, then rescripting is ultimately effective. In this way, we are engaging the identical processes that are responsible for the formation of the original self-shaming scripts (as discussed in Chapter 1), but now we are deliberately directing those processes in order to reverse their effects.

> *I decided to stick with the TV imagery. But instead of a big church, I switched the scene to my high school, where I had a great acting teacher who encouraged me to try out for parts even though I was shy. I was really fond of him, and whenever he critiqued my acting, it was never hurtful. I imagined we were doing a one-act play together. He'd offer the "good lines" when mine were critical, almost like we were playing tennis, and hitting the ball back and forth. So if I said, "You blew it again!" he'd say, "It's really not that big of a deal," or something like that. I got really into it, and it was kind of a reunion, a way of feeling close to him after all those years. It also made up for the fact that we never got to talk about anything personal, even though he was gay, and I'm sure he knew I was headed that way.*

Rescripting requires consistent practice over time. Don't despair that this process can take several years. Consider that you've been a prisoner of shame for a long time and that long-lasting change and growth takes time. You'll find that increased awareness is a huge first step that produces a feeling of improvement even when rescripting may take considerably longer. To complete the rescripting of our old shaming scripts takes years because these scripts have typically operated outside of awareness—hence, they've been largely invisible—and they were learned over a considerable length of time in our most formative years. Relinquishing these scripts requires consistent conscious effort over time, effort directed not just at changing the words we hear inside, but, more important, at transforming the affect-laden scenes in which those thoughts are rooted.

While the effects of self-shaming scripts are ultimately reversible, those scripts cannot be eliminated completely. We can become ever more vigilant, monitoring our scripts, gradually able to more quickly catch and replace them. But we cannot erase those entrenched scripts any more than we can erase the scenes from which they originate. Why? Because there is no delete key to consciousness. Scenes can be transformed, but not wiped clean. And shame is part of our lives. Some shame is healthy and appropriate, but the extreme level of shame surrounding gay and lesbian identity is not. *That* shame takes time to undo. And as long as society continues to shame our community, we will have to grapple with its effects and be prepared for its getting retriggered.

For instance, Lev had the misfortune to be humiliated at a junior high school graduation rehearsal for talking while the principal was explaining the procedures from the stage. He had to walk up the aisle from his seat while the principal contemptuously berated him for not paying attention, and the hundreds of students in the auditorium laughed. Sitting like an exile in the empty last row, he felt utterly crushed and exposed and couldn't even respond when a sympathetic teacher tried to whisper something to make him feel better. That scene comes back occasionally when he wonders after a party if he's "talked too much." Despite all his success at teaching and at public speaking, sometimes that uncertainty can still trigger the original scene. One of the ways he's learned to defuse that scene is through humor—exaggerating how much he must have talked at the party and how everyone was commenting about it, until his delight in the excess dissolves his shame, completely transforming the scene.

Shaming scripts can be profoundly altered, fundamentally rescripted into self-affirming ones, but never eradicated permanently. These distinctions are important because they establish the parameters of real individual growth without promising false security. We'll never be entirely free of shame, but we will be able to recognize shame as an affect that we all experience occasionally and *not* as the basis of our identity as gay men and lesbians.

Reparenting Imagery as a Way to Heal Shame and Transform Scenes

Since the early 1980s, we have been developing a process for healing shame by transforming scenes. This can involve contacting and integrating particular parts of us that have been previously disconnected. Think of the self as growing much like a tree grows, adding rings of growth that successively encompass all of the preceding ones. Within each individual there are many different "selves," beginning with the infant self, the young child self, even an older child self, then the early adolescent self, followed by the late adolescent self, continuing with the early adult self, and so on.

All these distinct and early phases of self are contained within each succeeding phase, and always remain potentially within awareness. While maturation usually brings enhanced power, powerlessness in adulthood always reactivates childhood scenes of helplessness because of their similarity. Experiences of powerlessness (being robbed, getting sick, losing a job, experiencing a lover's death) can reactivate any of these earlier phases of self, causing their immediate intrusion into present-day adult consciousness—whether or not we are fully aware of it happening. The self, then, actually functions more like a collection of selves, a perspective that our linear culture finds hard to accept and our language finds equally hard to describe.

Our focus here is not the inner child itself as much as *using reparenting imagery to transform scenes*. The "inner child" concept has been so widely popularized that it's no wonder comedian Kate Clinton has joked about her inner child "throwing up." Her mockery is a response to writers who give the concept far too much importance, even claiming that it's the key to all pathology and healing. Their writing is based on a static view of the self, not a fluid one. Not everyone possesses the identical inner child, formed at exactly the same point in time. And dealing with the concept isn't necessary for everyone.

The self is not composed of discrete states; rather, it is a *dynamic process* that is continuously evolving. Early phases of self, like the child or adolescent self, represent composite scenes that have become configured into enduring self-images. Just as what we hear as parental inner voices is the conscious, auditory residue of scenes, not simply "self-talk," the voices of our inner child or adolescent self are equally the product of scene construction. They are particular configurations of the self that have become separated in response to intense affect and for that reason are able to endure autonomously in consciousness.

When we encounter illness, death, or heartache, we can return to any child self, because it has been suddenly reawakened through the powerful governing scene of initial powerlessness. Even in the best of relationships and the most stable of individuals, powerlessness can reawaken the youngest child or adolescent self, which then will intrude directly into adult consciousness. Childlike and adult modes of experience actually coexist within the mature individual, and this is the normal course of development.

This perspective on how the self actually evolves, along with an understanding of scene dynamics, has given us an additional means for actively transforming early shame scenes that have accumulated around being gay or lesbian. This process directly engages *imagery*. In reading the words on this page, at this very moment, you are also making images because language is one of our most important methods for creating and using images.[7]

We are always operating in the mind with images of events that have already occurred, with images of events anticipated in the still distant future, and with images of things which are not yet present to the senses—this is the very stuff of invention.

These images are predominantly visual, but they also involve hearing, smell, movement, and touch. Scenes, as we've used this concept repeatedly, are based entirely in imagery. The scene itself is an image operating in the mind; or it may be a series of images that have coalesced into one. A child self is therefore created through imagery and composed of specific affect-laden images; it is simply a composite image formed during a critical period of intense affect.

This is the same imagery process we engage when we attempt to re-script self-shaming scripts into self-affirming ones. Now we mean to direct this same imagery process in another way: toward transforming early shame scenes.

In order to heal shame by effectively transforming scenes of shame, we must first recover the actual scene itself. We have to relive that governing scene as vividly as possible, fully reexperiencing and releasing all of the affect embedded in the original scene. The scene must come alive for us, here and now, and we must willingly reenter it, allowing it to surround us. We must picture the scene, visualizing its every detail. That enables us to reexperience and release all of the intense affect, however previously warded off, which is still embedded in that poignant shame scene.

Then we must transform the original scene by creating a new scene and changing it however we need to. We might have to take back the power if it was a scene in which we were powerless, or stop the abuse if it was a scene in which we had been abused in some way. Transforming the scene means bringing our adult self into that original scene to become the loving, respecting, protecting, nurturing parent to the child we were back then. In effect, we are creating a new inner ally. We must experience new words of comfort spoken by this newly created parenting self, experience new affects of safety, trust, and compassion, and also have an entirely new outcome occur. The old scene must be fundamentally changed.

During this transformation of the original scene, we must also experience the needs for touching/holding and identification as coming directly from the new parenting self which we are actually creating through this imagery process. We can reexperience old traumatic or shaming scenes and reshape them, transforming them into scenes of affirmation, healing, even celebration. Through reparenting imagery, we can exercise the power to fundamentally re-create who we are by giving ourselves new, more freeing messages. This transformation process must equally engage affect and imagery, together with language, in order to be completely effective.

The following is an example of a *reparenting imagery script* that you can utilize as a model. You can either use it as is or modify it to better suit you. You can read it and then engage the imagery by visualizing the scene, or you can tape-record the script so you can listen to it. You can even add music playing softly in the background. Be creative. As an additional aid, find a photograph of yourself as a child, one in which you are able to look at your whole face and directly into your eyes. Place it prominently in your home and gaze at it repeatedly over several days. Then, just as you are about to initiate the reparenting imagery, look at the photograph and gaze directly into your own eyes for a while before commencing.

Sit in a comfortable chair and close your eyes. Take a deep, relaxing breath and slowly let the air go, breathing out through your mouth. As the air releases, feel the tension in your body draining out of you. Imagine you are descending a staircase. All about you it's quiet and peacefully dark. Feel the smooth and comforting sensation of motion as you descend the staircase. Feel the banister against your hand. Feel the stairs beneath your feet. Now you're at the bottom of the staircase. You're standing at the end of a hallway. At the other end is a light. Walk toward the light. When you reach it, you're standing in front of a closed door.

On the other side of this door is your bedroom when you were a child. This is the room you grew up in, slept in, played in when you were twelve years old. If you had moved often as a child, pick one room that is vivid and easy to picture; then stay with that one image. If you did not have your own bedroom, or if you find yourself resisting this particular image, pick any room or place that you went to either to be alone or to feel safe. It could be a neighbor's or a friend's place, a tree house, your basement or attic, even a park or lake.

Now you are ready to walk into the room. You can see the handle on the door in front of you. Turn it and open the door. You're standing in the open doorway, looking into the room or place you've chosen to see.

Now walk into the room and let it surround you. Walk all around the room. Touch everything. Run your fingers across the walls, feeling the surface. Remember the color of the walls; were they painted or papered? Remember how you used to doodle or draw on the walls, in secret places? Where is the window in the room? Walk over to it and look outside. Remember how you used to stand there, wishing you could go outside and play? Is the floor carpeted or tiled? Is it bare? Remember what it smelled like in this room? Remember what it was like being young? Remember the games you used to play in this room, your favorite songs or stories? Remember what you felt like as a child in this room? Go over and pick up your favorite toy or book. Look at it. Touch it. Remember how you laughed and cried in this room? Remember it all. Entrances are all around you.

Your grown-up, adult self is standing there in that room, looking in on your childhood through the window you have now created. Slowly, you scan the room, but now you see a figure sitting on the floor off in the corner. Walk closer. Now you see who it is. It's a twelve-year-old child sitting there right in front of you, looking away, head bent, eyes downcast. That child, barely on the cusp of adolescence, is you. It's the young adolescent you were back then, still inside of you, who is now looking up at you as you walk closer. Say hello as you sit down beside your child. Remember how you used to dress, your favorite clothes, and how you combed your hair? When you have a vivid, clear image of yourself as a twelve-year-old, ask your child to hold your hand. Now be the gentle, older friend to your child that you needed back then. Put your arm around your child or touch your child's arm. Ask how your child is feeling on the inside. Get to know each other. Ask what your young adolescent self is needing at this moment. Then freely give it.

Now relive an old shame scene connected to your early awareness of being gay or lesbian. It could be a scene about touching and holding, or about looking into someone's eyes, or an explicitly sexual scene. Ask your younger self to take you through the entire scene once more. Relive the scene visually. Picture it vividly. Reexperience it as fully as you are able. Feel every nuance of affect. When the scene concludes, imagine yourself becoming the loving, compassionate parent to that adolescent that you needed back then. Say the words to your child now that your child needed to have heard then. You know the words—they've always been inside of you. You just have to speak them aloud. Be an ally to your child; change the old scene by continuing it, creating a new scene. Take back the power. When it is finished, simply hold your child on your lap for as long as your child needs, if your child wants to.

Now pick your child up in your arms and take your child outside, into the sunshine. Sit together on the top of a hill, watching the sun go down. Feel the warmth of the sun on your face. Your child is sitting cuddled up against you, feeling safe embraced within your enfolding arms. Now talk softly to your child about men who love men, about women who love women—how good it is. Talk to your child about being gay or lesbian the way you needed to be talked to by a parent back then. Talk to your child about the joys of women loving women and men loving men.

It's getting late now. It's time to come in, the sun's gone down. There's the hint of a chill in the air. Imagine bringing your child to a new, safe place that you are creating deep within you— think of it as a kind of kangaroo pouch right beside your heart. Be the protecting, nurturing parent to that child that you always needed and give your child a great big hug. Then tuck your child into bed in this new, safe place close to your heart. Sit on the edge of the bed for a while longer, and tell a story or sing a song to your child. Gaze into each other's eyes for as long as you both want to and smile. Then say to your child, "I'm pleased and proud to have you for my own." One last hug, one last kiss good night. Now tiptoe from your child, saying, "I will be with you always. I'll be back whenever you need me, whenever you call. It's safe now." Whenever you're ready, walk back down the hallway, up the staircase, open your eyes, and return.

This reparenting imagery process can be utilized to rework as many different shame scenes as necessary, scenes that occurred in the family, peer group, or school setting. They may have been scenes of mockery, ridicule, or disparagement connected to the early awareness of being gay or lesbian. These scenes could have occurred either before or during adolescence, even in adulthood. The greater the number of scenes actually transformed, the more complete the eventual healing of shame that is ultimately achieved. But remember, we can never eradicate those scenes; all we can realistically hope for is to transform them, knowing they might become reactivated. Even so, those scenes actually become integrated, and a changed relationship within the self gradually emerges through this transformation process.

Some people encounter real difficulties with reworking old scenes. This is not a pill to take or a cookbook recipe that's quick and easy to follow. You may find it hard or even impossible to do this without the assistance of a trained professional, or you may feel that this is something best done in the context of a safe and trusted group. Perhaps you simply do not feel ready, so don't force yourself to try it. Don't turn personal growth into an obligation. The pain of remembering can be great and our natural inclination is to avoid it, but through pain lies an opportunity for change.

CREATING A SELF-AFFIRMING GAY IDENTITY

Since identity itself is a relational pattern, a way of actually relating to ourselves, it is this inner relationship that we must ultimately transform. One of the principal dimensions of the self-esteem curriculum we have developed at Michigan State University involves first identifying and then transforming how people actually relate to themselves. This entails behaving in new and different ways which, taken together, actively strengthen the self within us. We must strive to behave toward ourselves as worthy and adequate beyond question. Accomplishing that objective is an active, conscious process.

Storing Self-Esteem

One aspect of this inner relationship is learning how to collect and store self-esteem. Unfortunately, most of us have been taught to base self-esteem in externals, in accomplishment, achievement, or performance. When we perform well according to whatever external standard has been imposed (like grades when we're in school), then we're permitted to feel good about ourselves—but only temporarily. If we fail on the next performance trial or do poorly, self-esteem plummets. Even when self-esteem is not directly tied to accomplishment, it is nevertheless contingent on the reflected appraisals of other people. How we feel about ourselves is too often determined by how others judge us—whether parents, teachers, colleagues, or bosses. Basing self-esteem either in external performance or in others' appraisals of us places self-esteem directly in the hands of others. Then, much as we might try to hold on to it, self-esteem will elude us.

The solution is to develop an *inner* source of self-esteem so that we can feel good about ourselves whether or not others do. We need to be proud of ourselves. By giving tangible feelings of pride directly to ourselves, and doing so on a daily basis, we actually develop an inner source of self-esteem. That's what self-esteem is: esteem for self, valuing of self, pride in self. Being proud simply means feeling joy about either yourself or your actual accomplishments; it does not diminish anyone else. Clearly, pride is not the same thing as contempt, which does indeed diminish others. Pride can be about how you actually live your life, the person you are inside, or how you handle difficult situations. Pride is about anything that leaves you feeling basically satisfied with you—it's not just about achievement or popularity.

To implement the transformation process, try keeping a daily list of accomplishments and achievements as well as situations you handled well. They don't have to be epochal events—that's too high and unreasonable a standard to hold ourselves to. Collect feelings of pride broadly: from performance as well as from the ways you live your life. Sometimes just getting through everything you have to do in a day can be a source of satisfaction. You can make your list at the end of the day, in the morning looking back on the previous day, or as things happen. Keeping a pride list is like keeping a focused journal; writing is helpful because it keeps you consistently aware and on track.

> *I'm always rushing through the day with eighty-nine million things to do. My mind's always thinking about the next task, and the one after that—I never stop to enjoy what I've done, I just obsess about everything that's left. I'm trying to slow all that down, to let myself really enjoy the sense of accomplishment. I know some people don't think stuff like getting shopping done is much to brag about, but why shouldn't I feel pleased with myself when it's over? It takes time, it's work. If the only thing I can get to feel good about is winning some kind of prize, then forget about it!*

Remember to consciously give yourself feelings of pride on a daily basis. When you do this, make the entire process conscious: make yourself aware of the event, experience the feelings of pride, and then store it internally as a scene. This is a way of creating and storing scenes of pride, resulting in an inner source of self-esteem. It's even more important when life seems overwhelming. We have to work harder then to find pride in the day.

> *After I got fired I was really depressed, and when I couldn't find a job it got worse. I'd just stay in bed and feel miserable. Nothing seemed important or worthwhile. But at a certain point I began to see that getting up and getting dressed were just as important as continuing the job search. There was no way I could be successful if I didn't get up and get my act together, so taking care of myself became part of the search.*

Most important, remember also to be proud of yourself every day for being gay or lesbian. Because we're constantly bombarded by antigay sentiments, it's essential to collect feelings of pride about being gay and then store those feelings inside. There's a great moment in the movie *Lianna* where the heroine stares in her bathroom mirror and joyfully proclaims, "I suck pussy!" What she's doing is turning the very thing that society condemns her for into a source of self-esteem. It's not just the words, but the affect too; she's creating a new scene about being a lesbian. We need to actively create these scenes in order to transform the negative messages we encounter daily about being gay.

Whenever participants in our self-esteem program attempted to engage this process consciously, they encountered difficulties. This is not surprising. Many people complain that they really haven't done anything major on any given day, certainly nothing that warrants pride. Their reactions reveal the very high inner standards by which most people judge themselves. Why not feel proud of the small successes, the little accomplishments, even the way you cope with difficult people or situations? Getting to work on time, making your bed in the morning, and caring for yourself during the day are all reasons to be proud of yourself. Look for ways you can be proud of yourself, like remembering to use this method.

Knowing How Much Is Good Enough

When self-esteem is based in performance or accomplishment, we unfortunately can end up feeling driven to excel, often in an ever-widening circle of activities, because that is the only means of acquiring good feelings about ourselves. The perfectionism that results is a treadmill. Teddy was a straight-A student in college and even graduate school, but he was always anxious. Could he keep it going? The longer he had a string of perfect grades, the more terrified he was of falling below "perfection," which made him work harder and harder, never letting himself off the hook. To get less than an A would have felt like a catastrophe to him. This attitude continued even when he was no longer in school, and in unexpected ways. He became obsessed not just with gardening, but with being the perfect gardener, with having the most beautiful flowers and shrubs, the best gardening tools, the healthiest lawn—it was endless. What started as a hobby began feeling like a job.

One way to get off the treadmill of perfectionism is to consciously determine how much is *good enough* in all of our pursuits. By developing an internal sense of how much is good enough, we are immediately released from the ceaseless striving for perfection. We actually maximize choice and thereby enhance personal power by independently determining how much is good enough in every activity we engage in.

Begin by simply asking yourself this question: "How much is good enough?" Consider it consciously over time as you continue through your various pursuits and activities, like particular tasks, your career, hobbies, even parenting. Undoubtedly, you'll need to ask the question repeatedly. Discernible answers to the question may not come immediately, but they will come only if you remember to consider the question.

Knowing how much is good enough is an antidote to perfectionism, and it's another dimension of this new relationship we are creating with ourselves. For some gay men, for instance, working on their bodies becomes a renewed source of shame, even though that may have started as a way of combating shame. After all, you can always work harder, get more muscular, have more definition and vascularity, make more people's jaws drop when they see you do chest presses. Where does it end?

Related to knowing how much is good enough in life's pursuits is believing that who you are is good enough. Some people may think that this is a formula for becoming complacent. Paradoxically, we are more likely to do our best and be our best when however well we do is good enough. The constant pressure to excel, even to better ourselves, can become an obsession. That preoccupation will undo us in the end. When we determine for ourselves how much is good enough, we actually maximize choice and thereby enhance our personal power.

Self-Nurturing

This inner relationship with ourselves must also embody essential elements of self-nurturing. We must become active, daily nurturers of ourselves —behaving toward ourselves in ways that are comforting, supporting, encouraging. While it is certainly important to have other relationships in our lives in which we can be nurtured, it is equally essential that we become able to provide ourselves with nurturing directly from within. That is the essence of true self-care. Remember: self-nurturing does not always have to cost money or add calories. The capacity to nurture ourselves must be cultivated through consistent practice over time. None of us are taught this in our society.

In a Puritan-based culture like ours, it's unfortunately too easy to interpret taking care of ourselves as spoiling ourselves, giving ourselves attention we don't deserve or should even do without. A further complication is the current cultural criticism of "yuppy narcissism," so that taking care of yourself may be unfairly mocked as bourgeois.

We must especially nurture the gay or lesbian aspects of ourselves in a particular fashion: by daily finding value precisely in our being gay or lesbian; by prizing our erotic desires for our own sex; by reading gay books, watching gay films, listening to gay music; by delighting in touching, identifying, and sexualizing with other men or with other women. Being lesbian or gay itself must be nourished in a comforting and encouraging way, and actively so, particularly since we have been forced to live in hiding at some time during our lives.

Many of us still live in hiding because we fear rejection or abuse or more shame. The people who have called us friend all too often have later betrayed us: parent, sibling, friend, teacher, employer. Even God has supposedly turned on us. We need to challenge and decry the Preachers of Hate around us and shout back at them that they don't speak for God. That *their* vision of God is wrong.

We need to rejoice in our sexuality, in our love for other women or other men, when we are repeatedly told that we are unnatural, an affront to God, an abomination. We need to sustain the courage to be that self we truly are and find within ourselves the determination to endure and even triumph.

We need to keep passion alive, to rekindle enjoyment and excitement daily. And we need to continue celebrating being gay or lesbian, especially when faced with threat or danger. Most of all, we need to be visible.

Self-Forgiving

Yet another vital aspect of this positive, new inner relationship that we are gradually but deliberately creating within ourselves involves developing a capacity for self-forgiveness. We have historically been taught, probably in all cultures and religions, to view the source of forgiveness as lying external to us. We're forgiven by our parents and teachers when we hurt someone; by our church or synagogue when we sin; by the state when we pay our debt to society after a crime; or by God. Even when forgiveness has, in fact, been received from outside, from another person in authority to dispense it, countless individuals actually continue to feel unforgiven because they have not taken that inner step to finally forgiving themselves. This drives them to continually apologize. Being able to genuinely experience forgiveness from within ourselves is a necessary psychological skill, one we must all learn if we are to heal our shame.

One way to forgive yourself is to close your eyes and imagine yourself with your arms embraced securely about you. Imagine your conscious awareness focused like a single beam of light, now radiating through you, throughout your entire body. In holding yourself, feel *one* with yourself. Next, relive whatever scene still haunts you, and then slowly repeat the words "Now, I forgive myself." Remember, we try to do the very best we can at any given time in our lives. Who we are is good enough. We must actively forgive ourselves, no longer looking for forgiveness to come solely from others, and thereby realize the power we possess to fundamentally re-create who we are.

By identifying with and embracing each and every single part of us, we actually become reunited, whole. That wholeness must also include being gay or lesbian: that is to be actively embraced, never cast adrift. Only then can we heal from shame.

Self-forgiveness is a process like making a quilt. Ultimately you're covered and warmed by it, but it takes work and grows a little at a time.

Eventually we need to try forgiving ourselves for all the things we've done which we regret doing; for all the things we've omitted doing or left unfinished; for the ways we've deserted ourselves, retreated or behaved cowardly; for all the ways we haven't lived up to others' expectations of us; for the ways we haven't been what others have needed us to be; for the ways we've deeply disappointed ourselves—only then can we truly let go of the past, begin to live life fully centered in the present moment, and thereby make a different future possible.

But in reshaping our future self, we do not need to forgive ourselves for actually being gay or lesbian because *there is nothing here to forgive*. Being gay is not wrong or bad. Only shaming from others has made it so. We can forgive ourselves for how we've been crippled by gay shame, but once we begin to come out of shame, we can forgive our past powerlessness, the years spent in the closet, the lies we told, the people we may have hurt by our dishonesty and fear.

What we must make inner peace with are the ways that our being gay has unfortunately collided with the expectations and judgments of others. Being gay is inherently worthwhile, valid in itself. Now we must embrace it by claiming our gayness as natural and right for us. Self-forgiving is only one part of the process for reuniting the self. What is of utmost importance with regard to being gay is *reowning* that aspect of our being—the part of us disconnected through shaming.

Reowning Disowned Parts of the Self

Probably the most difficult challenge we face in forging this brave new inner relationship is reowning all of the disowned parts of us, particularly the ones most disowned, our gay needs and desires. We must work diligently to integrate the gay part of us with the rest of our experience and identity in order to ultimately create a whole self. A self divided against itself cannot endure. As long as whatever is inherent to us is cast adrift, disconnected, placed beyond the bounds of the acceptable, we remain prisoners of our shame. But when we reach to embrace those rejected orphans within us, thereby transforming shame, we are at long last giving each orphan a home. Reclaiming the need to touch or identify with someone of our own sex—and to savor sexuality with this person who excites our interest, claims our touch —means that we are on the path toward the full integration of the self. It means we're truly out of the closet.

I grew up in a New England college town and as a kid I used to dread the spring because all the guys would be out in shorts and T-shirts. I felt assaulted, dizzy sometimes, like I had no control over myself. And I used to feel like crap, like whenever I looked at someone I was no good. I could hear my father cursing at me: "Faggot!" It was agony. Until I learned to drive. I noticed my driving instructor, who wasn't that much older than me, was distracted the same times I was! We were both looking at the same guys! At a stop light, he just grinned at me, and for the first time I felt safe about being gay, about wanting to look at men. Over the course of my lessons, we played a kind of game. When one of us saw a cute guy, we'd say a Star Trek–type line: Start the tractor beam. It cracked me up, and I felt like I wasn't alone anymore. He was the first gay man I ever talked to. It got even better because he was a great swimmer in high school, and we started doing laps together once I was done with driving lessons. He really helped me gain some speed on my kick turn, and I felt so powerful in the pool, on the road, whether he was there or when I just imagined him next to me. I wasn't weak or fucked up at all. He became a good friend, and that was exactly what I needed: reassurance, a kind of anchor. Even after he moved out of town, we stayed in touch, and he was never really gone.

Transforming self-shaming scripts into self-affirming ones, dissolving the various shame binds that constrict the expression of our gayness, and directly transforming shame scenes are the principal dimensions of the process that culminates in the active reowning of disowned parts of the self. Implicit here is a true rebirth of self.

Positive Identification as Gay or Lesbian

The path from gay shame to gay pride requires a positive identification as a gay man or lesbian. Most of us haven't grown up with positive models for gay identification. Feeling proud to be gay means being *positively* identified as gay, *positively* identified as lesbian. Pretend you're the woman from *Lianna* and shout out loud, "I love men!" or "I love women!" Do it looking into the mirror, your head held high, smiling triumphantly. Experience inside of you the joy of being gay or lesbian, then express it openly. Watch your face. Feeling it makes it more real, expressing it makes it a more permanent part of you.

The path to gay pride also requires positive identification directly with other gay men or lesbians, not only separately by sex but also together as people bound by shared experience. Of course, there are important differences between women's and men's experience, and these differences must indeed be recognized, actively remembered, openly respected. There are unquestionably real differences in the lives of lesbians and gay men, in their experience, even in what they cherish most. Lesbians have to deal more directly with sexism and the threat of violence and rape. Lesbians, like all women, also have more limited employment opportunities. Many lesbians face the question of whether or not to bear children. But differences can also be bridged. The central idea is that in healing gay/lesbian shame, we must achieve both a positive identification within ourselves as gay or lesbian *and* a positive identification with other gay men and lesbians.

It is, however, considerably easier to accomplish that identification within our own sex than to feel similarly identified across the great gender divide. The larger gender disparities between men and women in our society become even starker in the gay community. Gay men and lesbians don't have to communicate with the other sex—even minimally—to experience love. Yet that freedom from responsibility makes it more imperative to reach out to one another.

We have all observed, for example, how insular the gay and lesbian communities can be. What Thom Bean, the gay Black poet, writes about closing the racial divide could also be applied to gender: "we could be allies / unless we are too afraid / to find ourselves / in each other."[8] Reconciling the differences between the men's and women's communities does not mean ignoring or burying what's unique, but celebrating the distinctive cultural, social, and spiritual aspects in every community.

One way to begin healing the split between the sexes is by attending each other's events, whether comedy, music, or drama. Gay men and lesbians also need to read each other's literature, thereby entering each other's experience more fully. We can learn from our diversity only when we begin to respect it. The divisions existing between the men's and women's communities are perpetuated by a failure of positive identification between them. Those divisions can be overcome only through mutual understanding that is deliberately, actively sought and by the enhanced respect that it brings. Differences will always exist. But differences can become a source of strength, a basis for renewed identification, when we purposefully unite across them.

From Self-Affirmation to a Self-Affirming Identity

Through engaging the various interconnected principles explored earlier, we are able to create a whole, integrated self, a self able to find essential value in being gay, a self able to both prize and celebrate gayness. In so doing, we are fashioning a coherent, self-affirming gay identity.

To affirm the self is to openly value the self. We must learn to value ourselves whether or not others do if we are to build security within. Affirming ourselves also means admiring ourselves. Being able to affirm ourselves from within is the securest foundation from which to live life—with dignity, pride in self, and hope for the future.

With a secure and self-affirming identity as a gay man or lesbian, we are best prepared to freely encounter other gay men and lesbians, secure intimacy in our friendships, sustain strong relationships that are loving and erotic, and create new forms of community as an emergent people.

TRANSFORMING GAY SHAME INTO GAY PRIDE: A PERSONAL STORY

Coming out of shame is a process that happens ever so slowly over time. We come out in stages, never all at once. Coming to terms with the reality that we have not been what our culture, religion, and family proclaim to be right is a difficult, even tortuous journey. For we must discard fundamental assumptions received from past generations and walk an uncharted path. Embracing gayness requires us to learn how to nurture, forgive, and affirm ourselves from within—never an easy task for anyone. It is all the more challenging when the voices we hear all about us are condemning ones. Moving from a life of shame and self-loathing to one of positive identification both as gay and with other gays means actively creating a positive, self-affirming gay identity. Affirmation validates life as we have determined to embrace it. It makes our individual life more worthwhile and more vital.

Embedded here is a vision of new possibilities inherent in gay and lesbian existence.

But realizing that vision is far from quick or easy. How did *we* accomplish the various facets of the process we have been describing here as necessary? How did *we* come out of shame in our own lives?

We want not only to offer a personal confession, valid and useful as that might be, but more important to illustrate the process, we want to offer a model for others. Just as no two individuals' experiences of shame are ever identical, no two journeys out of shame are exactly the same either. But we offer ourselves as examples because we want to show that a new life is possible when you take the risk and begin the journey out of shame.

During adolescence, Lev was unable to look at men he found attractive without finding himself ugly and disgusting. Both of us engaged in invidious comparisons at one time or another: we would look longingly at other men, but then feel ourselves to be unmanly in comparison. Both of us felt rejected, humiliated, and devalued by our families. Both of us experienced sneering faces all around us until we absorbed and began to live with those faces inside of us.

Though each of us had grown up experiencing what were agonizing and deeply personal struggles with shame centered directly around being gay, our separate stories began to converge in 1981. Gershen was married at the time, living with his wife and two sons, even a dog, in a house in the quiet suburbs of a midwestern city—living the American Dream. Lev was planning to someday marry and have children of his own. Then we met at the university. Our relationship flourished in the context of teaching and writing together. That fateful encounter changed both of our lives. Four years later, after considerable inner turmoil and struggle, we were able to fully embrace our gayness. After Gershen was divorced, we decided to become a committed couple. Another year after that decision, we bought a house and moved in together. Those events are important signposts: they mark critical changes in the visible form of our lives.

But our relationship and the life we were slowly building together represent only the outline of the process of transforming gay shame into gay pride, and mainly the side of the process that is more visible to others. That process is always a complex one, occurring on many levels, both inner and outer. Now we'll sketch in more of the detail to illustrate how inner change must also become translated into lived experience.

One of the very first things we did was to seek out gay environments that we felt were nurturing. We helped form a study group at the university comprising gay men and lesbians. Our focus was on the thoughtful consideration of gay issues and ideas through literature and film. We also began seeking out gay society through forming gay friendships, both as individuals and as a couple. We immersed ourselves in gay life. Then we began to travel to gay communities, first the Castro in San Francisco and later Provincetown in Massachusetts. One year we ended up in San Francisco several times. Becoming immersed in an all-gay or mostly gay environment was deeply nourishing. What an experience to walk down the street holding hands or arm in arm, to not only feel free but validated and included with our gay sisters and brothers.

We attended Out/Write, the first national gay writers conference in San Francisco, and the one that followed it a year later. That conference was for us what gay sports leagues are for other people. We met other gay and lesbian writers there and at the Lambda Book Awards. These were people whose books we had read and enjoyed, new people whose work we became eager to explore. Hearing Kate Clinton and the Flirtations several times in different parts of the country opened up still another avenue to absorbing gay culture. With repeated trips to Provincetown, the Village, West Hollywood, and San Francisco, we steeped ourselves in the experience of being gay. And we found ourselves celebrating gayness as a result.

We were discovering a whole new world, and, like all explorers, we were entranced by it, captivated. The more we found, the more we hungered for. So we read even more widely than we had before in gay and lesbian fiction, history, magazines, comics. We saw every lesbian and gay film possible. We discovered more writers and professionals who were gay or lesbian. We began to network. No longer were we isolated or alone. We also began offering ourselves as speakers or workshop leaders at conferences and locally at the university. Gradually, we began to feel part of a rich community, and the feeling was electric.

Probably one of the most significant acts, and most transformative, was buying a house together. Not only did that cement our relationship in a very material way, but it rooted us historically. Now we were homeowners among other homeowners in a thriving community. We had neighbors. We were partners, lovers, soul-mates—and a *family*. Creating a home and family together itself is deeply transformative.

We celebrated not only home and hearth, but sexuality. Even though we had both previously enjoyed sexual relationships with women, nothing compared with holding the man you love and desire. Nothing was more satisfying than sharing erotic delight between us. Discovering each other's bodies and holding, touching, caressing each other felt as natural as breathing. We could laugh in bed and enter each other's fantasies. For the first time in our lives we each felt whole and complete.

Our involvement in and support of gay political action groups, at both the local and national levels, came somewhat later. Supporting lesbian and gay causes has become vital to us. So has the very public display of that support through writing, including articles, essays, opinion columns, and letters to newspaper editors.

Before coming out of shame, neither of us had ever marched for anything, but we've now marched in local Gay Pride parades and also attended a mammoth pride parade in San Francisco. Then came the 1993 national March on Washington. For us, the cumulative impact of those experiences was revolutionary, and we were not at all prepared for the empowering nature of being at the Washington March.

It started on the plane ride down. Very quickly we realized that more than half the plane was taken by gays and lesbians. With remarkable freedom and ease, people were sharing stories, laughing, joking even before the plane took off: one guy said he thought lesbians and gays should be served their meals first in honor of the event.

The sense of solidarity continued at the hotel, where almost everyone was wearing March-related buttons or T-shirts, and when we headed out the morning of the March it was like a pilgrimage to a holy site—everywhere we looked, lesbians and gay men were streaming toward the Ellipse, which was an explosion of color in banners, clothes, balloons, and streamers. People in the crowd were singing, shouting, hugging, calling out to old friends. We loved the feeling of celebration that was matched by fierce commitment; we loved the sheer numbers of lesbians, gays, and their supporters; we loved the excitement; we loved running into friends from around the country and around the world all day long; we loved the beautiful bodies and faces and spirits surrounding us. We were swimming in a sea of gayness.

We marched with the World Congress of Gay and Lesbian Jewish Organizations, and marching itself was even more exhilarating, especially as we sang in Hebrew, feeling completely immersed in gayness and Jewishness, politics and passion. There seemed no more triumphant way to be visible, powerful, *charged*. Time and time again, we wondered how we could ever have considered not going to the March, because of how deeply nourished we were just by being there.

If the flight home was somewhat sad, it was more than compensated at the Detroit airport. We were still wearing our March shirts and buttons: some people looked away, some nodded and even smiled. It was a kind of visibility we had never tried on in our home state.

When we bought a newspaper, the soft-spoken clerk who barely looked at us gestured vaguely at our T-shirts and furtively said she was "that way" too, but no one knew. Had we enjoyed ourselves? she wondered. With deep conviction, we said, "It was incredible!"

The March gave us rich rewards: feeling a part of history; feeling a part of the gay rights movement; feeling connected with our friends and community in entirely new ways; feeling we had stored up scenes of gay power and gay pride that would last our whole lives.

CHAPTER FOUR

Affect, Sex, and Relationships

L esbian and gay relationships have been typically viewed by the wider society as mere *caricatures* of heterosexual relationships. Relationships between women and men are seen not only as the preferred norm, but, more important, as the only true expression of love and sex. Maturity and psychological health have been equated with intimacy between a man and a woman that is also sustained over time. No other relationship is admissible to the realm of normalcy, or even imaginable. Our culture teaches us that the love shared between two women or two men can only be inferior, a lesser and laughable form of intimacy, and a mockery of real sex. Gay desire, affection, and intimacy are always described by society in terms of being lesser.

Our culture does not take gay relationships seriously—when they're considered at all. Usually, our relationships are seen as freakish and ridiculous. Gays are still asked, "Which of you is the man, which the woman?"— as if mature adult lesbians and gay men are merely little children play-acting and dressing up in the attic. With such a lack of knowledge, our culture reduces our deepest attachments to burlesque. That lack of respect causes us pain because we face obstacles that non-gay couples simply do not face. We have to deal with sodomy laws that can be used to brand us as criminals, with a profound lack of visibility and respect, and even hostility and violence. With such barriers to intimacy, many gays and lesbians end up feeling that their relationships are merely provisional, experimental.

Just as mainstream culture holds stereotypes about us, so do we: gay men are seen as obsessed with sex, superficial, and not interested in love, while lesbians are viewed as grim, enmeshed, and separatist.

Prevailing perceptions of gay and lesbian relationships profoundly mold the climate in which we grow up. Against these negative attitudes, lesbians and gay men struggle toward intimacy on their own, often living in anguished isolation, lacking visible images of successful relationships, too often lacking the belief that loving and lasting gay relationships are even possible.

Same-sex desire manifests in three ways. First is inner feeling, and our erotic feelings can be transitory or persistent. We may catch only fleeting glimpses of these feelings or instead find ourselves consumed by erotic desire. A second way involves spontaneous or deliberately constructed fantasies that are usually more intricate as well as enduring. These fantasies might accompany masturbation, or the sight of an attractive man or woman might spark a stream of interconnected scenes that are affectionate, erotic, intimate. The awareness of sexual feelings or fantasies also leads to sexual behavior that is either planned or spontaneous. An unexpected situation like a camping trip or sharing a dorm room might throw us together with another man or woman in a sexual encounter, or we might deliberately seek out such encounters at a bar, for example.

While sexual desire can be displayed in each of these ways, it may not be freely expressed; the degree of shame bound to sexual feeling, fantasy, or behavior determines which are inhibited, which are given free rein. When all the voices of our culture tell us that union between a man and a woman is the only natural one to pursue, we become deeply divided listening to our own insistent voice that calls us elsewhere.

THE SEXUAL IDENTITY SPECTRUM

Sexual identity, in contrast to sexual orientation, is an expression of self-definition. Further, sexual identity can either become fully integrated or instead remain disconnected from the larger fabric of your life.

The categories of sexual identity—heterosexual, homosexual, and bi-sexual—are the received wisdom of an earlier age, but the lived experience of real people is never categorized so neatly. The language we employ invariably shapes our perception of what exists. Because our language is rigid as opposed to flexible, our views of sexual orientation and sexual identity have been similarly limited.

A more useful and accurate view is to think in terms of a spectrum: *sexual behavior–sexual orientation–sexual identity.* For example, some people will engage in sexual behavior with other members of their own sex, but they won't experience or describe themselves as homosexual. That's true of men in prison or the navy who have sex with men but don't think of themselves as homosexual, just as it's true of a woman who is married yet drawn to affairs with women. Others will possibly experience themselves as either bisexual or homosexual in orientation but will not self-identify as bisexual, gay, or lesbian. Sexual attraction and desire for their own sex can be expressed fairly consistently over time, and it is fully conscious. Still, no matter how frequent homosexual sex is, they stop short of defining a sexual identity that gives shape to their lifestyle and direction to their relationships.

> *Sometimes I like sex with other women 'cause it livens things up. Like this woman at my gym. We became workout partners. I couldn't stop watching her. And the first time we went out for lunch after aerobics class, she made a pass at me. We go to her house twice a week now. But I'm not a lesbian. That's not me. I still have sex with men and that's what I really crave.*

Another group will not only self-identify as lesbian, gay, or bisexual, but will also openly identify with other lesbians, gays, and bisexuals. This latter group has found the answers to the perennial questions "Who am I?" "Where do I belong?" In every age, these have been the central questions that underlie the search for identity, the search for primary identification with some particular group which will then become the principal source of our identity.

Shame is another major influence on sexual identity. The degree to which we experience shame is actually a critical factor, often a decisive one, in determining where we fall along the sexual identity spectrum. Shame will constrict or entirely block the evolution of sexual identity, regardless of sexual orientation.

The sexual behavior–sexual orientation–sexual identity spectrum has another dimension: it stretches from the *heterosexually oriented*, through the *bisexually oriented*, to the *homosexually oriented*. Such a spectrum does not contain a set of fixed categories but instead reflects the various and changing directions of gender focus that sexual orientation actually exhibits. There are three primary directions inherent to sexual orientation: toward people of the other sex, toward people of both sexes, and toward people of your own sex.

Shame about any orientation will severely paralyze individuals in pursuing them. When the impact of shame spreads inward, erotic desire itself will be constricted, even banished entirely from consciousness. Such individuals will be barred by shame from pursuing their deepest wishes, their now only dimly perceived desires.

These three orientations also comprise a spectrum. When we use terms like *heterosexual, bisexual,* and *homosexual,* we are not describing a set of inflexible and mutually exclusive categories into which everyone can be classified. That's a far too limiting view of sexual orientation that simply ignores the marvelous plasticity of the human being. Thus, a lesbian who has always been attracted only to women and has a firmly established lesbian identity will be taken aback by the unexpected appearance of sexual attraction to a close male friend. She will likely be just as unsettled as a heterosexual woman who unexpectedly finds herself erotically drawn to women. Terms like heterosexual, bisexual, and homosexual are best viewed as coordinates, like those on a mariner's map; they enable us to better locate ourselves on the map of sexual orientation.

Similarly, parallel terms such as gay, lesbian, and bisexual identity must be treated as neither fixed nor unchanging. Categories are always restricting and invariably become mutually exclusive. If there is a single truth about the nature of identity itself, it is that identity is always in flux, evolving.

What keeps identity imprisoned is shame, whether it is the shame about being gay or lesbian directed from the wider non-gay culture or the shame about being bisexual directed from the gay or lesbian community.

HOW SELF-ESTEEM, IDENTITY, AND INTIMACY
REINFORCE ONE ANOTHER

The way to detect our true sexual orientation is by observing its actual pattern over time, a pattern that is expressed in feelings, fantasies, and behavior. Simply put, we need to become consciously aware of who we are spontaneously attracted to, the people we are immediately excited by.

If we're in doubt about our sexual orientation in adolescence or adulthood, then we need to observe the pattern of our erotic reactions over time: are we drawn mainly to women, men, or both? That is the only way to discern our true sexual orientation in terms of its characteristic gender focus. What constricts the natural flow and direction of sexuality is repeated shaming by family, culture, and religion.

Further, we must be prepared to allow into full consciousness all feelings, wishes, and fantasies. The only place to exercise control is at the boundary of action. We need to consciously decide whom we have sex with, when and how, and in what context. If we deny, suppress, or disown any affect, need, or drive, however, then the seeds of psychological disturbance are being sown. Psychological health depends on the full integration of all the affects, needs, and drives.

When being gay, lesbian, or bisexual has become previously bound by shame, then *owning* our innate sexual orientation is the key to psychological health. Owning is a threefold process. Owning means that a particular affect or need is first of all consciously *experienced;* then it is recognized and accurately *named;* finally, it is *owned* as an inherent, welcomed part of us. That's what must occur in the case of sexual desires for your own sex. For example, by owning your desire for other women, you're claiming those desires as natural, as valid in and of themselves. Owning is active, not passive, and self-acceptance is the direct result of owning. Reowning disowned parts of the self, including a previously shamed or disowned sexual orientation, is the principal path to psychological integration.

For years I could never admit that I craved women. I hated
myself every time I even looked at a cute woman. It was awful.

*Those crazy feelings tore me apart, until I began to face up to the
truth. I had this coach at college I admired. One day she just
grinned and said it out loud, plain as day: "God I just love
women's bodies. I love women." I couldn't believe it. But it felt so
damn good! So I began to say it too—to myself.*

The capacity to maintain self-esteem in the context of being gay or
lesbian depends on the balance between shame and self-acceptance. If self-
contempt is stronger than self-affirmation, then whatever inner conflicts are
present will only intensify further. But if you develop positive identification
with other gays, then your inner comfort grows and self-esteem, in turn, will
grow accordingly.

The coming out process—whether to family, friends, or co-workers—
can result in either enhanced inner comfort or even greater inner conflict
depending on how accepting and supportive those people are. It's not always
possible to know in advance how other people will respond to your coming
out. But their acceptance creates mutuality.

Intimacy, like self-esteem and identity, will expand and deepen in response to mutual enjoyment. But intimacy will become further constricted in
response to shame or fear.

*Before I met Roger, I was terrified of anyone finding out I
was gay. I was so lonely then, and hiding was my middle name.
But Roger and I had so much fun together, we laughed and par-
tied—and had great sex too. Everything changed. It's like suddenly I found this courage inside me to come out, to be myself.
Wherever I was, he was with me—inside, I mean. Encouraging
me, guiding me.*

Self-esteem, identity, and intimacy mutually reinforce one another, and
the outcome in one sphere can significantly alter the outcome in another. For
instance, if your gay relationships fail, then your self-esteem is likely to
plummet as well. Similarly, when your smoldering conflict over being gay or
lesbian is finally extinguished, both your self-esteem and possibilities for
intimacy will expand.

The ability to translate your homosexual orientation into a positive
gay or lesbian identity and then, in turn, translate that emerging identity into

a productive and flourishing life depends not only on developing positive self-esteem, but equally on the outcome of the pursuit of sex and love. And the pursuit of both is governed entirely by affect.

AFFECT AND RELATIONSHIPS

By carefully tracing how individual men and women become dominated by particular affects, we can more readily determine how the pursuit of intimacy in same-sex relationships becomes scripted. The expression of sexuality becomes equally scripted in this process, with or without intimacy. Some gay men seek intimacy in different relationships from those in which they seek sex, whereas other gay men look for both sex and intimacy in the same relationship. For lesbians, a dominant script is an increased level of merging within their relationships; coupled with this is a sharp decline in exciting sex. Lesbians are also more likely to remain emotionally involved with former lovers. The pursuit of anonymous sex, changing sexual partners, or sex solely within a committed relationship are other kinds of scripted patterns, for both gay men and lesbians. What's at work here is not necessarily a biological sex difference, but the operation of different governing affects and therefore entirely different scripted responses to affect.

Any *apparent* sex differences are determined by the gender shaming patterns we discussed in Chapter 1. There we observed how, both historically and cross-culturally, men and women experience shame differently, in that each sex has a specific set of affects and needs that are targeted for shaming. Affects and needs that are not targeted, and therefore remain free of shaming, are the only ones which are then allowed open expression. What varies by sex is only the specific *pattern* of affects and needs that is designated for shaming.

The "masculine" affects, those that men are allowed and actually encouraged to express, are excitement, surprise, anger, dissmell, and disgust. The remaining affects of enjoyment, fear, distress, and shame are designated as "feminine," the only affects that women are permitted to express.

Paralleling this separation, the spectrum of interpersonal needs also becomes partitioned into "masculine" and "feminine." Men are encouraged in the expression of only two, the need to differentiate and the need for power. Women, in contrast, are given free rein to express all of those remaining: the needs for relationship, touching/holding, identification, affirmation, and nurturing others.

PARTITIONING OF AFFECTS AND NEEDS BY GENDER

"Masculine"		"Feminine"
	Affects	
Excitement		Enjoyment
Surprise		Fear
Anger		Distress
Dissmell		Shame
Disgust		
	Interpersonal Needs	
Differentiation		Relationship
Power		Touching/Holding
		Identification
		Nurturing Others
		Affirmation

Shaming the overt expression of particular affects or interpersonal needs eventually results in suppressing them. The pattern of affects and needs that each sex is thereby allowed to give free expression to, in turn, plays a central role in shaping both identity and interpersonal relations.

Identity, in fact, becomes stratified in response to this partitioning of affects and needs. Men are scripted to pursue identity through differentiation and power, whereas women are equally scripted to pursue identity through relatedness and identification. The eventual pursuit of intimacy, sexual and otherwise, is itself equally governed by affect.

Affect Governs the Pursuit of Intimacy

Interpersonal relationships are fueled by affect, and the various relationships you form become patterned around particular affects or combinations of affect. When different affects become sufficiently magnified to the point that they begin to capture and dominate your life, the relational patterns you develop are in direct response to your predominant affects. When very different kinds of relationships coexist in your life, they do so because different affect combinations are operating simultaneously. When virtually *all* of your relational experiences become identically patterned, then a particular affect or combination of affects has gained a "monopoly" over you.

Any affect can become so magnified that it begins to dominate an individual, to monopolize that person's entire affective life. We've all met people who seem dominated by one particular affect—someone who's always annoyed and complaining (anger), for example, or people whose faces and voices are sad regardless of the situation (distress).

When enjoyment is your predominant affect, your relationships will be governed by continuity and commitment. Enjoyment affect will motivate you to invest in *sameness* over time, to enjoy reexperiencing the same person over a period of months and even years. Returning to the same place, to the same person, day in and day out—that's enjoyment affect in action.

> *I just love spending time with Grace. We can sit in front of the fire for hours, just cuddling and remembering things we've done over the past few months, places we've been, movies we've seen, even great dinners we had. It's like this Talking Heads song where "memories can't wait." That's us—we love remembering.*

The experience of mutuality is both deepened and renewed by the shared enjoyment felt when you and your friend or lover periodically relive shared events from the past: *Remember the time when—?* Mementos, letters, gifts, or photos can play a key role in nurturing this intimacy. Continuity in a relationship is fostered by enjoyment, just as the ability to sustain commitment to another person requires that enjoyment affect predominates.

When excitement is your predominant affect, however, then novelty and the pursuit of new lovers is the principle that governs intimacy for you. Excitement affect dictates an investment in change and novelty, which become increasingly required as excitement captures control of your affective life. If you are principally governed by excitement, then you will be scripted to continually seek out new relationships or lovers. In a relationship with the same person, excitement dissipates over time, and the newness inevitably fades. Your lover has now become too familiar, and so you must look for new lovers in order to experience the requisite level of excitement. Only strangers satisfy your hunger for excitement, because they're unknown.

I used to be so fascinated with Steven. Just seeing him—just thinking about him—made me hard. But now I'm bored in bed. He just doesn't turn me on anymore—I don't know what happened. I keep thinking about this new guy I just met who's really hot. I can't wait till it's over with Steven so I can move on.

When fear and excitement become conjointly magnified, then you become equally gripped by these twin affects and driven to always living on the edge where thrills and danger converge. In response to this combination of affects, you seek out relationships that are exciting as well as somehow dangerous in order to experience *both* affects in sufficient measure. Simple change or novelty alone is not enough; danger must be added to the equation. For some gay men, the danger comes from cruising in a park or having rest-stop sex, both of which involve the fear of being discovered and even arrested.

I can't get off unless I get that adrenaline rush going. I stopped at this rest area and there was a guy in the john, obviously cruising. There were all these people outside the building, and it was so blatant I loved it. I followed him into a stall. My heart was pounding I was so scared. We started jerking each other off right there. And then the outer door opened, there were footsteps—I thought I'd die. What a rush as I came!

When shame is the principal affect governing your affective life, then your relationships can be marked by hiding and the avoidance of intimacy. Individuals who are bound by shame hide from intimacy or even sexual encounters because there's nothing like intimacy or sex to awaken shame. The shame-bound woman or man is also particularly vulnerable to being drawn into abusive relationships. Because shame is self-validating due to the inevitable shame *about* shame, so are abusive relationships: you are apt to feel that you deserve whatever abuse you're receiving. If you're shame-based you're also more likely to stay in relationships that are abusive, or in which you're kept powerless, because shame leaves you feeling defective. Inevitably, then, you perceive the failing as your own: *It's my fault things aren't working out.* So you'll remain in relationships that are deeply unsatisfying, shaming, or demoralizing, always trying to make them work and never quite realizing that the only winning move is to leave.

> *I could never bear letting anyone too close—I was always getting hurt. Then I met Sally and we really clicked. I thought this was it. But after six months she started hitting me. I just freaked. I couldn't believe it was happening 'cause that's how my mother treated me. And I can't believe I'm still seeing her. I feel so awful.*

When fear and shame combine to govern your life, different outcomes are possible, depending on the strength of those affects. Seeking new contacts through personal ads is driven mainly by shame and fear for some people (though not everyone, of course), but these affects are not yet at a level that precludes all avenues to connection with others. You perceive less risk of rejection when you place or respond to an ad.

When shame and fear do reach paralyzing proportions, however, the prospect of being in a relationship itself becomes too costly. Fear is now magnified into terror, and shame into the deepest humiliation. The shame and fear can feel like insurmountable barriers to crossing whatever interpersonal bridges may be at hand. Increasingly you feel under siege, and you become a prisoner, isolated. When fear and shame are jointly magnified in sufficient measure, then you're likely to abandon relationships altogether.

> *I kept getting disappointed by guys I liked. It got so I dreaded even talking to anyone at the bar. So I stopped going. I just withdrew from everybody. I figured I could go it alone. That way I wouldn't get hurt anymore. But I got so lonely.*

When contempt is magnified and becomes your predominant affect, then your relationships will involve distancing people and superiority over them. You'll also be more likely to be abusive to others. In feeling contempt, you become immediately elevated above people, thereby perceiving yourself as superior. Contempt is the source of judgmental, fault-finding, and condescending attitudes that now infiltrate all of your relationships. You are least likely to identify or empathize with anyone you feel contempt for. Contempt also positions you to use people as though they were objects, so it is only a small step to actually abusing them.

I love cruising nerdy guys. They're always surprised that someone as hot as I am would even look at them. And I really get off on hooking them and then making them beg for sex, grovel and bring themselves really low. What a trip.

The following chart displays these different governing affects on the left side along with the various resulting relationship patterns on the right side. Keep in mind that these are not the *only* affects or blends that govern interpersonal relations, just those that occur most frequently. They illustrate the operation of very different affect patterns which over the course of a lifetime dictate different relationship patterns.

PREDOMINANT AFFECT	RESULTING RELATIONSHIP PATTERNS
Enjoyment	Continuity, commitment
Excitement	Novelty, new lovers
Fear and excitement	Pursuing danger
Shame	Hiding, avoidance, entering abusive relationships
Fear and shame	Abandoning relationships
Contempt	Distancing others, superiority, creating abusive relationships

Specific affects or affect combinations can become predominant very early in a person's life and then monopolize it for the duration. But the affects that predominate for a given individual need not remain constant over time. Governing affects are not necessarily fixed and unchanging. One affect may predominate during the first half of your life, but then an entirely different affect supplants it because of life events like an influential book or film, therapy, or a transformative relationship, which greatly reduces the first affect and magnifies the second. Your relational patterns will be discontinuous in this case because different intimacy patterns will dominate in direct response to your prevailing affects.

Vanessa had been physically abused as a child and most of her relationships with women were emotionally stormy and violent. Winding up in the emergency room one night with a broken nose, she met Colette, a nurse she knew casually from the bar. Colette urged her to get out of her current relationship and seek counseling. "I've seen the kind of women you go for," she said. "You're messing up your life." Vanessa not only was in pain but was stung and humiliated by her problem being so obvious. But Colette was persistent, revealing her own past history of abuse. Colette slowly brought Vanessa into a therapy group, where she began to face her shame. Eventually, Vanessa met someone new at work and they started dating; this was a woman who could truly care for her.

Other affect patterns over the life span generate different intimacy patterns. For Denise, three affects competed for dominance until she was forty: shame, fear, and excitement. During those years her relationships fluctuated depending on the particular affects in charge at any given time. When excitement was strong, she sought out new women for sex partners; when both fear and excitement captured control, Denise craved danger; and when shame became paramount, she avoided intimacy.

Each pattern lasted for a limited period of time, usually a couple of years at most. Around the time she turned forty, several things happened at once: she became acutely aware of her own mortality and, in response, became quite fearful of dying; and a series of very painful rejections rapidly magnified her shame into inferiority and worthlessness. At this critical juncture in Denise's life, shame and fear combined and then predominated. She gradually abandoned her search for intimacy with another woman because it had become too threatening. Even her prior excitement began to wane because she was no longer feeling so adventurous—fear and shame now overwhelmed her excitement completely and suppressed it.

If excitement had combined with fear instead of shame, however, her pattern of intimacy would have been governed very differently: she would have pursued some kind of danger in her relationships with other women, not abandoned them altogether.

There is another principal pattern for the emergence of affect dominance. Tom's first twenty years of life were dominated by shame, during which time he avoided all intimacy and had only sporadic sex with men that left him even more ashamed. The predominance of shame was eventually supplanted by the positive affects of excitement and enjoyment following a successful course of therapy in which he blossomed as a gay man. He began to approach life and relationships with hope. Eventually, Tom found a lover and they built a life together. Then at the age of forty-five, his lover of fifteen years died in an automobile accident. Tom had been following his lover home in a separate car and actually witnessed the accident. Now he felt devastated, his dreams destroyed. He abandoned hope, retreated from social contact, and kept to himself from that point on. With this tragic loss, shame suddenly intruded once again and recaptured him. Even though his initial avoidance of intimacy due to shame had given way to his active pursuit of intimacy, the sudden intrusion of shame in later life entirely reversed that. The intrusion of early affect, which had once been strong but then gave way to the dominance of other affects, can unexpectedly reappear and alter your relational patterns.[1]

Affect governs intimacy by scripting how you relate to others. Hank craves excitement and therefore new sex partners almost daily, while Ted enjoys his continuing involvement with the same man. Dave, in contrast, wants neither; he can tolerate only anonymous sex with men he picks up cruising on the street. These outcomes depend on the balance between the affects of shame, contempt, and fear on the one hand and those of enjoyment and excitement on the other.

Equally critical are the particular defending scripts that develop in response to shame. A power script utilized as a defense against shame, for example, would favor anonymous sex, particularly when coupled with the predominance of fear and shame as governing affects. Joanne craved control whenever she got close to anyone. She *had* to be in charge; otherwise she felt exposed. She had to run the relationship and run sex too. She was fearful of becoming vulnerable, so she always kept her guard up. Similarly, a gay man gripped by fear and shame, coupled with a power script, might find that the only type of intimacy or sex he could comfortably tolerate was anonymous: one-night stands or sex clubs.

But a power script might also lead you to pursue intimacy and sex in separate ongoing relationships instead of anonymous sex. Chris can be emotionally intimate with men, but not with the same man he has sex with; for him sex and intimacy have become split. This outcome is more likely when fear and shame are less intense. It's also more likely when sex has been disconnected from intimacy as a result of shame binds that surround the needs for touching/holding and identification as well as the sex drive itself. For Chris, trying to be intimate and sexual at the same time with the same man produces intense shame, and he becomes overwhelmed. Isolating sex and intimacy is his only recourse for keeping shame in check.

Governing affects, shame binds, and defending scripts all interact in determining how intimacy and sexuality become scripted.

AFFECT AND THE SEXUAL DRIVE

The sexual drive derives its power from the affect system. The drive must be amplified by excitement affect in order for us to experience complete sexual pleasure. This means that what we usually refer to as sexual arousal is not really a property of the drive at all, but a consequence of the amplifying nature of affect. What we're actually experiencing when we feel sexually aroused *is* the affect of excitement.

Because we've been taught, and therefore believe, that the excitement felt during sex of any kind resides in the sexual drive, we've failed to distinguish affect from drive and so have failed to accurately locate the source of that arousal. Why is that important? Because the sex drive becomes readily disrupted by affect, and understanding how affect governs sex gives us the means to release sex from the constricting effects of shame.

During sex we actually *experience* excitement in the face and nostrils and in the chest and breathing, not in the genitals. Of course, there are physical changes—like erections, tight nipples, and moistening vaginas—but these changes, even when they're genital, are not the same thing as excitement itself, which is an affect. The requirement that the sex drive be fused with excitement affect in order to function optimally has far-reaching implications.

Think of times when you and another person were sexually aroused together—and then suddenly you realized that the door was unlocked or the window shade was up or someone was in the next room. Excitement can be cut short by any negative affect like fear or shame. (That's different from our prior rest-stop example, in which fear actually *enhances* sexual excitement by providing an added rush.) In *this* case, fear cuts off excitement affect, and then the functioning of the sexual drive itself is interrupted.

Tara became sexual with another woman who turned out to have some hair on her breasts. The sudden disgust she felt at that unexpected sight swamped her excitement. She was simply no longer in the mood. Fortunately, her disgust was only temporary.

What if you become sexual with someone who unexpectedly criticizes or disparages you? Most likely, you won't feel in the mood for sex anymore.

What's happening in each of these examples is that the affect has changed. Excitement has been superseded by fear, disgust, or shame, and the sexual drive literally ceases to function.

Shaming Excitement Affect

Because excitement affect is targeted for shaming among young girls from an early age in many cultures, this particular shame bind produces a further complication for women when the sexual drive later matures during adolescence. The early shaming of excitement has no necessary connection whatsoever to sexuality. Girls can be shamed for *any* expression of excitement, for yelling too loud, playing too rough, running too fast.

Picture a girl whose parents, teachers in school, even her older sisters are perpetually trying to quiet her down or keep her from rough and tumble play. These people are responding to her natural expressions of excitement in ways that, in effect, produce shame. At times, the shaming of excitement is quite intentional. One five-year-old girl attended a neighborhood birthday party. Instead of joining the other kids in a game of tag, she remained on the sidelines, watching silently. When asked by an adult if she'd like to join the game, this youngster replied, looking shamefaced, "Oh no, I'm a girl—I'm not *supposed* to do that." By the age of five, she had already been sufficiently socialized by shame not to express excitement or engage in excitement-producing activities.

The overlap in time between expressions of excitement and shaming responses results in the fusion of excitement and shame, creating a shame bind that now constricts further expression of excitement. Once firmly established, such a bind operates to spontaneously and indirectly generate shame whenever excitement is later expressed outwardly, and in many instances even when excitement is only experienced internally.

The shame that is now bound to excitement affect then makes later manifestations of sexuality problematic, even without additional direct shaming of sexuality. The adolescent or adult woman will indirectly experience shame in her sexual life whenever excitement affect is activated, as it must be for the sexual drive to function. The shame connected to excitement now also invades her sexuality, interfering with the drive and disrupting its functioning.

> *When I was a girl, my big sisters and my mother kept me quiet by yelling at me. I wasn't supposed to laugh out loud or anything. Even outside, I always had to sit quietly and read or something like that. I wanted to run around, but they always stopped me. Later on, when I'd get the least bit excited in school or with friends, I'd suddenly feel awkward and just look down— like I'd done something really bad. Now I'm a woman. Whenever my girlfriend and I make love, I just freeze up. Like I can't let anything out or even move because something bad will happen.*

Because women have so often been silenced, many end up being inhibited sexually. The perception that women are not sexually active is a direct consequence of shaming excitement. While this particular dynamic can be most widely observed among both heterosexual and homosexual women, many men have also been heavily shamed for the vocal expression of excitement affect. Until his early twenties, Simon was extremely quiet during sex. From a very early age, his father had yelled at him incessantly about being a loud, noisy little boy. His father's constant vigilance in this regard made him hypersensitive about ever expressing himself too loudly. It wasn't until he had a sexual partner who cried out freely and wildly during lovemaking that he suddenly felt the freedom to cry out himself. At last he felt released.

In releasing the shame surrounding sexuality, it is important to also release the shame that inhibits the *cry of affect*. That is crucial to the experience of full sexual pleasure. We have all been taught to suppress affect from earliest childhood by constricting breathing and thereby inhibiting the vocalization of affect.[2] When we suppress the cry of excitement during sex, we actually have to hold our breath to inhibit it. By constricting breathing in this way, we invariably dampen sexual pleasure. That's inescapable. Reversing this suppression requires us to freely vocalize affect, like the cry of anger as well as the cry of excitement.

> *My lover and I have pretty good sex, but it really bothers me*
> *that he doesn't make a sound—ever. And when I go crazy when I*
> *come, he gets this real strange look on his face like I've done*
> *something wrong. It spoils it for me—I wish he could just let go.*

Vocalizing excitement during sex means crying out loud just as you would at a baseball game. Excitement affect is operating in both instances, and it must be expressed; releasing that cry is critical to complete sexual pleasure. As long as we continue to inhibit vocal expression of groaning and shouting, sexual pleasure is also inhibited. The key is being expressive instead of quiet during sex, particularly during orgasm. There are some exceptions, of course. Having sex in public places might dictate being quiet instead of noisy, but in this case excitement is intensified by the forbidden nature of sex in that setting. Likewise, some people's sexual fantasies involve having sex someplace where they cannot be noisy, and their excitement is intensified precisely by stifling vocal expression.

If your lover doesn't feel free to cry out during sex, it's true you run the risk of feeling embarrassed when *you* cry out; that additional shame can inhibit you further on the next occasion. Many people are thus forced to be content with some reduction in sexual pleasure if that means avoiding intolerable embarrassment. The key is working toward mutual release of the cry of excitement even if that means tolerating the momentary shame caused by being loud when your partner isn't.

Mutual Facial Gazing

Excitement has to be fused with the sex drive, and the cry of excitement also has to be vocalized, particularly during orgasm. Otherwise, sexual pleasure becomes muted. Enjoyment affect also comes into play, in the enjoyment of bodily caresses, in the relaxing glow after orgasm, and in the shared intimacy experienced directly during sex. Thus, it is possible to *enjoy* sex without necessarily being *excited* by it. Excitement affect is, however, critical for erection in men and orgasm in both women and men, yet sex can nevertheless be enjoyable even when excitement is reduced. In this case sexual enjoyment may predominate or, if intense enough, might actually evoke increased excitement.

Consider intimacy more closely. When we gaze continuously into each other's eyes during lovemaking, the resulting intensity of intimacy is dramatically heightened. On the other hand, when we make love with the lights out or with our eyes closed, so that we cannot see each other's face, the intensity of intimacy is immediately reduced to a more comfortable level—even though excitement still runs high.

Excitement Wanes with Sameness

One consequence of excitement being inextricably embedded in sexuality is that excitement actually diminishes in a relationship with the same person over time. Exactly how long it takes for that waning to occur will vary from person to person. Continuity kindles enjoyment, not excitement. That is why you can feel diminished sexual excitement around the person you're dating or living with, but you can feel instantly excited by a total stranger. This will be true even in the best of loving relationships. Being with the same person, seeing her or him often, or living together day in and day out produces such a degree of familiarity that you cease to even recognize that individual the way you did when you shared the excitement of mutual discovery. You may deeply enjoy your time together, but less often you feel like you're on a roller coaster or walking a tightrope.

Sexuality is thus "quite vulnerable to boredom which arises from excessive familiarity."[3] In any relationship that continues successfully over a period of years, then, the challenge is to rekindle excitement specifically in the context of the sexual drive. One way to accomplish this is to utilize fantasy. It is perfectly natural to imagine sexual scenes involving other people while you're sexually engaged with your lover of many years. People do this all the time, but usually feel at least some degree of shame about such fantasizing. Either they consider it being unfaithful or think, "I shouldn't *have* to do it to get turned on." Fantasy doesn't mean that there's something wrong with the relationship or either person in it.

To counteract this shame, bring the fantasy out of hiding and share it. Consider making love with your lover and, at the same time, utilizing fantasy in the form of mutual storytelling. Either person makes up a sexual fantasy involving an entirely different person and then "tells it as a story" during their lovemaking.

The use of written or visual erotica is another way to awaken or intensify excitement in the sexual life—it offers an entrance. Sexual fantasy is directly stimulated and excitement rekindled through either mode, written or visual. Erotica does not have to be abusive, debasing, or violent to be exciting. It's the inclusion of other affects like shame, disgust, and contempt —in addition to excitement—that turns erotica into debasing pornography.

Aging and the Sex Drive

While it has been observed that the aging process impacts men's and women's sexuality differently, the role of affect has been overlooked. The apparent decline of the sexual drive in men as they age, for example, may be as much a function of affect—particularly excitement—as of biology. The shackles placed on women's expression of excitement affect early in life are gradually dissolved over time, producing a later sexual peak, whereas sexual life peaks much earlier in men because in most cases excitement affect was never significantly bound by shame in the first place.

In both men and women, sexual excitement eventually dissipates as a function of sameness in a relationship over time and also as a function of aging. In the later years of adulthood as well as in old age, both sexes experience a decline in sexual excitement. That is particularly true when we have been in the same relationship that has endured over decades. Contrary to stereotype, this change is just as likely to occur for gays as non-gays.

There are also many sources of shame around aging as it connects to sexuality. In America, for example, old people are seen as sexless, and many of us tend to see ourselves becoming less attractive, less desirable to others, the older we grow. We may even find particular bodily changes quite difficult to deal with or even impossible to accept. Each of us is powerless to stop aging in its various manifestations: the spread of facial wrinkles, appearance of age spots on the skin, loss of muscle tone, loss of hair from the scalp, growth of hair elsewhere on the body, excessive weight gain, increasing thinness and frailty, changes in vision and hearing, memory loss. Any single one of these changes can create enough shame to bar intimacy in a culture that is so body-oriented and prizes youth beyond everything else.

Underpinning these attitudes are the ways in which our family responded to aging, which will profoundly shape the scenes we imagine around growing older. Zoe has always been looking forward to turning fifty. "We live till ninety in our family, and the women always settle down and get happier as they get older." This is not to say that she doesn't have some negative associations enforced by our culture's widespread loathing of aging and overvaluation of youth. But Zoe's predominant scenes have still been positive ones, based on her observations of women in her family and how they both spoke about growing older and actually experienced the changes that aging brought.

Attitudes about aging among lesbians generally seem more accepting and even celebratory. Lesbians are more likely to resist sexist images of what a woman should look and act like as she ages. Clearly recognizing the damage such notions do, they typically reject them.

Among gay men, however, there tends to be a lack of respect for older gays in the form of contemptuous remarks about "tired old queens" and similar comments. This contempt reflects a focusing of the wider cultural contempt and disgust specifically at aging gay men. Since there are still so few visible models of committed gay relationships, or even of individuals openly living gay lives, we have not yet seen sufficient numbers of gay men reach old age to provide us with different models for growing old. Nor do we yet celebrate such unions or individuals sufficiently in ways that counteract the shame of aging. The larger societal context is still dominated by a lack of recognition and respect for gayness and gay relationships, which unavoidably fuels that shame.

Maury recently lost his partner of twenty years and has not only had the loss to deal with, but also his sudden loneliness and feelings of not being able to fit into gay life. He feels conspicuous and out of place at gay bars and at many gay events because most of the men there are easily twenty to thirty years younger than he is. He doesn't live in a big city where there might be a group specifically devoted to senior gays and lesbians. He's not very politically motivated either, so the fervor and activism of many people who call themselves "queer" leaves him cold. He'd always imagined growing old together with his partner, and now those scenes have been shattered.

Some people have counteracted aging by throwing themselves into new sexual encounters with strangers, acquaintances, or persons significantly younger than themselves. Such conspicuous sexual excursions, either with or without intimacy, often occur in the misguided attempt to deny the inevitability of death. But these sexual encounters also occur because the stranger who is new and undiscovered immediately reawakens excitement affect, which then fuses directly with the sexual drive—producing a revitalized sexuality that had been dormant too long.

Expectations and Power in Sex and Intimacy

The feeling that sex or intimacy is expected and required can easily disrupt any kind of relationship, sexual or nonsexual. Only one of the people in the relationship has to *perceive* matters that way; the other person doesn't even have to behave in ways that communicate such expectations. Rita told us of an old friend, Kate, dropping by unexpectedly one evening on a drive out of town. They had dinner and later ended up having sex quite spontaneously. Neither one of them had ever talked about an attraction between them or was particularly aware of it either, though the evening was certainly a great deal of fun. The next time they were together socially, Kate seemed quite uncomfortable and uneasy, wasn't at all communicative, and over the following months fell out of contact with Rita. Eventually, Rita called Kate and they arranged to talk about what happened. It wasn't guilt that had made Kate put up a wall of silence, but the expectation of sex: "I felt you'd want to sleep with me from now on whenever we got together," she told Rita, who was surprised. Rita saw the situation quite differently: "I figured if sex ever happened again that was cool, but it wasn't essential." They decided to keep sex out of their friendship in the future, a mutual decision they both felt comfortable with making, and the friendship resumed.

Expectations about intimacy can also impede communication between any two people in a relationship. Wendy had a friend who loved to talk about intimate details of her relationship with another woman. While Wendy talked about her own lover when it seemed natural and comfortable, she began to resent the weekly phone calls in which she felt she had to delve deeply into her life with her lover, whether she wanted to or not. "Sometimes I just like to chat!" she said, feeling frustrated. She had come to feel that her friend expected her to be intimate on demand. Wendy increasingly resented this, and she found herself pulling back in response, revealing less and less.

Each of these scenarios has become scripted in a particular fashion, with the focus on sexuality in the first example and on emotional intimacy in the second. The focus could also be on sex and intimacy simultaneously. Richard and Michael have been lovers for almost a year. The closeness and erotic delight they shared early in their relationship gave way to gradually escalating arguments. Richard was very quiet and often shy around their friends. This left Michael uncomfortable with Richard's silence in public and with his lack of communication. Michael kept expecting Richard to talk more, to be more open about himself. But the more Michael pressured Richard to communicate, the more Richard felt bottled up.

Their sexual relationship was almost the reverse. Michael was extremely inhibited sexually. He had a strong distaste for sex and wasn't comfortable with doing much of anything sexually. He was always very tense and couldn't let go. Richard, in contrast, was much freer in bed, willing to experiment; he was more able to express himself nonverbally than Michael. As the months wore on, each time Richard initiated sex, Michael felt more and more pressured about having to have sex. Michael was easily turned off, became irritable, or just refused. When they tried to discuss the situation, Michael revealed his distorted perception: "You're always *expecting* sex from me. It just pisses me off!" This would leave Richard feeling helpless and confused because he wanted sex, probably even expected it some of the time. He couldn't understand what was so unreasonable about that.

For Michael, the scripting of sex included interpreting sexual surrender as a loss of power. When sex becomes equated with power, this signifies that power/powerlessness scenes have become fused together with sexual scenes. For Michael, the magnification of sexual scenes occurred only in the context of power scenes: both his real and imagined sexual encounters were reenacted along with power scenes, directly fusing them. Surrendering to Richard's sexual embrace meant becoming vulnerable to his desire and the sexual arousal it would unleash. For Richard, in contrast, intimacy meant permitting vulnerability of a different kind to occur, an *emotional,* not sexual, surrender. Michael could not surrender sexually, just as Richard could not surrender emotionally. Vulnerability unfortunately became equated for them with a loss of power that each felt was intolerable. When being either sexual or intimate comes to mean a loss of power, then the avoidance of sexual surrender or intimacy is the likely result.

Sex can also become a means of enhancing power. When the pursuit of sex and the pursuit of power converge, sex no longer serves the single purpose of pleasure. The power motive has captured the drive, and being sexual increasingly becomes a means to amassing power. The individual who must always pursue others sexually or actively seduce them—never allowing pursuit or seduction by others, never surrendering to another—is a person who is gripped by a power scene that has invaded the sexual life.

Carl likes to pursue other men, often older than himself. At the gym or bar, he'll usually spot someone he wants and then decide to go after him. He likes the feeling of pursuit and being in control. Usually, Carl gets what he wants. Once he has the man in bed, Carl wants only one thing: to penetrate the other man anally. After sex, Carl always returns to his own bed to sleep alone. Carl has no committed relationships, no true boyfriends either, but he has lots of men he has sex with. Whenever one of these men starts to desire him too much, or begins to expect more closeness or time together, Carl quietly fades away. He never makes a scene, never argues or even gets angry. He just becomes unavailable for a long period of time, while always promising that they'll soon be spending more time together. The other man's expectations are continually raised, and just as continually disappointed. Whenever a man asks Carl to spend an evening together, to go away for a weekend, even to meet for dinner, Carl always says, "Maybe we can do that." He never says no, but he never says yes either. When Carl reappears after an absence, he seems unusually intimate, as if he'd never really been away at all, and when he leaves again he's completely absent. One thing he can never do is be vulnerable. Thus his intimacy is only superficial, his ability to be close only apparent.

Carl is reenacting a power scene that is fused directly with sex. Why? When Carl was fifteen, he spent a summer away at camp. Even then he knew he was attracted to older boys and men. Carl noticed that his camp counselor kept looking at him, sometimes followed after him. Carl quickly realized that his counselor was attracted to him. So Carl became provocative, enticing. One night his counselor came to his bunk. Carl pretended to be asleep. His counselor fondled and then masturbated him. Carl loved it, and he felt in complete control. That scene was repeated on several more occasions. Then Carl began to elaborate the scene in his own imagination: he began fantasizing about penetrating his counselor anally, making him submit. It was that governing scene that Carl was reenacting in his adult life.

That power scene became fused with sex and completely captured him, fueling his current relationships.

For many gay men, giving or receiving anal sex unfortunately becomes experienced only in terms of power: who is doing what to whom, who is in control. If power is an issue generally for either man in a relationship, it will definitely surface sexually. Surrendering power means surrendering control, and too often that becomes equated with losing power completely to another person. Since surrendering to sexual pleasure always involves some letting go of control, power issues inevitably confound any sexual give-and-take.

When sex or intimacy become fused with expectations, then either can come to be interpreted as something that is *expected* by others. Some people do hold such expectations about sex or intimacy and therefore convey them, whether explicitly or not. Others are quick to perceive such expectations when, in fact, they're not present. Whether expectations of sex or intimacy are real or only imagined, a fusion of sex with expectations or intimacy with expectations has occurred.

Beth and Maggie have been lovers for about a year. Initially, they felt quite close and loving as well as able to share erotic delight. But recently their sex life has begun to deteriorate. Maggie began feeling less close to Beth because of unexpressed hurt feelings and a gradual buildup of resentment, both unrelated to sex. Without feeling the prior close connection between them, Maggie no longer felt much sexual desire for Beth. When Beth wanted sex, Maggie wasn't in the mood. Beth was always the more sexual of the two to begin with, and she was the one who usually initiated their lovemaking. Beth was beginning to feel rejected by Maggie's increasing lack of interest in sex. As Beth began expressing her sexual frustration more directly, Maggie began to feel that sex was being expected of her. Beth became silent and angry in response. When Maggie finally exploded and revealed how she needed to feel them connected emotionally before she could feel sexual, Beth understood but still felt sexually frustrated and also helpless. She didn't know what to do to restore the closeness that now seemed to her to be a prerequisite for sex.

Expectations about sex and intimacy do not have to be overtly stated to be present and potent in a relationship. The person who perceives expectations can react to them whether or not they *are* present. In either case, surrendering to sex or intimacy becomes invariably experienced as equivalent to being powerless. Becoming either sexual or intimate can then degenerate into a power struggle because any surrender is intolerable.

Sadomasochistic Scripts

For many gay men and lesbians there is considerable shame about sadomasochistic or S/M patterns even though they're widely observed in gay and lesbian life. The apparent prevalence of sadomasochistic activities is often used as a weapon by homophobes who argue that gays will destroy the military or the United States itself. Most gays find S/M anything from amusing to weird or disgusting because they can't understand why anyone would want to receive or give pain or participate in the domination of another person.

In sadomasochism, whether it actually includes the inflicting of pain or stops at the domination of one person by another, intimacy and sexuality are fused in a highly scripted pattern that is repetitively reenacted. Contrary to popular stereotypes, these scripts are not the province of gay men alone.

Many people, for example, as far back as early adolescence or even childhood, imagine explicitly sexual scenes in fantasy that also include important elements of either domination or submission. Judy had specific sexual fantasies in which she was tied to a ship mast by an abusive captain, a fantasy she had continuously from age six. This was her fantasy when she later masturbated, and as an adult this fantasy continually crept into her sexual encounters with women. When a lover suggested tying her to the bed, Judy became excited beyond belief. She was wild with anticipation. Now she got to live out what had only been a fantasy before. From that point on, she sought out lovers who would dominate her, both in their relationship generally and directly in sex. Being tied up became an obsession.

What is actually being reenacted here is a particular scene involving two people with precisely scripted roles, in which one is dominant and the other submits to domination. The submissive individual behaves so as to experience the affects of shame, distress, and fear whereas the dominant person principally displays anger and contempt. The submissive actor in the script also relinquishes power through submission to slapping, whipping, beating, or bondage. The dominant actor is scripted to express power to the maximum, and the power relationship itself is at the core of the sadomasochistic scene. That scene is reenacted over and over in order to relive it more completely—even more so, to *perfect* it.

People who are quite able to assert power in their jobs or relationships often become possessed by secret fantasies in which that power is completely reversed. They crave submission. This allows them to release fear, shame, and distress, affects that must otherwise be tightly controlled and suppressed. Similarly, those who feel powerless in other arenas often want power in the sexual one, which can lead to domestic violence and rape, as when unemployed men take out their frustrations on their wives.

Relinquishing power in the form of submission to domination is one of the features of these compelling scripts. Experiencing and expressing particular affects, such as shame, is another part of them. The third major feature is the degree of debasement that is actually scripted into the scene. We can be dominated and submit to domination without being completely debased, or we can desire to be dominated, shamed, and utterly debased, however we define it.

Another distinctive feature of such scripted scenes is the inclusion of pain, whether we desire to have it inflicted on us or to inflict it on others. For such people, pain has been scripted directly into the scene that is to be forever reenacted. Pain either may be utilized to heighten sexual arousal by further amplifying excitement affect, or it may have become a prerequisite for experiencing sexual excitement in the first place; or scenes of giving or receiving pain might simply have become fused with sexual scenes through reenactment in prior fantasy.

The presence of any of these features depends entirely on how the scripting of the person's various scenes has progressed. There are any number of originating scenes for sadomasochistic scripts. Judy illustrated one way in which this occurs. Such scenes can be entirely the product of fantasy, or they can be the result of actual experiences. In any event, these originating childhood scenes become relived internally and reenacted. Doug was spanked periodically by his stepfather and he found this both humiliating and sexually arousing. Later, his sexual fantasies began to incorporate the earlier spankings, and his sexual activities eventually expanded to include ritualized spanking. These are two ways in which sadomasochistic scripts develop.

If the scenes remain isolated, they become only occasional occurrences. But if those scenes become radically magnified and fused, they can capture a person's intimate relations and sexual life. The outcome depends on the degree to which sexual or intimate scenes become directly fused with dominance-submission scenes, or debasement scenes, or expression of suppressed affect scenes, or pain scenes.

While some people continually play out only one role and seek lovers to enact the other role, others will reverse roles with their lover from time to time. Other people live out their scenes in particular sex clubs set up expressly for that purpose. There are also people who do not actually enact their scenes overtly with anyone; instead, they relive their particular scenes internally in the form of scripted fantasies that accompany sex or masturbation.

Sadomasochistic scenes are neither primary nor even present for a great many gays. When sadomasochistic scenes are present, however, they reflect a distinctive history. They reveal a progression from one particular scene to another, from one form of expression to another. For some people the scenes grow and change over time, while others are left permanently fixed in a particular scene that they must relive over and over.

Such scenes are inherently shame-bound and shame-producing. Being shamed, expressing shame, or shaming another is deeply embedded in most sadomasochistic scenes. The purpose is to bathe in shame, release your own shame, or direct shame at another by reversing roles. These scripts reenact the scenes that govern your life, dominating sexual experience.

SHAME AND SEX

Shame about sexual addiction is probably the source of the greatest shame surrounding our sexual life. From an affect theory perspective, most addictions involve reliance on a particular sedative—alcohol, drugs, food, cigarettes, or sex. We increasingly use these sedatives in order to reduce negative affect that has become overwhelming. These are *sedative scripts*.[4] In addiction, the principal aim is sedation of disturbing affect, whatever it is: shame, rage, fear, distress. Virtually anything can become scripted for use as a sedative—exercise, gambling, working, or even buying clothing. The affect dynamics are the same regardless of the addiction. An addiction to anything, food or sex for example, will also generate further shame. Once you're addicted, you experience more shame as a result because you're now being controlled by your addiction.

Let's contrast two different types of cigarette smokers. "Positive affect smokers" use cigarettes to maintain or *enhance* positive affect, not to *become* happy. People like this smoke at the end of a meal they've enjoyed or to celebrate a special occasion.[5] Since having a cigarette *increases* their good feeling, giving up smoking doesn't usually create intolerable negative affect. Positive affect smokers characteristically have a low frequency of smoking, and that kind of dependency is more easily given up because they have many other sources of positive affect. They smoke only to maintain or enhance positive affect that they are already experiencing, *not* for sedative relief from negative affect or from addictive dependency.

"Negative affect smokers," in contrast, use cigarettes to reduce or *sedate* negative affect that they are already experiencing. As positive affect turns to negative affect and the scene turns from rewarding to punishing, dependence turns into addiction. Sedation actually becomes transformed into addiction when a particular sedative becomes increasingly necessary for remaining in or acting in any situation that has become permanently associated with negative affect. Further, if it becomes necessary even *before* entering that threatening scene, then the sedative has truly become a prerequisite to functioning. Janice feels threatened by her boss at work and smokes on the job to reduce her fear. She smokes more when she knows she'll have to interact with her boss. And Janice smokes heavily even when she's simply thinking ahead to such encounters. Before long, she has to have a cigarette even before coming to work, right before walking in the door, before entering the dreaded scene. True addictive dependency is setting in.

In *addictive scripts,* the sedative act—alcohol, cigarettes, drugs, food, or sex—has now been transformed into an end in itself. Initially, the sedative act must have been comforting in many different negative affect scenes—rejection by family, being in the closet at work, being in a disappointing relationship with a lover—in order for someone to become addicted. Later, we become perpetually vigilant about the absence or presence of the sedative. Its absence is punishing whereas its presence provides brief relief, but eventually its continuing presence provides minimal awareness and affect. That is why an addictive smoker can be lighting up a second cigarette while still smoking the first. The smoker has minimal awareness of the sedative act while it is continuously present. But take away all cigarettes—and the smoker becomes acutely aware of their absence! Panic sets in, and the individual immediately loses all sense of comfort that cigarettes once provided.

Reliance on a sedative—cigarettes, food, or alcohol—also begins to cloud emotional awareness and an awareness of what's important in your life. The sedative even *becomes* your life in some cases.

Consider the man or woman who becomes aware of being dependent on a sedative and then decides to renounce it. The *intention to renounce* the sedative act—alcohol or cigarettes—actually *increases* negative affect in a very specific way. The attempt to give up smoking or drinking paradoxically makes us overly aware of the absence of the sedative and generates a deep reluctance to give it up precisely because *now* we *must* have it. When we become increasingly aware that we're trying to do without cigarettes or alcohol, its absence is becoming rapidly magnified in our awareness.

What eventually happens is that awareness of the sedative's absence *and* the ensuing deprivation completely capture our attention, eclipsing everything else. The negative affect now produced by the absence of the sedative is both *preemptive* and *urgent*. If the attempt to renounce a particular sedative proves *ineffective,* then sedative scripts can become transformed into addictive scripts. But this is only one specific way in which that change occurs.

Critical to the shift from sedation to addiction is the degree of magnification of the *absence* of the sedative. However temporary, its absence produces intense negative affect in the form of panic. The resulting urgency then radically heightens awareness of its absence. Equally critical to this shift, the desirability of the sedative is further magnified as the *only* relief of its own absence. Only alcohol or cigarettes will relieve the panic produced by their temporary absence.

Lillian could not deal with stress at her job, where she was closeted, and began to drink as a way of tranquilizing herself. Alcohol became her constant companion, and she felt comforted when she had a drink in her hand. Drinking reduced her anger, fear, distress, and shame—no matter what their source was. Whenever these affects were triggered, Lillian immediately reached for the bottle. First it was only on weekends, next it happened after work too, then she had a drink or two on her lunch hour.

A critical change occurred when she was laid up in bed for almost a week recuperating from an accident. She discovered she'd run out of alcohol and couldn't get out to buy any; there was nobody she could confide in who could bring it to her. Suddenly she felt panic: *I've got to have a drink!* That panic wouldn't quit until she managed to obtain the only thing that would comfort her: alcohol. Lillian discovered that the panic she felt when alcohol was unavailable was far worse than anything she had ever experienced before. Now she *had* to drink in order to reduce the terrible panic that set in whenever she wasn't able to drink.

We become truly addicted when we learn that being without the sedative is much worse than any other negative affect that the sedative might reduce.[6] This is the unconditional urgency of the addictive script: the sedative is absolutely necessary to reduce the panic that is induced by its own deprivation. We drink or smoke to sedate the feelings that are generated when we're not drinking or smoking and to sedate any negative affect from any other source as well.

Addiction is always a scripted response to affect. Like cigarettes or alcohol, sex can also be used to sedate negative affect. In this case, *sexual addiction* functions just like other forms of addiction. Sex becomes a sedative that is used to reduce negative affect. Using sex in this way can block affect.

> *I'd rather have sex than deal with my feelings. If I get angry or feel bummed out, well, I just look for some guy to get off with. I've just got to do it then. There's no other way for me to blank everything out. The craving's so strong that almost anybody will do. I can't afford to be choosy.*

Other affect dynamics can also come into play when addiction enters the sexual life. Some people use sex not to sedate, but to *release* affect that they've suppressed; others seek sexual promiscuity in the pursuit of higher levels of excitement or instead displace affect from other contexts *into* sex.

Sex as a Way of Releasing Suppressed Affect

When the expression of affect is chronically inhibited, a condition of *affect hunger* is produced.[7] This is the need to release whatever has been tightly controlled. People have used alcohol for millennia to release suppressed affect. The man who stops at the neighborhood bar after work to "unwind" feels more relaxed after a few drinks. Now he can laugh or cry freely—neither of which he could release without a drink.

Engaging in sex can also permit the emergence of suppressed affect. Just like alcohol, sex functions as a *de-inhibitor* of suppressed affect—so there are many people who have sex in order to allow themselves just to feel affect of various kinds. The intensity and intimacy of sexuality can provide an opportunity, however isolated, for the free expression of affects that are otherwise overcontrolled.[8]

There is a cliché that women like to talk after sex and men fall asleep. Sam is different—he's a man who can't stop talking after sex. He is comfortable talking openly about himself only after he's had sex with another man. In every other context he keeps a tight rein on all of his affect, especially anger and excitement. Only the intensity of sexual release allows him access to those feelings, which he can then share at great length.

When sex is our only available means for releasing suppressed affect, then our pursuit of sex increasingly becomes governed by this single aim. We can become addicted to sex just to be able to openly express our feelings, and this is completely different from using sex to *sedate* feelings.

Affect Promiscuity and Sexual Promiscuity

In another kind of sexual addiction, we are indiscriminate about the people we erotically desire. To understand how sexual promiscuity can function like an addiction, we need to consider the more general case first—*affect promiscuity*.[9] Just as some people become passionate about a particular person or interest like photography, others become passionate about passion itself.

In affect promiscuity, you're addicted to a particular affect like excitement. In this case, you've become addicted to an intense level of excitement which requires varied and changing objects that, in turn, will pay off in perpetual thrills. Whenever there is a cessation of excitement, a lull, you feel compelled to search out new challenges that will rekindle excitement, such as mountain climbing, gambling, or finding new sexual partners. What governs the pursuit of objects is the affect payoff involved. In excitement promiscuity, excitement governs the quest for new objects that will generate the required intensity of excitement. But when the object is no longer exciting, the incessant search for higher levels of excitement resumes.

Sexual "promiscuity" is a special case of affect promiscuity. When excitement promiscuity enters the sexual life, we are forced into sexual promiscuity in the search for excitement. The quest for excitement now dominates our lives, overshadowing even strong ties of enjoyment in more enduring relationships. All other affects become eclipsed in the endless pursuit of greater thrills. Only perpetual excitement suffices, and that hunger governs the quest for new sexual partners because only sex with a stranger is sufficiently exciting to reach new heights. Here sex is not a means to sedate negative affect or to release suppressed affect, but instead a way of *maximizing* the affect of excitement.

If we want more enduring relationships, how do we reduce our dependence on sexual excitement? This problem is the exact opposite of someone whose excitement affect has been squashed and whose sexual life is bleached of erotic intensity. That person has to have excitement cultivated. In contrast, someone addicted to sexual excitement has to cultivate other affects, like enjoyment, and also learn to tolerate lessened excitement.

> *I never even spent a night at a trick's place—I always went back to my apartment, and I never saw him again. So going off for a whole weekend with Isaac was a first for me. We were backpacking and there wasn't anybody else around for miles I could have sex with. At first I felt marooned and was just dying to get away and have sex with somebody new, anybody. The horniness was driving me crazy and even by the first night I started feeling bored. But I had told Isaac this would happen, and he promised to help. He told me I had to tough out the craving if I was ever going to tame it, even a little. Isaac's a commercial artist, and before sunset each night he'd take out watercolors and do a little sketch. I was surprised how much I got into sitting there watching the sky and watching what Isaac did with it. And the first night, after we set up our tent and were having sex, he came up with this* Interview with a Vampire *fantasy where I was Tom Cruise and he was Antonio Banderas. It was really hot. So were the other fantasies the other nights. After a while I realized he could be different people even if he was the same.*

By becoming aware of our addiction to sexual excitement, we begin the process of lessening our dependence on it.

Displacement of Affect into Sex

Whenever we have to suppress affect in a particular situation, at work for example, and that suppression produces an intolerable intensification of this affect, we seek other people for its expression. If you are humiliated at the hands of your employer at your job, then you will likely return home and *displace* your shame onto someone else—your lover, child, or even a pet.[10] If you are enraged by someone you must be polite and courteous to, while still seething underneath, someone else will be found on whom you can vent your mounting furor. The affect suppressed in the original situation is now displaced onto others.

The identical dynamic can operate in your sexual life. For example, channeling a humiliating defeat at work, which must be suppressed in that context, into sexual experience which also degrades and humiliates is one instance of displaced, vicarious humiliation. A degrading sexual encounter actually permits the displaced expression of humiliation. We learn to crave sex if that is the only arena in which we can express certain affects, like shame, that are actually triggered elsewhere but blocked from expression where they originate. In this particular form of addiction to sex, the cycle is maintained by the intolerable intensification of shame that has been suppressed and that must find an outlet somewhere. Shame is displaced into sex and we, in effect, bathe in it.

This displacement dynamic may also be operating in the scripting of the various sadomasochistic patterns we considered before. In response to any experience of humiliation, we may want to reexperience that shame more fully by having someone else degrade and humiliate us in a sexual context. Conversely, we may want to change roles and humiliate the other person sexually, when that person is most vulnerable and we are more powerful.

The addiction to sex is multiply determined. Raymond was sixteen when he was followed into a bathroom stall at a shopping mall by a man who proceeded to force him to engage in oral sex. It was late at night, just before closing, and no one else was around. Raymond was short for his age and skinny, and the man pushed him into the stall and locked the door. He demanded that Raymond submit. Raymond felt scared as well as sexually excited. Afterward, he couldn't stop thinking about it. He had been sexual with other boys for several years, so he was no stranger to homosexuality. He had even begun to feel more comfortable with being gay. But now his sexual fantasies were completely taken over by the scene he had experienced in the bathroom. As he grew older, he began going to bathrooms in movie theaters and bus stations, looking for someone to have sex with. He even visited rest stops in his quest—always hoping for and equally fearing a repetition of his bathroom scene. He was captured by both fear and excitement. Often he met someone at one of these places and furtively engaged in sex, but he always felt consumed with shame and self-loathing afterward. He kept promising himself that he'd stop, yet invariably the craving compelled him to do it again. Raymond felt obsessed by his craving to relive that scene from his youth—it governed his life. And he was drowning in shame, yet the cycle always recurred. He felt powerless to stop it.

DISTINGUISHING FANTASY FROM REALITY

Sex addiction often mirrors other obsessions about particular people we encounter and then become preoccupied with, eclipsing everything else. To create satisfying and fulfilling relationships, we have to develop a conscious approach to all of our interactions with other people. All too often we become entranced by a virtual stranger and rush pell-mell into intimacy, or what we think is intimacy. We mistake infatuation for love, and think we know much more about our lover than we really do. Or we plunge into an intense sexual relationship, feeling erotically captivated, only to be abruptly disappointed afterward.

These forms of infatuation and true falling in love involve identical affect/scene spirals of enormous power that capture us totally. What captivates us so completely is usually the face of the person whom we suddenly encounter—a person whose face excites our interest, whose face we wish to visually explore, whose eyes we're immediately drawn into. We feel utterly consumed with erotic desire or with longings for intimacy at that very moment.

The face of that person can become a compelling preoccupation, eclipsing everything and everyone else. The person's face, along with his or her voice, gestures, and body, generate intense excitement and enjoyment in anticipation of reunion, coupled with intense longing and possibly equally intense distress, shame, fear, and even anger in response to that person's absence, however brief. The commonly expressed phrase "I can't get her or him out of my mind" therefore has a real basis in affect and scene dynamics. We have truly become possessed.

Scenes of enjoyment and excitement involving this person now spiral wildly, magnifying one another, greatly intensifying the affects we're feeling. The experience is electric. We begin to imagine all sorts of encounters with this new focus of our desire—sexual escapades, intimate moments, weekend getaways, even living together. We conjure up image after image, each fueled by growing excitement and enjoyment, which in turn are made stronger minute by minute—in this way fusing these images together in a never-ending cascade. These rapidly spiraling scenes, in fact, produce the sensation of *falling*. That is what spiraling, affect-laden scenes actually feel like. We come to describe this experience as "falling in love."

Just as depression is a negative affect spiral, involving shame and distress, falling in love is a *positive* affect spiral. One can fall into love, just as one can fall into shame, or even fall into hate.

Some individuals actually fall in love not with a particular person, but with the feeling of falling in love itself. What they crave is the experience of falling in love and seek it endlessly. In this instance the actual person is immaterial; almost anyone could do. Any actor can play this particular role in the script. When the feeling fades, they move on to another relationship, another person—always questing after that glow produced by affect/scene spirals, but never realizing that they're driven to repeat this scenario. They're hooked on the glow.

Distinguishing love from infatuation is absolutely essential. It requires effort to learn how to *detach* from these infatuation spirals by making them fully conscious. Only then can we accurately distinguish between falling in love with an actual person and falling in love with our *fantasy* of that person.

We can accomplish this detachment by learning how to *objectively observe* our expectations about other people, as well as the actual people themselves. Doing so will enable us to determine what we're needing *and* how capable those people are of actually meeting our needs and expectations.

To determine what you're looking for in any relationship, you first have to pay attention as your needs and expectations manifest in the form of recurring scenes involving either an actual individual or an imagined or idealized stranger. Your *relationship scenes* are often subliminal, operating at the periphery of awareness, drifting through your thoughts like a day-dream. By making them conscious and clear over time, you gradually bring them into sharper focus.

> *When I met Don, it was after two lousy affairs. I had told all of my friends I was just going to chill and not get involved with anyone for a while. But I kept finding myself picturing him—his big hands, the vein in his neck, those deep eyes. I'd be sitting at work and just space out. And it got to be more than just details. I'd imagine these long involved talks with him, really intense and exciting. I finally realized I wasn't just turned on by him, I wanted a really serious connection.*

A corollary of making your scenes conscious is objectively observing the other person in the relationship. Your individual needs and expectations must match reality, or you will be disappointed and thus shamed by the gap between what you hoped for and what you actually received. For a relationship to grow, each person's needs must be in harmony with what the other person is actually capable of providing. By stepping outside of our desires and hopes for a moment, stepping out of our scenes, and observing the other person objectively, we gradually become able to distinguish distinct patterns of interaction.

In response to the initial excitement we usually feel when we're getting involved with someone new—as friend or lover—we too often focus only on the positive aspects and screen out whatever contradicts that idyllic picture. The excitement we feel can completely blur our intuition. Later, when something goes wrong, we'll recall fleeting perceptions and doubts that were actually on target had we stopped to listen. But excitement clouded our judgment, and we allowed ourselves to proceed blindly.

> *The first guy I ever slept with was a party animal. I was wild about Nikos's energy on the dance floor and in bed, and I admired how experienced he was sexually. After our second date I found*

myself constantly thinking about him, wanting to call him, see him, stroke him, kiss him. I imagined us seeing shows, boating, going on trips, hanging out together all the time. But he was really hard to get a hold of, didn't return calls for days, and I was crushed when he told me he was going out with several guys. Here I was thinking I had a boyfriend, and he just wanted to party. I had even imagined how great it would be if he bought me a bracelet or something! I felt like such a dork.

To begin observing both your scenes and the other person, pick a particular relationship to begin working with. Before you see this person again, or even talk on the telephone, focus inward and pay close attention to your inner scenes involving him or her. Just watch for the recurring scenes that play out in your imagination. Tune in to your daydreams about this person. By consciously observing the flow of scenes, you clarify what you're actually looking for. And you create an entrance to identifying what you need or expect from this particular person at any given time. It usually works best to observe your relationship scenes just *before* you get together with this person; that's when you're likely to be more aware, and the scenes more active.

When you're with this person, practice objective observation to determine exactly what kind of person you're dealing with. Imagine you're a neutral, detached observer, and don't think of these observations as judgments.

Very consciously, consider the following dimensions: Do you really like, respect, or want to get to know this person further? What is this person's predominant affect—is it enjoyment, excitement, shame, or contempt, for example? Is she or he capable of admitting mistakes when they occur, of becoming vulnerable, of sharing the power in a relationship? Is this person dependable, trustworthy? How does this person talk about other people in general—critically, fondly, dispassionately? After leaving any interaction with the other person, consciously consider how well he or she was able to provide whatever you needed or expected.

You'll be confident about your observations if you make them over time during the course of becoming more acquainted.

Hannah dated Vicky for a few months, during which she grew increasingly uncomfortable with their relationship, wondering why it wasn't working the way she wanted. When she began to observe Vicky and herself consciously, she began to realize that she had great difficulty saying no to Vicky about virtually anything. Vicky could call her up at the last minute to rearrange a date or say she was inviting another couple to what was supposed to be an intimate dinner—and Hannah didn't object. Why not? Vicky was being manipulative and could charm her way around Hannah. Such behavior left Hannah feeling that her needs, her limits, didn't matter. Feeling powerless in their relationship, Hannah became increasingly resentful. When confronting Vicky didn't make a difference, Hannah gave up and ended the relationship. Vicky wasn't going to change, at least not for *her*, and so there was no reason to keep dating someone who disappointed her.

Focusing your attention on the other person in order to observe him or her is like the affect tool refocusing attention, which we discussed in the previous chapter, but now applied to your relationships. When your attention is focused directly on observing the other person, you make your intuitions conscious. All too often you'll say, "I knew there was something wrong with her!" after the relationship falls apart. Suddenly the clues and hints come rushing into consciousness and it's all laid out clearly before you. Well, why not develop that clarity earlier? Then the potential for shame is at a minimum. Instead of experiencing shame because you "should have known better," you can feel stronger for having entered the relationship with much more self-awareness and insight into the other person.

We all have to learn to match our expectations with the reality of the people we want to know, be close to, have sex with. By first observing our own relationship scenes, then the other person, and finally the soundness of the match between the two, we can learn a new approach to interpersonal relations. This approach is deliberately conscious in both its attitude and operation, and it preserves dignity and self-respect by minimizing our risk of shame.

SHAME AND RELATIONSHIPS

Because shame can bombard us from a number of directions throughout our lifetime, it can influence even the briefest of relationships. One of the most pervasive sources of shame stems from *not* being in a relationship. Many gays experience shame precisely because they're not part of a couple or even dating anyone. Single lesbians and gay men often feel enormous pressure to be in some type of ongoing romantic relationship, and it doesn't have to be long-term. The pressure comes from two sources: the wider culture with its model of monogamy and voices in the gay community itself that stigmatize gays who aren't dating. Gay men feel additional pressure to be sexual as a way of quickly dealing with their shame about being single.

Just having a relationship dissolves the shame that being single provokes, so many single gays pick poor companions because they feel they must pick *someone*. They cannot easily tolerate being alone or view solitude as an opportunity for enhanced intimacy with themselves. Being single may reinforce their sense of unworthiness or missing out on what everyone else is enjoying. Likewise, if we're growing older and see ourselves solely in terms of attractiveness, or market value out in the dating world, then aging diminishes our self-esteem and turns us into damaged goods.

We are all vulnerable to shame about our appearance, mediated by our images of beauty and how we feel about aging. We need to consider how to best handle this shame when it begins to surface directly between us and a date or a lover, so that shame can be transformed and we can restore the interpersonal bridge.

Embedded in our encounters with intimacy and sexuality are the attitudes of beauty that we inherited from growing up in a particular culture during a particular historical period. Though beauty may indeed be in the eyes of the beholder, so is shame. And we are always beholding ourselves, both in the mirror dozens of times each day and equally in our mind's eye. We not only have to deal with wider cultural attitudes about what is attractive and what isn't, but as gays and lesbians we also encounter different sources of shame around appearance, based on our own community's standards.

One lesbian told us that there were many "large" women in her circle of friends and she was often teased and even taunted for being such a slim, slight woman: "They act like I'm deliberately criticizing *them* by being the way I am!" We've also talked to other men who, like us, lament the fact that not only is youth held up as the most cherished physical ideal among gay men, but the young men in magazines and gay advertising mostly seem to be white, blond, and hairless. This preference can leave African Americans and other ethnic types, as well as older gays, shamed in the very subculture in which they seek refuge. Whatever ideal is held up as an image of beauty can unfortunately become a source of shame. In this way physical attributes become bodily indictments.

How we feel about our bodily characteristics and appearance is a continuing source of shame despite being in an affectionate or loving relationship that seems secure. These sources of shame do not have to "make sense" to others. Some people may feel ashamed, for instance, of freckles or moles that seem perfectly innocuous to anyone else, while others continue to be haunted by specific images of their bodies from early adolescence—images infused with shame. *Any* aspect of our body can strike us as shameful in ways that appear excessive and even irrational to others. So we may fear losing our lover to some young beauty with flawless skin. In many ways we judge ourselves by other people's standards, and we fear that our lovers will too.

Masturbation

It's perfectly normal for adults in sexually fulfilling relationships to masturbate, but it's unfortunately an all too common source of shame as well. The cultural presumption is that once you're in a relationship of any kind, you shouldn't need to give yourself solitary sexual pleasure. The relationship should satisfy all of your sexual desires. There's also the additional cultural and religion-based shame about masturbation itself at *any* time.

Your shame about masturbation may be a holdover from adolescence or even childhood, a consequence of ingrained sanctions in your family. If you think of masturbation as something childish or dirty, you're more likely to experience shame about it in a relationship.

Masturbation is a very positive, self-affirming, and self-pleasuring act. It gets us in touch with our bodies, our feelings, our fantasies. It can be a way of remembering and cherishing a sexual encounter in the past or a doorway to sex in the future. A friend of ours proudly put it, "I'm never giving it up—not when I've gotten so good at it!"

Sexual Fantasy

If fantasy has been a principal and recurring accompaniment to sexual release in adolescence, why do we believe that it will suddenly vanish when we're adults and have lovers? Once again, we face a highly unrealistic cultural assumption that our partner will fill every single corner of our lives and that we won't ever need to imagine we're in bed with someone else to feel excited.

Use of sexual fantasy can be a spontaneous occurrence, entirely unplanned, or it can be deliberately engaged by one or both persons involved in lovemaking. Such fantasy may be silent and internal, unspoken by either person, or it can become a direct and invited part of the couple's lovemaking. More often, what prevents this from happening naturally is shame about having such fantasies in the first place, shame about voicing them in the presence of another person, shame about revealing our secret desires, shame about being sexual itself. Once again, ideological norms are at work behind the scenes, reinforcing shame and constraining sexual freedom.

Dissolving that shame is a gradual process. You need to openly express your sexual fantasies directly to your lover, however secret or shame-bound they may have been. Try it first when the two of you are lying quietly together with the lights out; then try sharing your sexual fantasies with each other with the lights on; and, finally, try it during lovemaking together. The way to dissolve that shame is by not letting it prevent either the use of inner sexual fantasy that remains silent or the overt sharing of fantasy directly during lovemaking.

Feeling Neglected

Feeling neglected or taken for granted by a lover is a commonplace source of shame. This rarely happens when love or lust is young, when a relationship is new. Then you savor every moment and seize every opportunity to treasure and enjoy each other. But later you become so familiar to each other that you don't always appreciate what attracted you in the first place.

Even the person you care most about, who is central in your life, can become so familiar that you take her or him for granted, or you simply don't behave in the ways you did at the beginning of the relationship.

I loved how Melissa was so attentive when we first started dating. She was always sending me cards and little presents, leaving cute messages on my answering machine. And when we fell in love she almost went overboard. Champagne, flowers. Some of my friends said it was corny, but I felt really special. After a year or two, though, all that stuff kind of disappeared. It wasn't that she was any less enthusiastic or loving when we were together, but I felt like she didn't care that much when we were apart.

Our response to feeling neglected is often to withdraw or be angry in small, unexpected ways, to bristle. What's happening is that the perceived neglect is triggering scenes from childhood. That's a time when we rely on our parents for an incredible amount of attention and validation: *Look at what I did! Look at me!* If our need for feeling admired, appreciated, and recognized wasn't met sufficiently back then, neglect from someone we care about in the present can easily trigger those scenes.

Feeling neglected may even make us feel childish, and we end up criticizing ourselves, further inducing shame. In that case, it's likely that when we reacted to feeling neglected as children by pouting or getting upset, we were criticized: *Don't be such a baby!* That history may make it difficult to even admit how we're feeling to our boyfriend or girlfriend. One unfortunate response is waiting for the other person to figure out how we feel.

It's more effective to take the risk and *say* you feel neglected and try to work out a solution.

I told Melissa I felt like we had to start dating again. She laughed and asked what I meant. When I explained I didn't feel as special anymore, she was surprised seeing it from my point of view. She had no idea I had been feeling this way. We did start dating again—going out dancing once a week, or for dinner, but what helped us the most was starting to talk about how things were going between us, how she felt, how I felt.

Jealousy

The problem of jealousy will never be permanently solved by denial of its presence. You have to acknowledge it exists and be prepared to deal with it honestly. Jealousy is invariably sparked by the sudden, unexpected appearance of a "rival" on the scene. You'll perceive that person as a rival for your lover's affections, someone who may eventually displace you.

Jealousy is a blend of shame and anger and frequently occurs in triangular scenes, or what are commonly called "love triangles." Those scenes go back to our childhood, and usually involved either a parent or a sibling. One of them was seen as a rival for the favored parent's interest and love. The birth of a sibling always creates a triangular scene, a new potential rival. The shame of jealousy is rooted in the comparisons we make between ourselves and the "intruder," as well as the fear of impending displacement or abandonment. Anger is a typical response to shame in these instances.

Jealousy is natural, though most of us have been shamed for feeling jealous. Think back to your childhood. When your brother's or sister's birthday arrived, for example, didn't you feel jealous? Or how about watching a teacher fuss over another student who had done much better than anyone else in the school play? Classrooms are common breeding grounds for shame because many teachers think they're encouraging students by holding up the achievers as models.

In your family and in the classroom, weren't you invariably and publicly shamed for expressing jealousy openly? Every child is jealous when someone else is receiving something or being singled out for special attention. It's no wonder that now as adults we feel shame about feeling jealous, which only makes matters worse. Given how American culture encourages competition and comparison making, jealousy is a common hazard.

Being in a relationship you value, only to find your lover suddenly looking at and obviously feeling attracted to someone else or becoming the focus of someone else's attention, can immediately reactivate those earlier scenes involving rivals. Those compelling scenes now intrude directly into consciousness, invading the encounter taking place, confusing the present circumstance with the earlier situation that first gave rise to the scene. Consciously distinguishing between the governing scene that has been unexpectedly reactivated and the current situation is vitally important. Otherwise, we are forever caught in our scenes, compelled by them, and driven to reenact them.

My younger brother was the family star: straight-A student, terrific baseball player, confident, funny, talented at anything he did. Kids liked him, teachers liked him. My parents were always raving about how wonderful Barry was, with the unspoken criticism that I was mediocre. After college, I turned out more successful than him, so I felt like all that jealousy was in the past. Then my boyfriend Drew started talking to me about this new neighbor of his, how cute he was, how sexy, how fascinating. I couldn't believe I was so furious. Instead of asking for details and enjoying them, I was like a little dictator telling Drew to shut up.

Jealousy may be triggered by nothing more than a look on your lover's face, a look clearly aimed at someone else. But however it's triggered, and whatever role your old scenes play in it, jealousy must be consciously acknowledged first to yourself, then openly expressed, and finally listened to and heard by your lover. This three-fold process validates the feeling and lessens its power to damage the relationship.

Sexual Attraction to Others

Both lesbians and gay men struggle with experiencing sexual attraction to others while they are in an intimate relationship with a particular person. It's misguided to deny the reality of such attractions when they occur or pretend that they're not happening. The problem most often occurs when the couple is together in a social or public setting. When either person in the couple is out somewhere alone, then attractions to others may still occur, but the boyfriend or girlfriend is not present to notice them and be disquieted, though suspicions might indeed arise afterward. This may be more troublesome if one lover is more likely to attract other people, whatever the reason: personality, looks, age, status.

How do you navigate these turbulences? Instead of hiding them, try *sharing* your attractions to others directly and openly with each other—even when you are in public. This will require trust. The important thing is not to hide or deny what may be inevitable and not to feel shame about feeling those attractions in the first place. Ideological norms are what constrain us. By sharing attractions to others openly between the two of you, either when they occur or afterward, you bring them directly into your relationship. Sexual attraction to others now becomes something to be shared and need no longer be a threat dividing you from one another.

Sexual Betrayal

Despite all precautions and preparation to the contrary, sexual encounters with other people may take place. When your girlfriend or boyfriend has "transgressed" and violated agreed-upon rules of sexual conduct, it only serves to confirm the presence of an unwanted rival. Now we have truly been displaced by another, or at least we feel that way. Trust is shattered; we feel betrayed. The deep, abiding shame that ensues can potentially consume any relationship.

When you have violated your own or your lover's rules by having sex with someone else in a manner *you* disallow, the shame you will experience as a result invariably will take the form of *immorality shame*. That is because of the ethical judgment of transgression that has been added to the experience of shame in this instance. The affect is still shame, though you will most likely call it guilt.

> *Jerry and I had really worked hard at making it as a couple. Neither one of us had ever had a long-term relationship, and they always fell apart because somebody started sleeping around. We were determined to make it work and keep sex at home. Well, Jerry was away on business one weekend, I went to a friend's birthday party, got high, went dancing, and I ended up in bed with somebody I just met. I couldn't believe how I could throw everything away in one night! I felt like a real failure, like I was hopeless and was never going to grow up. It turned out better than I thought, though, because Jerry was mad and felt really betrayed, but said that if we broke up, we'd be back where we started. Shouldn't we try to deal with the consequences, together?*

Honestly confronting the shame that each person feels in this situation and then dissolving shame through mutual sharing and understanding is the only viable course to restoring the relationship. Each of you will experience shame in any instance of sexual betrayal, and each of you must be able to express your shame to the other, however painful that may be. Unexpressed shame only divides you further. By facing shame together, and supporting each other through it, you'll come to a new place in your relationship.

Coming out of shame individually enables you to deal more effectively with shame in your relationships.

DEALING WITH SHAME AS A COUPLE

Even if they haven't been together that long, couples should be prepared for shame to burst into their most intimate moments. Each lover must also understand how to respond to shame the other person is experiencing and, most important, how *not* to respond.

Most of us have learned to handle shame the way we saw it handled in our own families. Remember when you were little and complained to your mother or father: "Nobody likes me"? Parents typically deny such expressions of shame by saying, "Of course they do!" rather than help their children neutralize and counteract shame directly. Parents are likely to have their own shame triggered in such a situation and their denial serves to protect them as well as their children.

Shame must be approached, acknowledged, and validated. Never deny your lover's feeling of shame, and never try to "fix" it either. Make it clear to your lover that you recognize his or her shame, you see how badly he or she feels. Be compassionate and understanding, and also be prepared to experience shame yourself because affect is contagious. Your lover's shame will likely trigger your own scenes of shame.

> *Karla's mother was a model, so she always felt like she would never be as beautiful and classy as her mom. Well, I didn't care because I liked going out with her and I thought she was fine just the way she was. But every now and then she'd have these attacks where she'd kind of shut down, at dinner or something, after saying, "God, I feel so fat! I feel ugly!" I was embarrassed— it was so out of place, and unexpected. She'd get louder and I'd worry about what other people thought and try to shut her up. It seemed crazy, because Karla runs ten miles a day and is really slim. First I tried to kid her out of it by making faces, or saying I was the one who was a fatso, but that didn't go anywhere. She felt even worse. It was like she'd fallen down this well and nothing I could do could reach her. Then I started to feel really annoyed,*

and told her she didn't know what she was talking about, and should stop acting like a little kid.

When body shame erupts, don't tell your lover he or she *shouldn't* feel that way because you think he or she is beautiful or handsome or whatever. Of course, you need to convey those sentiments at some point, if they're genuine, but you must first allow shame to be given full expression in order for it to be ultimately released. That is not an easy task. Tolerating someone else's shame demands patience and a willingness to be uncomfortable, even through empathy.

Try to enter your lover's experience by imagining yourself inside his or her skin. For a moment, try to feel what it's like to actually be your lover. Listen to your lover's feelings of shame in order to understand them, and allow those feelings to be expressed fully.

Remember, shame becomes healed through new experiences of identification; therefore, share a parallel shame experience drawn from your own life, if you feel comfortable doing so.

Shame can divide us because we often push others away, feeling too exposed, so be prepared for what may seem like an angry response like: *What do you know about how I feel!*

Remember to touch or embrace your lover throughout the interchange, so that you stay connected.

> *I wanted to see Karla more, so I decided I should try something different, when I realized that her complaining about how she looked really unnerved me. She was so much more attractive than I was, that when she said she felt ugly, I started feeling bad myself. One night I showed her my family pictures from one of the worst periods of my life—when I was eleven, buck-teethed, with thick glasses, and looked like a troll. I told her about how kids at school had made fun of me. At first she said, "It's not the same," but then she started talking about how her mother was always dropping these little "hints" about ways Karla could make herself more beautiful. It was the same, sort of, because we both had this stuff inside of us, and we could relate to each other's experiences. We cried together, and managed to laugh some, too.*

Sometimes, *we* can unfortunately be the source of our lover's shame, even in the best of relationships. And too often, we either dismiss our lover's feelings by saying, "It's no big deal," or even *blame* our lover by saying, "You're too sensitive."

Ruben and Elliot met at the gym and started dating. They had so much fun, in bed and out, that Ruben suggested they start working out together. Elliot was uncertain, because he was new at pumping iron, and Ruben had competed in bodybuilding. Unfortunately, the gym became a minefield for their relationship. Ruben was a perfectionist, and when he spotted for Elliot, he had so much to say that Elliot felt like he was being lectured. Ruben was also pretty loud in his comments, and Elliot thought that everyone at the gym was watching and mocking him. He protested: "You're making me crazy—this is just a workout, not a job!" But Ruben was dismissive and critical: "Hey, if you want to look like a geek, feel free."

When your lover's shame has been triggered by something you've said or done, don't deny your part in what happened. Instead, admit whatever mistakes you might have made—which, in turn, requires you to be able to tolerate shame yourself. We invariably react to our own mistakes with feelings of shame, which often makes apologizing difficult. When we're able to tolerate that shame, we can more freely admit our mistakes.

The most important thing is to *own* your own part in triggering shame in your lover, however that happened.

Though it's very challenging, be prepared to accept and absorb your lover's anger in response to having been shamed by you. Say something like "I know you're pissed off now, and you're right, but I hope you'll end up forgiving me." The aim of what you say is to acknowledge your lover's feelings without rushing your lover to "get over it"; you're also showing you want to stay connected. This message restores the interpersonal bridge and heals shame in the relationship.

Understanding the way shame plays out between you and your lover can help you chart such situations and explore their solution in all relationships, especially when your commitment becomes long-term.

CHAPTER FIVE

Partners in Intimacy

A ll of the foregoing shame dynamics and strategies for dealing with them
apply to the entire gamut of interpersonal relations, from superficial to
more intimate ones, from casual friendships to erotic encounters, from very
brief to more enduring connections, from family to work relationships. Now
we want to narrow our focus and consider the unique challenges faced
whenever two men or two women decide to join together in a loving part-
nership that has become primary for each of them. Here a gay couple is truly
crossing a border. Just as we have lacked necessary models for being gay or
lesbian and for gay and lesbian relationships in general, we have lacked
equally essential models for committed relationships that are meaningful
and mutual, intimate and sexual, loving and lasting.

We have already explored a number of critical dimensions of lesbian
and gay relationships that need to be carefully considered in the context of
creating a relationship. But even when these questions are consciously delib-
erated and mutual resolution is finally attained, they will resurface repeatedly as a couple continues together over the years. The answers reached at
any given time in our lives will not necessarily carry us forever. Our vital
needs and expectations change as we grow into maturity, as our most deeply
cherished loving relationships continue to evolve—making this a process

that must be continually engaged in over time by every couple seeking to preserve an enduring commitment.

FAMILY RELATIONSHIPS

The place where we first learn about having relationships and where we first see models of intimacy is the family: that's where we first strive to belong and feel connected. Parents are the first people we want to be like because we experience them as central in our world. Children have no greater wish than to emulate and identify with the parents they love and need. But the dawning awareness of being gay or lesbian—which itself begins with the early awareness of gender difference—collides with that wish. If we have witnessed antigay and heterosexist attitudes or behavior within the family, then who we are alienates us from these individuals whose love we need most. The awareness of being so fundamentally different from everyone else generates shame and bars further identification. Suddenly, a barrier rears up in our family about who we are on the inside, about our deepest wishes and dreams, while on the outside we start hiding. As soon as we begin recognizing our true desires—at whatever age—the necessity of hiding may unfortunately come to govern our relationships with those people who have been central in our formative years.

In the best of circumstances, the unequal power relationship that exists between parents and children evolves with the attainment of adulthood into a new relationship where power is *shared*. To the extent that we're crippled by shame about being gay and afraid of being disowned, we're mired in an unequal relationship with our parents. For lesbians and gay men, coming out to our family can be a way of assuming equal power. If this happens when we're financially and emotionally independent, then the risks of coming out are lessened.

It wasn't until I was out of school, away from home, and holding a real job that I told my folks I was queer. They always used money and access to the car and things like that to keep me and my brothers in line, so I knew that I'd be sunk if they were hateful and wanted to punish me. There was no way I could earn enough money to pay my college tuition by myself, and I sure wasn't going to put up with any of that stuff about "This is my house, and you do as I say." So even though it was painful, I waited.

It takes a great deal of inner work to reach a secure level of self-esteem, which then enables us to come out to our parents and feel protected against an adverse reaction. If we apologize for who we are or plead for acceptance, then we're still acting out of shame, hoping that our parents will ease our shame for us. We have to do that work ourselves and present our gayness to them as a gift of honesty, a way of furthering closeness.

IDEOLOGY AND RELATIONSHIPS

Since our parents are the first models we have of being in a couple, their example casts a long shadow on how we form couples in our adult life. For better or worse, we inherit our family's *ideology*, or organized set of feelings and ideas *about* feelings, which determines how we conduct our relationships. People relate according to two main opposing ideologies, and these ideological scripts develop directly from the way their families handled affect.[1]

If the family has worked from a *normative* ideology, then it used punishment to socialize affect during childhood. Normative parents show an intolerance for their children's negative affect (shame, distress, fear), along with an overriding concern for punishment if their children have violated a norm. Rigid rules guide life, and there aren't any exceptions.

By contrast, in a family operating from a *humanistic* ideology, rewards are used to socialize affect. These parents empathize with their children's distress or shame. They also feel that punishment for violating norms isn't as important as how their children feel. Such a family is guided by flexibility in enforcing children's compliance with rules.

Why is this distinction significant? The different family patterns produce distinct sets of ideas about which affects are appropriate and when. Every couple will struggle with similar ideas about which affects to express and how and also about interpersonal needs. Conflicts may additionally break out for any gay couple about sex, politics, religion, and social action; such conflicts are rooted in clashing ideologies.

> *Martha has got to be one of the most concerned and politically active women I've ever met. She's just like her parents—her dad was a doctor, her mother a social worker. Martha must be on the board of seven different lesbian and gay groups in our city, and when we first moved in together, I admired her energy. After a few years, though, I've gotten jealous of all the time she devotes to other people, to strangers. It's like she feels the whole world is her responsibility. And it hurts me that everyone else takes precedence over anything in our life together. She's always coming home late, meeting me late at restaurants or shows, because there's always some emergency, someone to take care of. Once she even missed my daughter Becky's birthday—how do you explain that to a little girl? Even when she promises it won't happen, it does, and that's the worst part. I was raised to always keep my word and never break a promise to someone you love, no matter what. Martha and I keep trying to work it out, but I'm discouraged, because we just see the world so differently.*

If the couple, gay or lesbian, is also engaged in raising children, then the possibilities for ideological clash over childrearing practices become endless. One parent might be much more concerned with empathizing with the child's feelings in response to misbehavior, whereas the other parent will be more concerned that the child violated a rule and has to be punished.

> *Even though my parents were driven at work—which is why I'm such an overachiever—they were pretty easygoing at home, pretty even-tempered. They never really punished us, and that's why I can't be strict with Becky. I mean, she's only five. She can't really help it when she does stuff like lie about breaking a vase, or take money from my purse. She's too young to really know what she's doing. I can't stand watching the big song and dance Annette does when Becky's misbehaving. She acts like she's the Supreme Court or something, instead of trying to figure out why Becky did it, what's really bugging her underneath. I don't think I'm too*

lenient with her, but her mother is always criticizing me, saying I'm teaching Becky to be irresponsible. Last time we got into a big fight about it, I was furious that Annette said I was sloppy and didn't care enough about Becky to put my foot down. Her parents are German, so I called her a Nazi, which was awful. But I wanted to hurt her.

Two people whose ideological orientations sharply differ will inevitably become embroiled in conflict throughout the course of their relationship. If you want an intimate relationship to last, it's vital to consciously examine your own and your partner's ideological orientation. Such an examination will illuminate how you feel about a whole range of issues like politics, parenting, attitudes toward social welfare, law and order, sex, abortion, religion, and even dividing areas of responsibility in your relationship. The quality of the match will determine how well you can create a future together.

When Shay and I first got together, I was really turned on by his passion for me, and how single-minded he was. He'd say things like "I never look at anyone else anymore, ever. You're the only man I even think about." Well, I was just coming out of a rocky relationship with a guy who just wouldn't commit to me, so I thought this was terrific. Things changed when I started traveling for my new job. I went to lots of trade shows, and Shay was always putting me through an inquisition before I even got back home. On the phone he'd ask where I ate, who I ate with, who I talked to, if there was anyone cute there. And he sounded suspicious no matter what I said. I just couldn't stand that I had to call him at a certain time every day I was away no matter what. It didn't make sense. But that's how he organized his whole life— everything was on schedule, planned out, perfect. We started arguing about money, too. If we budgeted a certain amount for a vacation, for a new computer, or whatever, he would throw a fit when I wanted to go over the amount. And forget trying to surprise him with a gift—he'd ask how much it cost and then tell me it was too expensive! The longer we lived together, the more I felt like I was in prison. He was always watching me when we went out, to see if I was checking out other guys. Of course I was. I love looking at men—I always have. But he tried to make me feel like I was a criminal, that I didn't really love him. What I thought was devotion in the beginning turned out to be possession.

When differences between ideologies can't be bridged through effective compromise, each partner is likely to either feel shame in response to the comparison or try to shame the other person as a way of controlling the situation.

DEBATING SEXUAL MONOGAMY

Perhaps the area of greatest ideological conflict is sexual monogamy versus multiple sexual pairing. Early on, partners in a committed relationship ought to openly discuss the reality of their attractions to other men, to other women, or to both if either of them is bisexual. Avoiding this matter will not solve it, but instead will only make potential problems more likely later. The only course is to consciously face the reality of sexual attraction to others, both as individuals and as a couple, and then determine together how to best handle such attractions when they in fact occur.

Shame plays a critical role in this process, however unexpressed, because shame inhibits such open acknowledgments when they are truly felt. We feel ashamed of feeling them in the first place. Shame plays another role in the couple because feeling an attraction to another individual, whether it is expressed openly or not, is a common source of jealousy. And the direct expression of jealousy by the jealous partner will very likely trigger shame in the other partner, typically accompanied by anger in both. Shame breeds shame, while anger breeds anger. Eventually, silence by either or both partners becomes the rule followed in future incidents.

But silence and denial solve nothing. Sexual attraction in one partner and jealousy in the other will only be further magnified when affects are forced underground. The suppression of affect always backfires. That is why the healthiest course, both for individuals and for couples, is the free expression of affect, including sexual attraction to others.

Conscious attention by each person to the other's feelings, jealousy included, is the way to preserve the intimacy between them. Though it can be very painful, each must strive to understand and empathize with the feelings and needs of the other.

> *Donna is much more outgoing than I am, and she's an ex-model, so women are always flirting with her. Even when I'm right there in the room or holding her hand. They act like I don't exist. Donna loves the attention and flirts right back. That's what I have so much trouble with. We've been working on it, because Donna was a sickly child who blossomed really late, so she's always felt unattractive no matter what the mirror says. Flirting makes her feel great, so we're trying to figure out how we can handle this with both of us feeling comfortable. It's a tough one!*

Striving for empathy with your partner's feelings is the soundest basis for reaching a mutual decision that you can both live with amicably. When these attractions to others are revealed in a relationship where both partners feel secure in their *mutual* desirability, such open expression need not be disruptive. In contrast, Miguel had a relationship in which his partner continually pointed out other men he found "humpy," but he never expressed genuine desire for Miguel or said he was attractive. The hidden message always seemed to be *Now* that's *someone I'd really like to sleep with—unlike you.* For Miguel, the result in each instance was silence and shame.

Actual sexual involvement with other people outside of the committed relationship poses a greater challenge. Postponing conscious examination of this volatile issue will only invite the intrusion of affect storms later. We cannot leave reality out of the equation. Each partner must confront their expectations about how each would prefer to handle sexual encounters and also each person's true limits. One partner may actually expect to have other sexual liaisons while the other expects nothing of the kind. Or neither may consciously expect sexual encounters with others to ever occur—believing sexual monogamy to be desirable—yet each knows that such occurrences are at least possible, if not likely.

Shame creates silence and may inhibit frank exploration in this area. You may even feel diminished when your partner talks about finding other people attractive. Or your partner may shame *you* when you reveal your own attractions. It's important in a conversation like this to be aware of the various ways you might trigger shame or experience shame—from comparison making, scene intrusion, or unintentionally critical comments—and be prepared to deal with shame as it comes up. Look for the signs of shame—blushing, turning away, eyes down, head down. It's difficult territory, but you need to find the courage to talk about sexual desires for other people, and consider how you truly feel about it—before something happens.

The potential for shame through sexual betrayal in a long-term relationship is enormous. If you're polar opposites, and one of you lives by strict rules (the normative ideology) while the other is more flexible and situation-focused (the humanistic ideology), then your reactions to each other's sexual liaisons will be vastly different.

> *Val didn't understand. All I did was spend part of one night with another woman. I didn't even sleep with her! We were in Lori's hot tub, and she started massaging my shoulders and kept massaging. . . . It was no big deal, but when I told her, Val was screaming at me, throwing books and dishes and calling me a slut. I thought she'd be glad I was honest. When I told her I wouldn't mind if she had a little fun with someone, that made her even madder.*

Having *similar* ideological postures leads to other possibilities. If both of you have a normative framework, neither of you will be able to see past the violation of trust. Punishment for betrayal is apt to be swift and merciless. When partners both display a humanistic orientation, there's a greater likelihood of mutual understanding and eventual forgiveness.

Is monogamy a viable model for interpersonal relations as we move forward into the twenty-first century? Most people wonder what other model there *could* be for maintaining loving relationships. The principal terms we have inherited from prior generations to describe alternative forms of relationship are pejorative: *promiscuity* or *adultery*.

We lack a meaningful, coherent model for viewing relationships other than the model of heterosexual monogamy—which, not coincidentally, developed at a time in our evolution when the life span was considerably shorter and the universal goal in all cultures was to be fruitful and multiply. Even though we've all observed that sexual practice deviates sharply from the espoused ideal of sexual exclusiveness, monogamy (whether in heterosexual marriage or in gay unions) continues to function as a paramount social value, never to be questioned. People often claim they want a sexually monogamous relationship even when they don't practice it, or know from experience that they won't be able to sustain it.

We must discover how to sustain intimacy over time, how to keep passion alive, how to weave together the vital threads of sexuality and intimacy into an interpersonal tapestry that will endure.

To do this, we must first honestly confront the reality of the situation facing us. Lesbians and gay men are first of all separated by the difference in their sexual orientation from the heterosexual community at large, and are also prevented from participating directly in the institution of marriage. We are therefore *somewhat* freer from the constraints imposed by the dominant cultural pattern of monogamy. That freedom is limited because the values of sexual constancy and monogamy operate in gay culture every bit as much as in heterosexual culture. Wedding sex to love is part of our Puritan legacy.[2]

But as a people, we are already immersed in the difficult task of inventing new forms for our relationships, our families, and our communities. As outcasts, we have been more able to stand apart, to see mainstream heterosexual culture a bit more objectively.

Monogamy simply may not be possible or desirable for many gay men and lesbians who find it impossible and oppressive to remain exclusively sexual with just one other individual over the course of life. What is needed is a deliberately conscious approach by each couple to determine how best to deal with inevitable sexual attractions and desires for others and with potential sexual encounters.

Lois and Marie have been together in a committed relationship for well over ten years. They fully expect theirs to be a lifetime commitment. They own a house together, have joint bank accounts, and have even granted each other power of attorney in the event of illness. They've also coparented Marie's son from a prior marriage and have had a church service with their respective family members and friends assembled to publicly celebrate their union. The commitment these two women have made to each other is an enduring one, comparable to any heterosexual marriage.

Two years into their relationship, they decided that they would try to avoid anything that would threaten it, and they wanted to be as honest with each other as possible. But they knew that sooner or later they would find themselves either attracted to someone else or in a situation with another woman in which something sexual was possible. They wrestled with this dilemma over many months. They did not want to proceed naively, blind to events that were likely to occur. Nor did they want to rule any sexual encounter with another woman absolutely off limits for all time. That seemed foolish and misguided. Besides, it rarely worked. They knew other lesbian couples in which one of the partners had furtive sexual liaisons. Not for them. Neither woman felt comfortable with the other becoming sexual with anyone else, as their lesbian friends had arranged things: *Do it, but don't tell me about it.*

What was the answer? The decision they arrived at mutually was that neither of them would ever become sexual with another woman on her own. But if they met a woman they both liked, felt close to, and were sexually drawn to—and who responded—then they would invite her to bed with them. Over a period of four or five years they experimented with this form of sexual nonexclusivity on several occasions. But after each time they did so, they carefully explored their individual feelings about and reactions to including a third woman in their sexual relationship.

Several rules emerged to guide them. First, they would only proceed when they *both* freely wanted to; if only one of them wanted to be sexual with another woman, it went no further. Second, they never did anything sexually with another woman unless both of them were present at the same time. Third, by mutual agreement they kept certain sexual practices private, only to be shared between themselves. They wanted a clear way to mark their own sexual relationship as distinctive and special. Fourth, if the woman whom they both felt drawn to responded strongly only to one of them but not the other, then the experience usually was a disappointment and was not repeated with that woman. With practice they learned to distinguish beforehand when that was likely to occur. Of paramount significance to them both was preserving the love and commitment between them. *It's not something we talk about with our other lesbian friends. It's hard for them to accept—if you sleep with someone else, then that's the end of everything.*

For this particular lesbian couple, occasional sexual encounters with a third woman became a vehicle for absorbing the inevitable sexual attractions that each of them felt toward others. Honesty was preserved, and trust thereby maintained. Each knew she had veto power over any subsequent sexual liaison. Their commitment to each other and the bond of intimacy between them never felt threatened or in jeopardy. *It wouldn't work for everyone, I guess, but it works for us.*

The approach that this couple discovered is simply one way to confront the problem of multiple sexual pairing within the confines of commitment. It won't necessarily be an answer for other couples. Nor is it the only way to proceed on this vital matter. Some couples, for instance, may choose to allow each other outside relationships or encounters, but only when one partner is out of town, or providing neither discusses it.

What is important is that gay men and lesbians who are creating a life together as a committed couple remember to *consciously* explore how they want to handle their inevitable attractions to and desires for others. Even if you're not expecting a lifetime commitment, the openness of your relationship to outside sexual contact needs to be carefully considered beforehand. Otherwise, the potential for shame disrupting and even ending the relationship goes ignored.

REENACTING EACH OTHER'S SCENES

Throughout our analysis of the impact of shame both on individuals and on relationships, we have discussed the critical role of *scenes*. All affective experience, shame included, is stored in memory in the form of specific scenes. When these scenes become interconnected and fuse directly, they magnify one another greatly. They take on a life of their own and govern our relationship patterns. Those governing scenes operate either entirely out of awareness or at the periphery of awareness.

Any life event or interpersonal situation that is sufficiently similar to a governing scene can reactivate the scene and prompt its return to consciousness. This is one of the most frequent and volatile causes of reexperiencing shame throughout adulthood, particularly in intimate relationships.

> *I was a shy kid and always short for my age, and kids in grade school were always making fun of me no matter how much I tried to be invisible. I didn't have a lot of friends, and basically just did my homework. They even made fun of that, calling me "teacher's pet" and "brown-nose." I moved away in junior high,*

and I thought all that was over. Years later, my lover was watching me organize notes for a class I was teaching, and he said, "You're a good little boy, aren't you?" I know he didn't mean it as an insult, but I felt like I'd been buried in a sandstorm. I couldn't move, I couldn't talk. And then I just exploded at him, screaming and crying.

Even well-intentioned and affectionate teasing by present-day friends can cause you to reexperience a governing scene along with its deeply embedded shame. This will be more disturbing if it's a lover who is the inadvertent trigger: in a relationship where you feel safe, this sudden unexpected exposure can be shocking and disorienting. It can feel like a betrayal.

Activating each other's early governing scenes is inevitable in every couple relationship, however secure, trusting, and satisfying it may be. It's increasingly likely to happen as you spend more time together and grow more intimately connected.

When governing scenes are reactivated, they immediately invade the present interaction, usually without any awareness that it's happening. At that moment, we are trapped in our scenes. We reexperience them fully with all of the original affect reawakened, and we reenact those scenes in the present, right at that moment, directly with the person who reactivated them. This process is universal, occurring in all individuals, in all relationships.

Embedded in the scene are any people who were present during the original situation when it occurred, any words that were spoken, feelings you experienced, actions that you observed or suffered, sounds, and even smells. Occasionally, all that remains conscious from the entire scene is a voice, often the voice of a particular individual in the scene. This is the actual source of inner parental voices that can be directed inward against ourselves or turned outward against others. When we suddenly realize we're reacting like a child, what we are experiencing is a set of interconnected scenes in which we were actually that young, needy, and insecure.

It is critically important that we consciously map our scenes so that we can help our partners avoid triggering them and even enlist their help in muting their impact. Each partner needs to distinguish both persons' scenes from their present-day interactions whenever those scenes intrude. That is the only way to sidestep automatically reenacting each other's scenes and being caught up in the ensuing affect storm. Scenes cannot be eliminated, but they can be transformed by first making them conscious, then learning to recognize them with increasing skill, and finally rescripting them.

Here is one scene that we had to confront almost immediately upon moving in together. Before we lived together, the situation never arose. Lev returned home from grocery shopping one day, and Gershen innocently asked, "Did you get the tomato sauce we like?" This casual question unleashed an unexpected affect storm. Lev became suddenly enraged, feeling his judgment called into question. He was experiencing shame, which in turn prompted rage. But Gershen wasn't questioning or intending to question his judgment; he was simply asking whether Lev had bought the sauce, and he didn't understand the response.

Several stormy repetitions of this scene forced us to examine it more closely. After some reflection, Lev recalled scenes from childhood and adolescence in which his judgment *had* been questioned or criticized by both parents for being so forgetful—like losing or misplacing his keys or wallet. That was why he invariably shouted at Gershen in response to that particular question or any question like it: "Was it on the list? Then I *bought* it!" Lev's scene had been reactivated and had invaded their interaction. Lev was actually raging at one of his parents who was embedded in his governing scene. These early scenes were the source of Lev's feeling that his judgment was now being criticized and of the shame he felt in response.

But the interaction was even more complex. Gershen was reliving scenes of his own during this everyday interchange that started so innocuously but ended in both of us being captured by our scenes. Whenever young Gershen returned from grocery shopping for his mother, she would invariably ask him, "Did you get—?" While Gershen had *recast* his scene and now was playing the part of his mother, Lev was playing out his own scene directly: Lev was responding to Gershen *in the present* in the identical way he had always felt toward his father in the past. We were both relieved to finally see what was actually transpiring beneath the surface of this unexpectedly troublesome interaction.

Now that both sets of scenes had been identified and the cast of actual characters expanded, what was the solution, since somebody still had to do the shopping? The scene itself had to be *rescripted* in order to transform it.

We began by experimenting with using humor and also changing the actual dialogue—in advance. When Lev next returned home from grocery shopping, Gershen was ready with some new responses: "Did they *have* any tomato sauce today?" or "Were they *able* to sell you tomato sauce at the supermarket?" or, to paraphrase Oscar Wilde, "Was there any tomato sauce to be had for ready money?"

We broke out laughing and the dreaded scene did not return. We had found a way to navigate successfully around it so as not to be drawn into the scene like a psychological black hole. In fact, humorous exchanges about shopping became one way of healing shame as well as transforming the original scene. From then on, that old scene returned less and less often, though we always had to remain vigilant; rescripting became a conscious, ongoing part of our lives.

Ultimately, we came to view all of our interactions as vulnerable to unexpected intrusions by governing scenes. Though such scenes can involve virtually anyone who ever played a significant role in our lives—including siblings, relatives, teachers, and peers—in the great majority of instances, these are scenes in which interactions with our parents are deeply embedded. After all, we spent many years observing the ways in which our parents interacted in the family, even before we acquired language.

These "visitations" have led us to think of our parents, somewhat fondly, as the "Gang of Four." We often realize that one or another of our parents, or even all four for that matter, have suddenly returned to invade our living space. They seem to like the kitchen, as when Lev will watch Gershen chopping something and ask in unconscious imitation of his father's criticism, "You couldn't find a *smaller* knife?"

Announcing the Gang of Four's arrival makes us laugh, and we immediately unhook from the negative affect. Humor releases the hold of the scene. Sometimes one of us will say, "I didn't know you were inviting your folks to dinner" or "It's getting kind of crowded in the kitchen, isn't it?" Playing with the scene has also helped us quickly identify who our unexpected visitor is, and so sometimes one of us will say "That's my dad!" as soon as the critical comment pops out.

RESOLVING ARGUMENTS AND ANGER AS EQUALS

Many couples are frightened of anger or assume that arguing at all is a sign of a troubled relationship. Part of what makes anger so problematic in relationships is the way it seems to tear apart and trample love, affection, and commitment—however momentarily.

When people in a relationship disagree with one another, or when arguments break out, anger can quickly ignite and magnify. Anger can rapidly *polarize* two individuals despite their mutual, loving relationship, and each person will begin to assert more extreme positions on whatever issue they're at odds over.

> *Jackie and I were really worried about money one year because there was talk of the state laying off workers because of a budget crunch. So this perfectly calm conversation about how we could trim things for a while got completely out of control. We agreed on spending less money on clothes. Then I suggested we eat out less, which she loves to do. Jackie said I should stop buying so many books. That made me mad because I'm a journalist—I have to read a lot. Then I said we should cancel our summer vacation and she was yelling at me that we had to sell our cars. I topped that with saying we had to sell the house! None of it made sense— we just got louder and more ridiculous till we ran out of stuff to threaten each other with.*

Anger not only turns partners into opponents, but it can quickly recruit past grievances. Prior scenes of feeling wronged, neglected, taken advantage of, misunderstood, shamed, or powerless—however unrelated to the present argument these may be—become imported directly into the fray.

Of utmost importance is that power between the two individuals remain equal throughout the ensuing affect storm. It is precisely by this dynamic, well known to every couple, that people are most severely taxed. Affect is contagious. Virtually anything, however innocent or well intentioned, can unexpectedly reignite rage that has already begun to subside. Power must be equal in order for the affect storm to abate.

How? First, let's consider the verbal expression of anger. The tendency to bring up unrelated past grievances in the midst of a current argument is something we've probably all experienced. This pattern of handling anger is one that many of us have learned. In fact, we are typically taught this way of arguing by our parents during similar confrontations. Either these disputes occurred directly with us or else we observed them happening between our parents or between a parent and a sibling. Observational learning is just as potent as direct experience in this case.

> *When my parents fought, it would start with something kind of mild, like a disagreement about one of the kids, but then they brought out the heavy guns. It didn't take long before Mom was telling Dad he was a bum, drank too much, and couldn't support us decently. She'd hammer him with all the jobs he ever lost. He'd tell her she was a bitch and nobody liked her, not even her own family, and he'd snap out all these terrible things her sister and her father told him about her temper. It was like they'd say anything to get at each other. It was brutal.*

There is another important reason why arguments quickly dissolve into *grievance retrieval* from the past, and this concerns the very nature of affect and scene dynamics. Anger that is magnifying rapidly through verbal and facial expression will itself recruit other anger scenes stored in memory that originated in prior relationships or encounters. Embedded in those scenes are specific affects, particular verbal expressions, actions, even actual people. An offense perceived in the present will automatically recruit similar past offenses because of the similarity between them. Our highly developed skill in similarity detection guarantees that past analogous scenes will be reactivated, and those scenes then become directly imported into the brewing affect storm.

What is required in handling such storms is conscious awareness by both partners that resists the tendency to bring up past events in the midst of a current argument. Doing so only triggers powerlessness in the other person, prompting shame followed by retaliation. Unfortunately, grievance retrieval by one partner will invariably spark an identical response by the other. Therefore, we need to make an explicit agreement not to bring up past events. Then, ideally, either partner can gently remind the other whenever continued or persistent grievance retrieval occurs. We need to remember to acknowledge such slips when we're reminded; apologizing for having slipped restores the interpersonal bridge.

Equally important is to remember to *own* your feelings during a disagreement or ensuing argument by saying, "I feel angry," "I feel jealous," or "I feel hurt." Always give "I" messages instead of "you" messages, which are inherently blaming and therefore invariably activate shame. Say, for example, *"I'm really pissed off at you!"* as opposed to *"You're making me so pissed off!"* Worse than that is character assassination like "You're such a lazy jerk! I always have to do everything around here!" What is critical in expressing anger is the avoidance of unnecessarily shaming the other person by fixing blame. Most of us have not been taught to claim our feelings and assert them as our own. Rather, we have been taught to blame or accuse. Why? Because those have been the principal models we've witnessed growing up in our families.

Remember to avoid generalizing from one specific occurrence. Saying something like "You *always* ignore me" or "You *never* say you're sorry" is a global accusation that will directly activate shame in your partner if such comments reactivate similar scenes from your partner's childhood. Stand back while another affect storm erupts.

The tendency toward making such global indictments also reveals affect dynamics at work. When an event ceases being a single occurrence and instead becomes interpreted as universal or global, occurring always or never, then distinct scenes have in fact become magnified into a closely knit set of interconnected scenes. Words like *always* and *never* are important signs of magnification. Once unrelated and separate occurrences have become fused in this way, any subsequent occurrence merely becomes *proof* of the universal case, further validating its existence. The careless child is no longer occasionally but *always* careless, and each new instance of carelessness only confirms this fact. The neglectful partner is no longer occasionally neglectful but *always* neglectful, and each new instance of neglect only proves the point.

In navigating these turbulent situations, conscious awareness is of utmost importance: an understanding of how to avoid generalizing from the specific to the universal, along with definite knowledge of alternative ways of communicating during the heat of anger. In contrast to the blanket accusation, saying something like "When you don't give me the attention I've asked for, I feel hurt and mad" is not *inherently* shaming. Instead it conveys clear ownership of your own feelings coupled with their direct connection to your partner's specific behavior at a particular time. It is not a global accusation, and it doesn't lend itself to being interpreted as a universal indictment. Striving for this latter form of communication avoids or lessens shame and preserves mutual respect, thereby maintaining equal power. You can't guarantee that what you say *won't* shame your partner, but you can make a conscious effort not to use shame as a weapon and to always remain alert to its manifestations. It's important to commit to not wielding shame against our partners, because the more we know their vulnerabilities, the easier it is to say something wounding and vicious.

Another tendency during outbursts of rage is to take all the *power* by making threats of various kinds, including ultimatums. The most dangerous is the threat to leave. In the midst of rage, one person may be driven to utter futility or exasperation and, feeling powerless, may threaten to leave or walk out.

> *There was a period in our relationship, about seven years after we met, when Matt got obsessed with work, and he was always at his desk at home. At first I tried kidding him about it, but it pissed me off that he'd just mumble and keep working when I'd say dinner was ready. I told him it bothered me, but nothing changed, and one night I just told him to go to hell, and that I was fed up and would move out. Well, did he leave that desk in a hurry! He was boiling mad, shouting at me, waving a fist in my face. I almost started heading for the door, but I thought, I don't want to walk out, I love him, I just want to feel like I'm as important as his work. I could feel all my hostility melt away, and I just grabbed him and started crying. That's when he told me he had been passed over for a promotion and was working like crazy because he was feeling desperate. I promised I would never threaten to leave when I was angry, and he promised not to keep trouble to himself anymore.*

The result of an ultimatum is that our partner is immediately rendered powerless and will have to issue an equally volatile threat to offset his or her sense of powerlessness. Such threats ought never to be made in the midst of anger because they invariably up the ante, guaranteeing further shame and retaliation.

One of the unfortunate consequences of such deteriorating confrontations is the use of force. Rendering one person utterly *powerless* in these instances is the most frequent trigger of physical violence. Physical abuse of one partner by the other partner does indeed occur in both gay and lesbian relationships, in spite of claims to the contrary. The source of such denials is the considerable shame felt about the occurrence of abuse itself. None of us is immune to the dynamics of affect. That is why productive and healthy relationships depend on an understanding of those dynamics and how best to handle them. Maintaining equal power is the best safeguard to avoiding the resort to violence, verbal or otherwise, and to defusing rage. Whenever arguments appear to be deteriorating, partners ought to discontinue the argument and separate until the boiling affect subsides. Cooler heads reason better. But disengaging from a heated quarrel itself will require conscious effort and the prior agreement of both partners that doing so is the wiser course.

MATCHING EXPECTATIONS IN COMMITTED RELATIONSHIPS

Expectations are critical whenever two men or two women become involved in a committed long-term relationship (however they define it) or are seriously contemplating one. It is vitally important for the couple to make fully conscious each of their individual expectations for their current and future relationship together. Then they need to determine how well their individual expectations actually match.

Whenever two individuals, lesbian or gay, create a life together as a couple, each person brings into the relationship two entirely different sets of expectations. Each has certain expectations about how the other person is actually going to behave in countless situations, but each also has other expectations about herself or himself. We thus have four distinct sets of expectations operating behind the scenes, but always capable of spontaneous intrusion directly onstage whenever either person's expectations become unexpectedly disappointed or thwarted.

At work here are both scene and affect dynamics. Expectations manifest themselves in the form of imagined scenes, usually involving the positive affects of enjoyment or excitement. When we expect someone to behave in a certain way, whether we're fully conscious of having that expectation or not, we actually imagine scenes involving that person behaving how we need or expect. Expecting a response and experiencing a need are two sides of the same experiential event. Whenever our expectations are disappointed and needs aren't met, shame is directly and immediately activated. That is why first making each person's expectations fully conscious and then determining how well they actually match form an indispensable foundation for the life of any couple.

Commitment to the Primary Relationship

If commitment is an important value in your relationships, make sure that it is an equal value for the other person with whom you're building a relationship. That sounds obvious, but we can often *assume* our partner feels or believes something, based on our own needs. We need to know *for sure.*

Commitment is a promise for tomorrow through which we define who we are, who we will be. To make such a commitment to another person is to willingly bind ourselves to that person for the future. But commitment always involves a fundamental trade-off. In committing ourselves to one person, we inevitably give up all of the infinite possibilities of commitment with numerous other individuals, whom we have not yet met, and choose from among all of those possibilities *one future* alone.

Not everyone looks for committed relationships, nor is everyone necessarily even capable of commitment to a relationship. Some people treasure their independence and see commitment as giving up freedom. Any exercise of choice can be seen as a limitation (even though each choice opens up others). So people who prize their freedom above everything else will be likely to partake of as many possibilities as they can, postponing commitment until a more convenient time, if ever.

Sharing the Power and Negotiating as Equals

Maintaining equal power is essential for sound, mature relationships in which each person's feelings and needs are to be respected.

Josh moved into Adam's house after they dated for a year, but he didn't feel at home amid the very stark postmodernist furniture. As he put it, he wanted to "humanize" the place. Adam, who had lived there for eight years and thought the house was perfect, vetoed any change Josh suggested, however minor. "You're a hick with terrible taste" was Adam's refrain, leaving Josh feeling ashamed and powerless.

Whenever our partners disagree, *how* they do so offers a clear indication of whether they are capable of sharing the power by respecting our rights.

Does your partner argue, wheedle, or mock you: "Boy, that's a really stupid idea!"? Do you get bombarded with incessant questions like "Why won't you drop this?" or "Why won't you change your mind?" Does your partner go ahead and overrule you or ignore your decision anyway? Power needs to be shared in a relationship in order for two people to experience themselves as equal partners.

The situation between Josh and Adam deteriorated when Josh wanted to use an unexpected inheritance for a lavish trip to Europe and Adam refused, insisting that they should invest the money for the future. Josh felt stymied, unappreciated, and angry: "You're a cheap bitch!" Adam felt that Josh wouldn't listen to good advice and was far too impulsive and emotional.

Couples need to discover, preferably early in their relationship, if they can negotiate as equals to resolve essential differences with respect and to their mutual satisfaction. Otherwise, they won't be able to create a relationship in which each cares about the feelings and needs of the other. Issues like where to live, how to pursue a career, what to spend money on, how to deal with family and friends are just some of the questions every couple will have to negotiate. If they can do so as equals, then shame will not undermine either person's self-esteem.

Josh and Adam could not compromise on the feel of their home or on what to do with Josh's inheritance. Adam hated Josh's suggestion that if they didn't move to a house they both liked and could create together, then Josh should at least have one room in the house to make his own. Josh likewise utterly rejected giving up his fantasy of blowing all the money on a European trip. Their "discussions" were tense and hostile and degenerated into abusive name calling; it was clear they had reached an impasse.

Sexual Compatibility

Sexual tastes are as free and various as imagination allows and as rigid and restricted as shame demands. Sexual compatibility is important to the life of every couple. Knowing each partner's sexual desires and boundaries will enable a couple to determine the soundness of the match between them.

If one partner continues to hunger for a particular form of sexual expression but the other partner is unwilling or refuses—for whatever reasons—to participate in that specific form of sexual encounter, then the potential is great for disappointment, eventual shame, and a deepening resentment.

Bob had come to really enjoy protected anal intercourse, particularly the experience of having his lover inside of him. When he and Walt began their committed relationship and moved in together soon after they started dating, their very different sexual tastes became a source of growing contention between them. Walt refused to participate in anal intercourse, feeling it was dirty, and rarely even participated willingly in oral sex of any kind. That too was disgusting to him. This left Bob feeling repeatedly frustrated sexually and also increasingly drawn to other men. Attempts to openly discuss their different desires went nowhere because Walt was adamantly opposed to trying anything different in their sexual life. Even the frank discussion of sex was too embarrassing for him; Walt was *that* completely held prisoner by shame. His shame, and the excitement Bob felt when they met, had kept both of them from talking about sex *before* they moved in together.

Sexual practices must be mutual; each partner has to be willing to participate or experiment. That is why open and honest discussion of each partner's explicit sexual desires, as well as secret sexual fantasies, is absolutely essential at the outset of a relationship and also continuously throughout. It is the only way to reveal the inhibiting power of shame and then determine how able the partners will be to dissolve their sexual shame.

The HIV status of both persons must also be openly discussed at the outset, and such a discussion can often activate shame. Admitting that you're HIV positive can generate shame, just as being HIV negative can also trigger shame in some circumstances. If you're a mixed status couple, then the negotiation of safe sex and the presence of shame remain ongoing.

The admission of other types of sexually transmitted diseases like herpes or genital warts can also trigger shame. You may feel unclean, diseased, disgusting by making the confession, or even by hearing it. But avoiding such disclosure because of shame or fear of rejection is not a viable solution. When the other person discovers the truth, whether about a previously undisclosed positive HIV status, genital herpes, genital warts, or some other sexually transmitted disease, that person will feel betrayed as well as threatened. Honesty about this issue is the only way to preserve relationships.

Safe sex practices need to be addressed directly and examined consciously by both persons as a couple. Failure to do so courts disaster.

> *Since Jack and I were both negative and monogamous, we never bothered about safe sex, and that was a relief after other relationships. We never even talked about it. But then I found out from a friend that Jack was seeing somebody else. I was furious, and terrified. If he was hiding an affair, maybe he'd hide if he got infected, too.*

Relating to Other Couples and Friends

Couples have relationships with other couples as well as with individuals, just as each partner in the couple can also have numerous separate relationships with other people without the partner being directly included. Not all relationships need be, or even ought to be, "couple relationships." If everything that two people do is always done by both of them as a couple, then the danger arises of each person losing his or her separate identity as an individual by submerging it within the dual identity. The need to identify takes over and swamps the opposing need to differentiate.

Karen and Mandy met and fell in love at work, but it wasn't until they moved in together that their closeness became a problem, at least for Karen. They both liked running, so they not only lived and worked together, but wound up exercising together. Mandy craved being with Karen every minute of the day, would even follow her around the apartment to be near her, no matter what they were doing. When Karen wanted to go out with friends, alone, Mandy would look so miserable that Karen asked her along. There was almost no time for Karen to feel she had her own life—except in the bathroom!

It's important for couples to find a way to balance fusion and merging with separateness, identification with differentiation. Complete separateness in all endeavors and relationships is just as out of balance, just as likely to produce difficulties as total submersion of individuality within a couple identity. In the process of forging intimacy bonds that are to endure over time, equal attention must be given to maintaining each person's separate identity as a unique individual. Identity and intimacy are coequal developmental tasks, and they remain equally paramount throughout the course of life. They're not confined to just one particular phase of development.

Lesbians and gay men creating a committed relationship need to periodically attend to balancing a separate identity with intimacy. Jeff had a number of close friends whom he saw regularly, both women and men. His partner, Howard, knew some of them but was rarely a part of their usual socializing, which revolved around tennis, a sport Howard didn't like. Howard was involved in directing amateur theatre, and lots of his friends were actors and writers.

Jeff and Howard also had many friends whom they socialized with together as a couple. They knew the importance of continuing to have individual and separate relationships with others, and each also enjoyed some activities the other didn't. Neither one felt they had to do everything together, and neither felt threatened by the other's separate friendships. But they always talked about their separate activities, bringing the experience back into their relationship.

Separate Interests, Separate Time

Balancing the need for autonomy and individuality with the need for identification plays out in what may seem like less serious arenas. Not everyone embarking on a couple relationship is able to tolerate a partner's having interests, hobbies, and avocations in which the other person is not involved. Some people feel they should be included in everything their partner does; some resent the feeling of being excluded; and others feel vaguely threatened or even abandoned by the presence of competing interests of any kind.

> *I've always enjoyed photography, and when I moved in with Dennis, it was great to finally have a big apartment with a good darkroom. It's something I'm really passionate about, and I especially love taking photos of Dennis. I know on some weekends I spend a lot of time in there, but it relaxes me. Dennis was so generous in helping me set things up that I was completely unprepared for how critical he got. He started complaining to all our friends about how he never saw me, how I spent all my free time locked up away from him, how I probably didn't love him. It wasn't really true, and I didn't know what to say.*

Two people may have very different unspoken expectations about how a committed relationship will be conducted. Those expectations are rooted in scenes that originate in the past, beginning in the family but continuing through countless other contexts. We also actively construct such scenes in our imagination. We additionally absorb the limited cultural scripts we receive about how a romantic relationship is supposed to operate, and too often we aren't aware of their power over us.

> *When we started arguing about how much money I was spending on film, paper, and chemicals, I knew Dennis and I had to clear this up. Once we started talking, it all made sense. He felt neglected; I felt invaded. I was spending too much time alone, but that's because when I was growing up, my family was so crazy and intrusive, so that I always dreamed of having a place where no one could bother me. And Dennis grew up an only child with really cold parents, so he felt isolated from them, shoved away. Now that we know how we're vulnerable to being hurt by each other, things are a little easier. We talk about our families more, and we try to talk about how we're both feeling together, with each other.*

Both partners bring into their relationship different sets of scenes and scripts about how to be a couple, how to spend time together. The clash of expectations means that their scenes collide rather than converge. Usually, shame is the reaction triggered by such collisions between divergent scenes, between markedly different expectations regarding intimacy and separateness.

If one partner believes that being a couple means spending all available nonwork time together, but the other doesn't share those expectations, then the ground is laid for affect to erupt whenever those widely differing sets of expectations collide. Disappointed expectations always cause interpersonal strife.

Intimacy itself is a fluctuating experience. People in any couple relationship do not feel equally intimate all the time, but are actually more likely to experience periods of distance that fluctuate with periods of closeness. Distance is not necessarily a sign that something is wrong in the relationship.

Our individual needs for identification and differentiation oscillate over time, and so do intimacy and distance, which spring directly from these needs.

Couples must realize that they also differ in the relative strength of those needs in the first place. Some people simply need more time by themselves than others do. The important thing is not to experience our partner's distance as rejection. It's a challenge to handle circumstances whose potential for activating shame is seemingly unavoidable. We need to be able to openly converse about our expectations and about feeling separate or close in an atmosphere where such conversations don't breed shame or resentment.

Handling Finances

How money is handled in a relationship and how financial decisions are made reflects the power dynamics within that relationship. Will you and your partner merge finances, for example, into joint bank accounts and checking accounts, or will they be kept separate? If all of your money is going to be jointly held, who'll have control over spending it, and what about money that you earn separately? Is money earned separately but spent jointly?

If all your financial decisions must be joint ones, how will you and your partner reconcile different spending priorities and spending styles? Finally, how will you deal with large discrepancies in the actual income of each partner? Conscious attention to these important issues must include the maintenance of equal power within the relationship. That's especially important if one partner earns less, whether because of age or career. That partner may feel shame because of not contributing as much. The failure to carefully consider the handling of finances as a couple can result in powerlessness, with shame generating unnoticed.

This is an issue that we had to examine in our relationship and resolve on two different occasions. When we first bought our house and moved in together, our incomes were significantly different, requiring deliberate attention to how we would handle the inequality so as to avoid generating resentment. Initially, we decided to apportion each of our financial contributions to our joint living expenses in accordance with our actual incomes, though they were so different. Since Gershen earned more than Lev, Gershen simply paid more. But we divided the tasks of living and managing the home more or less equally, and the entire arrangement worked.

Several years later, Lev wanted to make a career shift from university teaching to writing full-time. We discussed this at length. Gershen willingly offered to assume the major if not total financial support for both of us. In the first year of this new arrangement, Lev was more dependent and felt he had to constantly explain what he was accomplishing now that he had more free time in which to write. We had to monitor and deal with the emergence of powerlessness and shame caused by Lev's sudden excessive dependence and also any possible resentment Gershen might feel. We found ourselves having to balance the unequal financial situation by finding other viable ways of contributing to the joint enterprise. Lev now took on the full responsibilities of shopping, cooking, and yard work as his reconfigured contribution to the household.

Our attention to the financial realities had to be matched by attention to the emotional realities. Being fully conscious as we went about the whole process helped us make major adjustments in our life together while also maintaining and preserving equal power.

Dividing Responsibilities at Home

Who will do what around the apartment or home? Dividing responsibilities for managing the shared home is partially influenced by each partner's expectations and scenes about those arrangements. Usually, those scenes were inherited from our families. There are basic tasks of living that either need to be designated for one partner to handle or must be shared. But a conscious focus on deciding the issue, even if the partners have to keep revisiting and deciding again, will ensure that disappointed expectations do not unexpectedly intrude.

Before Tamara moved in with her, Joyce almost always ate out because she was too tired after work to cook for herself. She was also accustomed to eating out a lot with her family and took it for granted. Tamara loved to cook, so she took on the responsibility for cooking without any discussion. Joyce quickly got used to coming home from work to find dinner ready, but she wasn't very appreciative, and Tamara grew resentful of all the time she spent shopping and planning meals. One night she just exploded: "Why don't you ever lift a finger around here! I'm sick of being your slave!" They had fallen into a pattern that ended up creating shame for Tamara because they had never bothered to talk about how they would handle things like preparing meals.

The question of sharing responsibilities is different when partners have separate residences. They may live and work in different cities, or they may not be ready to move in together. One or both of them may actually prefer to continue maintaining separate residences in order to preserve a measure of independence while also continuing to build a life together as a couple. Occasionally, questions of career may take precedence over living together in the same locale. In every instance, each partner's scenes will play a decisive role in influencing or even entirely determining the desired outcome.

Managing Dual Careers

Managing dual careers in any relationship is challenging, particularly in a society of increasing mobility and competition. Balancing the pressures and demands of two careers can present unexpected difficulties. Even the degree of involvement or commitment to their respective careers can be very different for the partners, leading to potential conflict over priorities, available time to spend together, even the perceived importance of their relationship versus their individual careers.

> *Nick is always pushing me to "make something" of myself, to do more than just wait tables. But I'm good at it, it's fun, and I make a lot in tips. He's a lawyer, everyone in his family is a professional of some kind, and he thinks I'm a failure. I'm not, I just don't think a job should be the focus of your life. I work to make money, that's all. I get my kicks elsewhere.*

Individual expectations about how we're supposed to blend career and relationship are also important. If one partner wants to move to another city because of better career opportunities and the other partner either does not wish to relocate or is already well established where they now live, how can the couple resolve this predicament to their mutual satisfaction? Whose career comes first? And if the second partner agrees to the move but later comes to feel he or she has given up too much, then powerlessness and resentment will likely breed. There are real dilemmas ahead however the couple proceeds on this issue, but talking about it openly and planning for it consciously is the only likely approach to preserve mutuality and equality in the relationship.

> *Stephanie spent so many years on her doctorate that when she got it, and got a college teaching job right away, we agreed to move together. I was really happy where I was, but since jobs were so scarce in her field, we both came to the decision that this time, her career would lead the way. It was great to move to Boston anyway, which was so much gayer than where we were. But we also agreed that if something solid came up for me down the road in another city, she would try to find a job there too, so that we'd both feel like we had a say. Her job led to our first move, so the next move would have to be connected to my career.*

There are also times in any person's career when we feel particularly powerless and thus more vulnerable to shame. We can be burdened by a homophobic boss or co-workers and feel trapped in a work environment in which we have to be closeted. This situation not only can be demoralizing for the person who's stuck but also can undermine the relationship.

Another source of division occurs when one partner is far more successful or satisfied in his or her work, which can leave the other open to shame-inducing comparisons: *How come I'm doing so badly?*

Mutual Interest in Having Children

It's no longer necessary for every individual to bear or raise offspring so that this species will survive. Becoming a parent, whether biologically or through foster parenting or adoption, requires a conscious desire to participate actively, directly, and consistently in raising children. That desire should be more than just looking to children to meet our own needs, but actually having something useful to give to the next generation.

Not everyone is interested in becoming a parent or especially suited to the unique frustrations and demands of parenting. Having children ought to be a free and equal choice—for everyone. With the decision to become parents, both partners have to be willing, interested, and prepared for the changes in their relationship that raising children inevitably brings. For lesbians and gay men, all of these questions are complicated by the ways in which society makes it difficult for them to adopt or raise children.

Lesbian or gay parenting is inevitably branded as a parody of family life because two women or two men are seen as incapable of providing a complete relationship in which to nurture children in a healthy fashion. Like intimacy and sexuality, parenting ostensibly requires two persons of different sexes.

But what children require more than anything else is to be demonstrably wanted and loved as persons in their own right and also to have their own love received and accepted as worthwhile. Children must be wanted by each parent involved; further, they must feel convinced of this love. Otherwise, they will experience shame.

For lesbians and gay men there are very real questions beyond foster parenting or adoption if they want to have children. If you're a lesbian, will you use artificial insemination with the aid of sperm donors? Will the donor be a stranger, someone you know, maybe even someone in your own or your partner's family? Will the donor be involved in coparenting? If you're a donor, will you tell your family? If both women want to bear children, who goes first?

The issue of ideological orientation and the existence of conflicting orientations between the partners will have an enormous impact in the arena of childrearing. This is where ideological clashes will erupt for a couple even when they were quiescent before. Exploring and sharing individual ideological stances is therefore vitally important for every couple desiring to become parents. It is these ideological postures that will determine, more than anything else, what your actual childrearing philosophies will be in the course of parenting. Will you govern your child by adherence to rules—and how strict will you be? Or will you be more concerned about your child's feelings of distress and shame than about breaking rules? If both partners operate from strongly opposed ideological positions, how and when will you be willing to compromise? And how do you raise a child to not feel that there's something wrong with one of the parents—the one who's "too strict" or "too soft"? How will you keep the child from trying to manipulate either one of you *because* of your different ideologies?

Being "Out" Versus "Not Out"

The question of how "out" each partner is becomes a potential source of divisiveness primarily when the two partners are at opposite ends of the continuum: one is very closeted while the other is very out, either in the community or politically. If the couple is to thrive precisely *as* a couple, then each must respect the other's comfort level and readiness to come out. Timing is everything. Each must be fully supportive of the other's personal decision on this profoundly important matter, even when fear and shame are what dictate hiding and secrecy. Encouragement is vital for the partner who is not ready to come out, but so are understanding and respect.

Angel is an AIDS activist and has been out since he was a teenager—he's never known any other way to present himself, and there isn't anyone in his family or life who doesn't know he's gay. His partner, Phil, teaches music in a high school across town and is paranoid about being "discovered" and falsely accused of molesting one of his students. Angel is dismissive of those concerns, saying they can always sue the school if someone files phony charges or if he's fired—or Phil can just get a job somewhere else. Angel's never lived with that level of shame about being gay or that intense fear of exposure, and he finds it hard to empathize.

The decision to self-identify as lesbian or gay is as deeply personal a decision as any you can ever make. Publicly claiming a gay or lesbian identity involves a deliberate choice to come out of the closet and, in doing so, to come out of shame. Sensitivity to shame in the more closeted partner by the partner who is already out will be of greatest benefit to both.

Having Relationships with Each Other's Family

If relationships with your own parents and family can be problematic when you're gay or lesbian, so are relationships with your partner's family. Exactly how to relate to each other's family is complicated by the question of how out each partner is to his or her own family. In a real sense, the partners must give one another permission to even *have* a relationship with each other's family. Then the possibilities for connection can be more freely explored by each person directly.

I have to admit that the first time Monica told me my mom had called when I wasn't home, and that she and my mom had a really long talk, I felt very uncomfortable. It was like a small invasion and I felt kind of paranoid—what were they saying about me? And because Monica's so established as a speech pathologist, while I'm still struggling with writing freelance, I felt jealous, like my mom would think better of her, would admire Monica, and think less of me. Whenever my mom called after that, and asked to chat with Monica, too, I got steamed. Finally we had it out, and Monica said that if I didn't like it, she would back off and not try to be friends with my mom. Her saying that made a difference and made me see I was being unreasonable. Now they talk on the phone a lot, and it feels much better to me.

Relationships must be reciprocal in order to be genuine. Whether the other partner's family is truly receptive to having a relationship also has to be carefully and sensitively explored. The families of gay men and lesbians may have their own shame to contend with, and, when present, that shame is the principal impediment to their relating more freely. But carefully approaching such matters as a couple, first with each other and then with each set of family members, is a good way to facilitate a relationship between each partner and the other's family.

It wasn't easy growing up an only child, so it amazed me that Monica had six brothers and sisters and a battalion of aunts, uncles, cousins. Christmas was like a show at Radio City Music Hall—you practically had to have a ticket! I sometimes felt overwhelmed by all the noise and commotion and how open they were about us being a couple. Then the birthday cards I got, the presents! After the stuff with my mother on the phone, Monica told me she had no trouble with my connecting to anyone in her family, to go ahead if it felt right. So I'm closer to some of her relatives now than she is, partly because of work interests, but for lots of other reasons, too. I feel like a member of her family for sure.

Sometimes we can relate much more easily to our partner's family than to our own. That's because we have no history with them, no troubled past of resentments, disappointments, or hurts. When this happens it can sometimes result in shame if we see our partner relaxed and confident with the very people we have struggled against: *Why can't I do that? Why can't I be that laid back?* Many of us have also probably experienced moments when a friend says, "I really like your parents" and we wonder how anyone could possibly come to that conclusion.

The way your partner's family reacts to your being gay can be even more puzzling. Your partner's family may find it much easier to accept your homosexuality, and even talk more openly about it, because there is some distance and safety for them.

> *Monica told me that my mother asked her if she thought being gay was genetic, and was there anyone in her family Monica thought was gay, too. It blew me away! My mother's never even mentioned anything like that with me, and I was depressed until Monica said, "At least she's talking to somebody, right?"*

Including Non-Gay Friends

Usually, gay and lesbian couples also have friends who are non-gay, but who are gay positive to varying degrees. How to include those friends in the couple's life, along with their other gay and lesbian friends, isn't necessarily a problem but will likely require at least a measure of reflection. Again, this is best handled by considering the matter together as a couple. For example, one partner may want to include both gay and non-gay friends at the same social events, whereas the other partner may feel uncomfortable doing so and actually prefers to keep the two circles of friends entirely separate. There is no right or wrong answer, and no way that will necessarily work equally well for all individuals. Each partner's own comfort level, along with the comfort of both their gay and non-gay friends, will be decisive.

Patrick didn't like straight men and stereotyped them as the bullies and thugs he had grown up with in his family and at school. He was very uncomfortable around Ivan's best friend from work, who was straight. *Why does he want to hang out with us? Is it a freak show for him—or is he really a closet case?* The simple friendship Ivan enjoyed seemed suspicious and even threatening to Patrick, so they agreed that Ivan should socialize with his friend on his own.

In certain parts of the country, it's quite possible to have mainly gay friends or even to be surrounded entirely by gay neighbors. Some lesbians and gays are so used to being in an all-gay environment that they feel totally out of place and exposed when they leave their enclave. They may be surprised to experience shame elsewhere when they feel suffused by gay pride at home.

But in most parts of the country it's not possible to live as you would in the Castro, for instance; you're far more likely to be in the minority. Where we actually live influences to some extent how we interact with others, gay and non-gay alike.

Friendship with non-gays is complicated further by how out each partner is in various settings like work, church or synagogue, and the community at large. Even when both partners are out to everyone they know, some of their lesbian or gay friends may not be out; that fact must be considered when bringing together gays and non-gays at the same social event. The presence of someone who is non-gay, however gay positive they may be, can still cause discomfort in gays who are closeted. An innocent social gathering can unintentionally become an occasion for outing someone.

Being Politically Active

Some gays and lesbians join causes, march in public demonstrations, and participate actively in gay or lesbian community events. But many others do not affiliate in such public ways or seek involvement in activism. Not everyone is a political activist, nor should every person be expected to become one. Certain people come to social and political activism quite early in life, others arrive at it much later, while some never do. Unfortunately, some stay closeted because of the fear that coming out will *require* them to be an activist.

If one partner is inclined toward activism but the other is not, strain can generate in their relationship unless there is mutual respect for the differences. *Invitations* to participate are never experienced the same way as *pressure* to participate. We can offer encouragement, but we have to do so with respect.

Jim was my first lover and the first man I lived with. I was swept up in finally coming out, in the excitement of being in love, but he scared the hell out of me. He was beyond out. There wasn't a lesbian/gay committee in our town he didn't serve on. He was always organizing protests, getting petitions going, testifying at hearings, appearing in the paper and on the radio. It terrified me. He was this Gay Avenger, and I felt like a little country mouse. But right from the start, I told him that I wasn't ready to picket or protest. He just grinned: "Not yet, you aren't." It was cool with him; he didn't expect me to be him.

When the two partners are at opposite ends of the spectrum on this issue, regardless of the reasons, the involvement in activism by one partner might become a cause of resentment and even shame for the other. That partner may feel less out or less gay, or like a "bad" gay. This can happen when political activism actually supersedes other common interests or is perceived to do so. If the nonactivist partner is also deeply closeted, then the other partner's activism can be perceived as a threat: *People recognize her all over town—if they see us together, they'll know I'm a lesbian!*

Only conveying genuine respect for essential differences and granting each other the right to self-determination for such questions can ever be the basis of equal power in a relationship. Examining this issue openly and honestly as a couple is the best way to forestall difficulties later.

Religious/Spiritual Expression

Given the rejection that lesbians and gay men have largely experienced from organized religion, barring certain exceptions, the issue of faith and religion remains problematic for many of us. There is a spiritual dimension to human experience and, like every other quality, the need to express it will vary from person to person. The need to identify with something larger than ourselves—with Nature, with humanity as a whole, with whatever we conceive of as the divine—though universal, can be stronger in one person and weaker in another. Much depends on each person's prior encounters with religion, both through particular teachings and specific individuals. Each person's experience of the spiritual or the divine is always a deeply private affair.

The two partners can also come from very different religious faiths, for example one Catholic and the other Jewish, and their levels of religious observance and depth of faith can be quite different as well. They can also be of the same faith, but still from very different backgrounds.

Mary and Sharon were both raised Protestant, but only Sharon still goes to church regularly. Her pastor is gay positive and even blessed them as a couple. But Mary always resented being force-fed religion as a girl, and her resentment bars any church involvement. They have been quite open with each other about their religious differences, particularly since Sharon feels a strong need to share this part of her life with Mary and wants them both to participate more actively in various church activities. This has caused a great deal of tension between them which they have had to face head-on. Being open about the tension has not resolved it, and questions like this may not be resolvable. But it hasn't divided them as a couple, even though it's a source of real difference.

Ideally, couples are in harmony on this matter, but more often they experience varying degrees of discord. You may try to impose your own way on your partner, or you may look down on and disparage your partner's views or preferences. Either approach will only generate conflict and sow dissention through inducing shame.

SHARING DREAMS, CREATING A FUTURE

We construct our lives around dreams of enjoyment and excitement. What we imagine for ourselves and anticipate in the future pulls us forward in different, sometimes changing directions.

From as far back as I can remember, I wanted to go to France and rediscover my family's heritage. It really bothered me that we had a French name but nobody even spoke it anymore. I studied French on my own before I could even take it in school, eventually got really good at it, and in college my dream started to come true. I spent a whole year studying in France, traveling around the country, and discovering women. I think I knew I was a lesbian as early as first grade, but I'd always been afraid to do anything about it. I was so exhilarated

*by being in France, though, that I had the courage to try. I
loved it there, was determined to come back, but in my senior
year back home, I met Barb, and the idea of a life together
took over. That meant more to me than anything. Eventually
the two dreams converged, because Barb convinced me to go
into education and become a French teacher, which is what I
did. Now I take classes of mine to Paris every year. I feel so
lucky to have my new dream, and the old.*

Through the scenes we envision in the future, we experience purpose
and meaning in life. Then we command into being those compelling scenes
of deepest and enduring affect in which we cast ourselves as hero. We're
compelled to enact those dreams for our future. They're like dramas we first
"write" by imagining ourselves playing them over and over. They shape the
contours of our lives.

In any couple, dreams may be a source of tension, impossible to reconcile. While two sets of dreams envisioned by the partners may be closely
aligned early in their relationship, later their dreams may change and begin
to pull them in very different directions. In any relationship, dreams have to
be expressed openly in order to see how well they converge, both at the
outset and throughout. Ideally, for the relationship to flourish there have to
be certain shared dreams that are significant and highly prized. Shared
dreams are vitally important agents of bonding for the future.

For gay men and lesbians, the whole question of dreams is complicated
by the nightmares we've grown up with. Our society has told us we're sick,
evil, perverted, child molesters, superficial, promiscuous. Not so long ago,
the culture told us that gays ended up committing suicide: "Show me a
happy homosexual, and I'll show you a gay corpse." Now we're told we'll
all die of AIDS or be damned to hell.

It's important to fight that vicious undertow by recognizing its force,
its ability to shame us, and by transforming those scenes of doom into scenes
of strength, commitment, love, creation, power, pride, and hope.

*The first time I ever heard anyone say the word "homo" I
was ten and my parents were making fun of this older male couple
sitting on a park bench. I remember they wore neck scarves and
lots of jewelry, and their pants were too tight. My parents sneered*

at them like they were disgusting, and my mother said, "They'll end up stabbing each other—they all do." I thought about that years later when I started coming out. It was so hard for me to look in the mirror and not feel like I was as gross as my parents thought those two guys were.

When my first lover wanted us to get an apartment together, I freaked. Sex seemed so different from thinking of us as a couple. A couple of men? I just couldn't picture it—it didn't seem possible. And I kept wondering what my parents would say. I couldn't do it, and we broke up.

It took me years of building a life I was proud of to feel that I could live with another man, that I had a right to be happy, to be myself. Alex and I have even become role models for younger gay couples we know. They think we're amazing because we've been together twenty years. Given where I came from, I guess I am pretty amazing!

Revisioning Our Lives, Reinventing Ourselves

On this journey out of shame we have explored the interplay between shame and gay experience on many levels: societal and cultural, family and peer group, individual and interpersonal. Shame is a dynamic that operates, silently or visibly, in each one of these domains, just as each domain, in turn, influences and shapes emerging gay identity. These different domains are, in fact, embedded within one another, making shame a distinctive multilayered phenomenon of enormous significance.

All human beings stand equal in the sudden exposure wrought by shame, women along with men, gay and non-gay alike. Shame shadows each of us, and everyone encounters the alienating affect in some form, at some time. Entering that experience long enough to endure it, deliberately and consciously in order to transform it, is a challenge which knows no bounds.

Yet only by facing that challenge can we ever hope to re-create who we are. To finally triumph over shame requires fundamental inner resources: courage to suffer and determination to prevail. With these in place we can launch the process of reinventing ourselves with confidence assured, but never certainty.

What we have attempted to do in this book is to show a way, create choices, reveal possibilities—illuminate *how* to revision our lives. But grave challenges still await us as we speed toward the coming millennium.

Foremost is the continued advancement of gay rights toward full equality. But even that argument can be reframed by asking a different question: What is a civilized society's responsibility to its members? Does society have a responsibility to include *all* of its citizens equally?

Another challenge will be creating new community, viable new forms for gay and lesbian relationships, families, and social organizations. Related to that task is continuing to find ways of celebrating gay and lesbian life. We must actively work to transform shame scripts into celebratory scripts. Coming out groups, support groups, and youth programs for lesbians and gay men directly facilitate the celebration of being gay and the dissolution of shame along with it. Pride marches are still another major way to generate enjoyment and excitement about being gay or lesbian, to publicly celebrate gayness. Other avenues to celebration are through the arts and the media, such as literature, painting and photography, music and comedy, television and film.

We need new images of ourselves. We need to see ourselves in films and on television so we can have new images reflected back to us—positive images that are freeing, enduring. We need them desperately as we go about the task of reinventing ourselves. The burgeoning lesbian and gay film festivals are an example of creating our own images in a medium where they're all too scarce.

We continue to face challenges in the exercise of political power, in gay activism. This is true in regard to AIDS, gays serving in the military, state ballot initiatives aimed at excluding gays from civil rights protection, and appropriate inclusion of gay-related subjects in various public school curricula. Ideology prevents people from embracing new knowledge, and ideology will continue to hold sway in the ensuing national debate over gay issues. Ideology will play out in every corner of society because the long-standing silence about homosexuality has been broken, and breaking that silence is irreversible. The debate over gays in the military or including homosexuality in the curriculum will be equally fueled by fact and fiction, by both knowledge and ideology.

At an entirely different level, the recent emergence of gay studies programs in colleges and universities is a more hopeful sign. It is through our educational system, particularly at the level of higher education, that we have the greatest opportunity to effect change in societal institutions. Here we can impact the educational system directly in order to normalize and legitimize gay experience. But despite some encouraging signs, the process has only just begun and obstacles inevitably remain.

The celebration of gay life must include an intimate understanding of gay shame if we are to place gay pride on a solid, secure footing. We can't ignore or underestimate the impact of shame in our community, whether through addiction, political infighting, denial, or contempt for other gays and lesbians. The pursuit of gay activism must be informed by an understanding of shame, particularly at the societal level; otherwise gay power will ultimately be undermined. Attaining a measure of power may deceive us into believing that shame has been vanquished, when it still operates to undermine our resolve and self-esteem. We need to neutralize shame in order to have real power.

Confronting and counteracting homophobia and heterosexism is a case in point. Ideology dies hard. Individuals will cling to their beliefs about homosexuality as matters of fundamental faith just as they do about abortion. They will sometimes even die or kill for their ideological beliefs. What we must do is actively confront homophobia directly whenever it appears, in whatever guise, and confront it specifically in terms of affect. We can expose ideology, *name* it for what it is, and unmask the particular affects that are being communicated or engendered directly in other people. That exposure will help make those ideas less powerful, less attractive, and hopefully less prevalent.

When others seek to shame us by quoting the Bible, they are hiding behind ancient religious texts whose equally strident rules they often choose to disregard in other contexts. We can use the knowledge gained from an understanding of shame to our advantage. We can sidestep the attempt to embroil us in ideological debate by focusing directly on the actual affects on the homophobes' faces and in their words. We have to uncover and *name* the disgust, the anger, the contempt—and call attention to their intention of inducing shame.

Since religion remains a persistent source of shame about being gay or lesbian, it will be a continuing challenge into the next century. All those who claim that God hates sin but loves the sinner have to be made to face the consequences of their rhetoric. Gay bashers and murderers of gay men or lesbians do not make such elegant distinctions. All those who denounce us in the name of God are fueled by hatred masquerading as compassion. It's time we stand up to them and say, "You will shame us no longer."

There is some hope in the fact that evolution is the essence of religion, as any student of the great religions knows. From our own cultural/religious vantage point, there is a movement within Judaism called Reconstructionism that conceives of Judaism as an evolving religious civilization. Gay and lesbian Jews have been openly embraced by two branches of American Judaism: Reconstructionism and Reform. In the process of creating bridges with Judaism, gay and lesbian Jews have been immersed in a profound transformation.

Through the leadership of Jewish lesbians and women generally, new liturgy is being written to reflect the general experience of women and to include the more specific experience of gays and lesbians. Even Torah (the Hebrew Bible), which Jews have historically referred to as a "Tree of Life," is being reinterpreted, given new meaning in the light of the contemporary needs of the Jewish people. The telling prohibitions recounted in Leviticus are undergoing reinterpretation by Judaic scholars, just as the Torah was reinterpreted by the rabbis in every age. The meanings we have been given are based only on translation over the centuries, translations *of translations.* Much of the original meaning is lost, so that those specific prohibitions must also be read in the context of the Torah taken as a whole. For example, Leviticus includes the infamous verse (18:22) "You shall not lie with a man as with a woman; it is an abomination." But that injunction must also be read in the context of another famous verse in Leviticus (19:18): "You shall love your neighbor as yourself," a transcendent injunction that can be used to counteract messages of intolerance and put them in an entirely different perspective.

A revitalized and re-created Jewish community is in the making, one that includes Jews who are lesbian and gay. As a rabbi argued several years ago in his Rosh Hashanah (New Year) sermon, "Our attitude towards gays and lesbians is a *true test* of the depth of our commitment to the Torah's human values. Judaism's moral strength is tested not by how narrowly we may define its parameters, but rather how broadly we can draw its circle."[1] The same could be said about the values of every faith.

. . .

We have our own deeply personal story to tell in this challenging context of bridging sexuality and religion. We are two Jewish men who had felt alienated from Judaism and other Jews throughout our lives, in large measure because we knew we were gay. That secret awareness always barred full entry into the Jewish community, full inclusion. Where we could have felt most at home, especially during religious services, we felt most like strangers.

Our story begins about five years ago in Toronto, Canada, where we attended our first Conference of Gay and Lesbian Jews. There we were introduced to the World Congress of Gay and Lesbian Jewish Organizations, of which this was a regional meeting. For the first time in our lives, we entered a room with over a hundred other Jewish men and women who were also gay. Slowly we looked about us for a long while, silently drinking all of them in with our eyes, knowing we were about to join in prayer as we had done so many times before. But this time was different.

We were the congregation. Even one of the rabbis was gay. Then we opened our prayer books and prayed together as a community, the way Jews have prayed together for over two thousand years. Our unique experience as gays and lesbians was openly included and celebrated in the prayers we read out loud during the service. We had been written directly into the liturgy.

At times we stood in silent prayer as a congregation, at other times we joined our voices together to sing our prayers out loud, in unison. We sang the ancient melodies that transcend time.

As the two of us slowly entered into prayer that fateful evening, embraced in a new congregation, feeling first surprised and then astonished, we were drawn ever more deeply into the service, and to each other. We gazed into each other's eyes. We felt unashamedly overcome by emotion, our arms tightly about each other, and we felt immense awe, struck by the enormity of what was happening—with tears streaming down our cheeks, and joy in our hearts.

At long last, we had come home.

Deep inside, we felt whole.

Such wholeness is difficult to describe, and the inadequacy of our language reveals one of the lasting barriers to dealing with gay shame: a failure to articulate our experience as one without shame. To break our shame binds and release our identity from the shackles of shame, we have to be able to name who we are and who we love. Sadly, the language we have all inherited for describing same-sex relationships restricts those relationships to an erotic basis, an endless source of discomfort and shame.

The term *lover* is a case in point, which we have not been able to avoid in this book. What we need is a new language to express loving and sexual relationships with persons of the same sex, but a language that does not merely mimic heterosexual relationships. Terms like *husband, wife,* and *spouse* are derived from heterosexual marriage and generate a sense of shame and inadequacy when used in a gay context.

Unfortunately, *lover* still defines our relationships primarily in sexual terms. Even though we like to think we have invented a new meaning for this term, that meaning is not generally shared, either in the lesbian and gay communities or in our wider society. An alternative is *companion* or *partner,* though the former makes the relationship appear less meaningful than it actually is and the latter almost makes it sound like a business relationship. Lev once introduced himself at a local community social gathering as Gershen's partner, and the woman he was speaking to said, "Oh, I didn't know Gershen had gone into business with someone!" Life-partner is a somewhat more accurate term, but unwieldy, and its other form, partner-in-living, sounds like the parallel of partner-in-crime.

Why so much bother about a few words? Because language invariably shapes perception. It is also one of our most important methods for making images, for actively engaging imagination. How we envision both ourselves and our relationships is inevitably molded by the language we use for describing them. Every language must remain alive, open, and changing. It has to invent new words and also experiment with new usages for old words, thereby discovering entirely new meanings in what it has to say.[2] The language we use, therefore, can either limit the possibilities we see or else set our imagination free.

What we need at this point in our evolution is a new language for sexual orientation, sexual identity, as well as intimate relationships between persons of the same sex—a language that is not limiting but expanding. To release gays and lesbians from the chains of their culture, to free the gay and lesbian imagination from the oppression of silence, to imagine new possibilities for gay communities and new forms for gay families, we must invent new words and create a new language.

But until new words evolve, we must reclaim the words we have. By transforming shame, we can begin to reclaim the words *lesbian, gay,* and *lover.* In this context, we understand one of the most painful words we know: *queer.* If we can be cultural workers by being out and proud, then we can transform what these words mean and dissolve the shame surrounding our identities.

By transforming our lives through coming out of shame, we transform the culture's perception and understanding of our lives, finally breaking the equation that *gay = shame.*

Notes

NOTES TO PROLOGUE

1. Holleran, A. "Linoleum City." *Christopher Street,* 13 (No. 3, Issue 147): 4–7.
2. Collins, Mark R. "Making a Scene." *10 Percent,* January/February 1995: 65.
3. Fay, R. E., Turner, C. F., Klassen, A. D., and Gagnon, J. H. "Prevalence and Patterns of Same-Gender Sexual Contact Among Men." *Science,* 243 (1989): 338–48. See also Rogers, S. M., and Turner, C. F. "Male-Male Sexual Contact in the U.S.A.: Findings from Five Sample Surveys, 1970–1990." *The Journal of Sex Research,* 28 (1991): 491–519.
4. Personal communication.

NOTES TO CHAPTER ONE

1. Kaplan, R. D. *Balkan Ghosts: A Journey Through History.* New York: St. Martin's Press, 1993.
2. Tomkins, S. S. *Affect, Imagery, Consciousness: The Negative Affects,* vol. 2. New York: Springer, 1963, p. 118.
3. Tomkins, S. S. *Affect, Imagery, Consciousness,* vols. 1–4. New York: Springer, 1962, 1963, 1991, 1992.
4. Ekman, P. "Universals and Cultural Differences in Facial Expressions of Emotion." In J. K. Cole (Ed.), *Nebraska Symposium on Motivation,* 19 (1971): 207–83. See also Ekman, P. *Emotion in the Human Face,* 2nd ed. Cambridge: Cambridge University Press, 1982, pp. 147–53.

Notes

5. Tomkins, S. S. "Shame." In D. L. Nathanson (Ed.), *The Many Faces of Shame.* New York: Guilford Press, 1987, p. 137.

6. Tomkins, S. S. *Affect, Imagery, Consciousness: The Negative Affects—Anger and Fear,* vol. 3. New York: Springer, 1991, p. 6.

7. Tomkins, 1963, pp. 3–6.

8. Tomkins, 1987, p. 138. See also Tomkins, 1991, pp. 9–13.

9. Tomkins, 1991, p. 7.

10. Tomkins, 1991, pp. 15–18.

11. Tomkins, 1962, p. 27.

12. Tomkins, 1991, p. 74.

13. Tomkins, 1991, pp. 74–77.

14. Tomkins, 1991, pp. 87–88.

15. See *Shame: The Power of Caring; Psychology of Shame: Theory and Treatment of Shame-Based Syndromes;* and *Dynamics of Power: Fighting Shame and Building Self-Esteem.*

16. Ekman, 1982.

17. Tomkins, 1963, p. 133.

18. Tomkins, 1991, pp. 22–23.

19. Tomkins, 1991, pp. 22–23, 534.

20. Tomkins, 1991, pp. 51–54.

21. This is demonstrated, for example, by the discovery that shame is a compelling theme in the life of Edith Wharton, the early-twentieth-century American novelist, as well as in much of her fiction. See Raphael, L. *Edith Wharton's Prisoners of Shame: A New Perspective on Her Neglected Fiction.* New York: St. Martin's Press, 1991.

22. Tomkins, 1987, p. 137.

23. Alter, J., and Wingert, P. "The Return of Shame." *Newsweek,* February 6, 1995: 20–25.

24. Tomkins, 1963, p. 123.

25. Tomkins, 1963, pp. 123–28.

26. Kaufman, G. *Shame: The Power of Caring,* 3rd ed. Rochester, Vt.: Schenkman Books, 1992, pp. 12–17. See also Kaufman, G. *The Psychology of Shame: Theory and Treatment of Shame-Based Syndromes.* New York: Springer, 1989, pp. 32–35.

27. Piers, G., and Singer, M. B. *Shame and Guilt: A Psychoanalytic and a Cultural Study.* Springfield, Ill.: Charles C. Thomas, 1953; reprint, New York: Norton, 1971.

28. Kaufman, G., and Raphael, L. "Shame as Taboo in American Culture." In R. Browne (Ed.), *Forbidden Fruits: Taboos and Tabooism in Culture.* Bowling Green, Ohio: Popular Press, 1984. See also Kaufman, 1989.

29. Gilligan, C. *In a Different Voice.* Cambridge, Mass.: Harvard University Press, 1982.

30. Tomkins, 1991, p. 229. See also pp. 229–53.

31. Tomkins, 1991, p. 236.

32. Tomkins, 1991, p. 236.
33. Tomkins, 1991, p. 236.

NOTES TO CHAPTER TWO

1. Bayer, R. *Homosexuality and American Psychiatry: The Politics of Diagnosis.* Princeton, N.J.: Princeton University Press, 1987.
2. Goldstein, R. "A Geshrei." *Voice,* November 1, 1991: 34.
3. Tomkins, 1963.
4. Leites, E. *The Puritan Conscience and Modern Sexuality.* New Haven, Conn.: Yale University Press, 1986.
5. Ng, V. W. "Homosexuality and the State in Late Imperial China." In M. Duberman, M. Vicinus, and G. Chauncey, Jr. (Eds.), *Hidden from History: Reclaiming the Gay and Lesbian Past.* New York: Meridian, 1990, pp. 76–89.
6. Williams, W. L. *The Spirit and the Flesh: Sexual Diversity in American Indian Culture.* Boston: Beacon Press, 1992, pp. 131–40.
7. Wood, F. G. *The Arrogance of Faith: Christianity and Race in America from the Colonial Era to the Twentieth Century.* New York: Alfred A. Knopf, 1990.
8. Wood, 1990, p. 250.
9. Bissinger, H. G. "The Killing Trail." *Vanity Fair,* February 1995: 145.
10. Boswell, J. *Christianity, Social Tolerance, and Homosexuality: Gay People in Western Europe from the Beginning of the Christian Era to the Fourteenth Century.* Chicago: University of Chicago Press, 1981.
11. Al-Khayyat, S. *Honour and Shame: Women in Modern Iraq.* London: Saqi Books, 1990.
12. Crompton, L. *Byron and Greek Love: Homophobia in 19th-Century England.* Berkeley, Calif.: University of California Press, 1985.
13. Monette, P. *Becoming a Man.* New York: Harcourt Brace Jovanovich, 1992, p. 2.

NOTES TO CHAPTER THREE

1. Dunlap, D. W. "Gay Leaders Resist Attacks on Gains." *New York Times,* February 12, 1995: 16.
2. Welsh, P. "It May Be the Safest Sex, but It's Risky to Talk About It." *Washington Post National Weekly Edition,* December 26, 1994–January 1, 1995: 25.
3. Tomkins, 1963, pp. 157–59.
4. Tomkins, 1963, pp. 171–83.
5. Tomkins, 1991, pp. 96–100.
6. Sullivan, H. S. *Clinical Studies in Psychiatry.* New York: Norton, 1956.
7. Bronowski, J. *The Identity of Man.* Garden City, N.Y.: Natural History Press, 1971.
8. Bean, T. "A Love Poem for White Boys Who Don't Know Who I Am." In A. Saint (Ed.), *The Road Before Us.* New York: Galiens Press, 1991, p. 15.

Notes

NOTES TO CHAPTER FOUR

1. Tomkins, 1963, pp. 301–48.
2. Tomkins, 1991, pp. 13–15.
3. Tomkins, 1962, p. 346.
4. Tomkins, 1991, pp. 254–58. See also Tomkins, S. S. "Script Theory." In J. Aronoff, A. I. Rabin, and R. A. Zucker (Eds.), *The Emergence of Personality.* New York: Springer, 1987, pp. 185–96.
5. Tomkins, 1987, p. 195.
6. Tomkins, 1987, p. 193.
7. Tomkins, 1963, pp. 267–70.
8. Tomkins, 1963, p. 269.
9. Tomkins, 1963, pp. 270–72.
10. Tomkins, 1963, pp. 272–76.

NOTES TO CHAPTER FIVE

1. Tomkins, 1991, pp. 25–36, 230–38, 250–51. See also Tomkins, S. S. "Affect and the Psychology of Knowledge." In S. S. Tomkins and C. E. Izard (Eds.), *Affect, Cognition, and Personality.* New York: Springer, 1965. See also Tomkins, S. S. "The Right and the Left: A Basic Dimension of Ideology and Personality." In R. W. White (Ed.), *The Study of Lives.* New York: Atherton, 1963.
2. Leites, 1986.

NOTES TO EPILOGUE

1. Sternfield, M. P. "A Greater Judaism in the Making." San Diego, Calif.: Congregation Beth Israel, 1990.
2. Bronowski, 1971.

Selected Bibliography

Al-Khayyat, S. *Honour and Shame: Women in Modern Iraq.* London: Saqi Books, 1990.

Broucek, F. J. *Shame and the Self.* New York: Guilford Press, 1991.

Ekman, P., Levenson, R. W., and Friesen, W. V. "Autonomic Nervous System Activity Distinguishes Among Emotions." *Science,* 221 (1983): 1208–10.

English, F. "Shame and Social Control." *Transactional Analysis Journal,* 5 (1975): 24–28.

Fossum, M., and Mason, M. *Facing Shame.* New York: Norton, 1986.

Jacoby, M. *Shame and the Origins of Self-Esteem: A Jungian Approach.* London: Routledge, 1994.

Johnson, G., Kaufman, G., and Raphael, L. *A Teacher's Guide to Stick Up for Yourself.* Minneapolis, Minn.: Free Spirit Publishing, 1991.

Kaufman, G. "The Meaning of Shame: Towards a Self-Affirming Identity." *Journal of Counseling Psychology,* 21 (1974): 568–74.

———. "On Shame, Identity, and the Dynamics of Change." Paper presented at symposium, Papers in Memory of Bill Kell: Issues on Therapy and the Training of Therapists. The Meeting of the American Psychological Association, New Orleans, 1974.

———. "Dynamics and Treatment of Shame-Based Syndromes." In *Proceedings of the Eighth and Ninth Annual Adult Psychiatric Day Treatment Forum.* Minneapolis, Minn.: University of Minnesota, 1986.

———. "Disorders of Self-Esteem: Psychotherapy for Shame-Based Syndromes." In P. A. Keller and S. R. Heyman (Eds.), *Innovations in Clinical Practice: A*

Source Book, vol. 6, pp. 53–62. Sarasota, Fla.: Professional Resource Exchange, 1987.

―――. *The Psychology of Shame: Theory and Treatment of Shame-Based Syndromes.* New York: Springer, 1989.

―――. "The Role of Shame in the Differential Patterning of Gender Socialization: A New Psychological Perspective." Paper presented at the National Conference on Re-Visioning Knowledge and the Curriculum: Feminist Perspectives, Michigan State University, East Lansing, Michigan, 1990.

―――. (Speaker). "From Shame to Self-Empowerment: Origins, Healing, and Treatment Issues." Newton, Mass.: Lifecycle Learning Cassettes, 1990.

―――. (Speaker). "Shame-Based Syndromes: Theory and Treatment." Robesonia, Penn.: Logan Audio Publishing, 1991.

―――. *Shame: The Power of Caring,* 3rd ed. Rochester, Vt.: Schenkman Books, 1992.

―――. *The Psychology of Shame: Theory and Treatment of Shame-Based Syndromes.* London: Routledge, 1993.

―――. *Journey to the Magic Castle.* Sepulveda, Calif.: Double M Press, 1993.

―――, and Raphael, L. (Speakers). "Listening to Your Inner Voices" (Cassette Recording No. 20275). Washington, D.C.: Psychology Today Tapes, 1983.

―――. "Relating to the Self: Changing Inner Dialogue." *Psychological Reports,* 54 (1984): 239–50.

―――. "Shame as Taboo in American Culture." In R. Browne (Ed.), *Forbidden Fruits: Taboos and Tabooism in Culture.* Bowling Green, Ohio: Popular Press, 1984.

―――. "Shame: A Perspective on Jewish Identity." *Journal of Psychology and Judaism,* 11 (1987): 30–40.

―――. *Stick Up for Yourself! Every Kid's Guide to Personal Power and Positive Self-Esteem.* Minneapolis, Minn.: Free Spirit Publishing, 1990.

―――. *Dynamics of Power: Fighting Shame and Building Self-Esteem,* 2nd ed. Rochester, Vt.: Schenkman Books, 1991.

―――. *Defiéndete!* Col. Sta. Cruz Atoyac, Mexico: Editorial Pax Mexico, 1992.

Lewis, H. B. *Shame and Guilt in Neurosis.* New York: International Universities Press, 1971.

―――― (Ed.). *The Role of Shame in Symptom Formation.* Hillsdale, N.J.: Erlbaum, 1987.

Lewis, M. *Shame: The Exposed Self.* New York: Free Press, 1992.

Lynd, H. M. *On Shame and the Search for Identity.* New York: Harcourt, Brace, 1958.

Morrison, A. P. *Shame: The Underside of Narcissism.* Hillsdale, N.J.: Analytic Press, 1989.

Nathanson, D. L. (Ed.). *The Many Faces of Shame.* New York: Guilford Press, 1987.

―――. *Shame and Pride: Affect, Sex, and the Birth of the Self.* New York: Norton, 1992.

Peristiany, J. G. *Honour and Shame*. Chicago: University of Chicago Press, 1974.

——, and Pitt-Rivers, J. (Eds.). *Honor and Grace in Anthropology*. Cambridge: Cambridge University Press, 1992.

Piers, G., and Singer, M. B. *Shame and Guilt: A Psychoanalytic and a Cultural Study*. Springfield, Ill.: Charles C. Thomas, 1953; reprint, New York: Norton, 1971.

Raphael, L. *Edith Wharton's Prisoners of Shame: A New Perspective on Her Neglected Fiction*. New York: St. Martin's Press, 1991.

Scheff, T. J., and Retzinger, S. M. *Emotions and Violence: Shame and Rage in Destructive Conflicts*. Lexington, Mass.: Lexington Books, 1991.

Schneider, C. D. *Shame, Exposure, and Privacy*. New York: Norton, 1992.

Tomkins, S. S. *Affect, Imagery, Consciousness: The Positive Affects*, vol. 1. New York: Springer, 1962.

——. *Affect, Imagery, Consciousness: The Negative Affects*, vol. 2. New York: Springer, 1963.

——. "Affect and the Psychology of Knowledge." In S. S. Tomkins and C. Izard (Eds.), *Affect, Cognition, and Personality*. New York: Springer, 1965.

——. "The Phantasy Behind the Face." *Journal of Personality Assessment*, 39 (1975): 551–62.

——. "Script Theory: Differential Magnification of Affects." In H. E. Howe and R. A. Dienstbier (Eds.), *Nebraska Symposium on Motivation*, vol. 26, pp. 201–36. Lincoln, Nebr.: University of Nebraska Press, 1979.

——. "The Quest for Primary Motives: Biography and Autobiography of an Idea." *Journal of Personality and Social Psychology*, 41 (1981): 306–29.

——. "Affect Theory." In P. Ekman (Ed.), *Emotion in the Human Face*. Cambridge, Mass.: Cambridge University Press, 1982.

——. "Affect Theory." In K. R. Scherer and P. Ekman (Eds.), *Approaches to Emotion*. Hillsdale, N.J.: Erlbaum, 1984.

——. "Shame." In D. L. Nathanson (Ed.), *The Many Faces of Shame*. New York: Guilford Press, 1987.

——. "Script Theory." In J. Aronoff, A. I. Rabin, and R. A. Zucker (Eds.), *The Emergence of Personality*. New York: Springer, 1987.

——. *Affect, Imagery, Consciousness: The Negative Affects—Anger and Fear*, vol. 3. New York: Springer, 1991.

——. *Affect, Imagery, Consciousness: Cognition—Duplication and Transformation of Information*, vol. 4. New York: Springer, 1992.

Wurmser, L. *The Mask of Shame*. Baltimore: Johns Hopkins University Press, 1981.

ABOUT THE AUTHORS

GERSHEN KAUFMAN is the author of two previous books on the subject of shame. A professor at Michigan State University, he lectures widely on shame and self-esteem. LEV RAPHAEL is the author of a collection of stories, *Dancing on Tisha B'Av*, which won a 1990 Lambda Literary Award, a novel, a mystery, and a book of essays. Together, they have authored three books, including *Stick Up for Yourself!: Every Kid's Guide to Personal Power and Positive Self-Esteem*. Life partners for ten years, they live in Okemos, Michigan.